VCs OF THE FIRST WORLD WAR

ARRAS & MESSINES 1917

GERALD GLIDDON

WRENS PARK

A Sutton Publishing Book

First published in 1998 by
Sutton Publishing Limited · Phoenix Mill
Thrupp · Stroud · Gloucestershire · GL5 2BU

This edition first published in 2000 by Wrens Park Publishing, an imprint of
W.J. Williams & Son Ltd

British Library Cataloguing in Publication Data
A catalogue record for this book is available from the British Library

ISBN 0-905-778-618

Typeset in 10/13pt Sabon.
Typesetting and origination by
Sutton Publishing Limited.
Printed in Great Britain by
J.H. Haynes & Co., Sparkford.

CONTENTS

ACKNOWLEDGEMENTS

I would like to thank the staff of the following institutions for their assistance during the six-month research for this book: the Commonwealth War Graves Commission, the Imperial War Museum, the National Army Museum and the Public Record Office. In addition, I would also like to thank the archivists and curators of the many regimental museums and libraries who have responded to my requests for information.

Where recently taken photographs have been included, their owners have been acknowledged with each individual illustration.

As was the case with my three earlier books in the 'VCs of the First World War' series, Donald C. Jennings of Florida has been immensely kind in supplying me with pictures of many of the graves or memorials included in this book.

Many of the maps used in this book are from the British military history, *Military Operations France and Belgium, 1914–1918*, edited by J.E. Edmonds and published by Macmillan/HMSO from 1922 to 1949.

For the fourth book running, Maurice Johnson has once again spent many hours in the Public Record Office in Kew on my behalf, checking the *War Diaries* of the units involved with the men who won the VC in the first half of 1917. Other individuals who have also given help in many ways include Peter Batchelor, who also compiled the index, John Cameron, Jack Cavanagh, Colonel Terry Cave CBE, Peter Harris and Steve Snelling. Other people who provided either material or assistance but whose names are not mentioned here have been acknowledged in the Sources section at the end of the book.

INTRODUCTION

At the Allied Conference at Chantilly in November 1916 it was agreed by the British and French delegations that a joint Allied offensive would be carried out in the New Year, beginning on or about 1 February 1917. However, in December certain political changes took place which affected this agreement. First, David Lloyd George replaced Herbert Asquith as British prime minister, and in France General Joffre was replaced by General Nivelle as Commander-in-Chief of the French Northern Armies. The latter had become a new French hero owing to his recent success at Verdun.

While it was always the intention of Field Marshal Haig, who was Commander-in-Chief of the British Expeditionary Force, to conduct a campaign in Flanders, General Nivelle, seemingly brimming with confidence, had other ideas. He wanted the British to take over another 20 miles of front and to relegate them to carrying out a secondary role containing the German Army. While this was happening, Nivelle's army would deliver a knock-out blow against the German Army on the Aisne with the use of twenty-seven divisions.

In Germany the politicians were in favour of negotiating a peace, while Marshal Hindenburg and General Ludendorff wished to bring the Allies to their knees. The German Army had also decided to change their tactics and planned a new line of defence in depth, divided up into a series of zones which they would 'invite' their opponents to attack, thus luring them into a trap that would be difficult to escape from. This line was known to the Germans as the 'Siegfrid Stelung'.

Work on the new line had been progressing for several months and on 4 February 1917 orders were given to the German troops to begin to retreat to this new defence line. Five days later a 'scorched earth policy' was introduced in order to hinder the Allies, who naturally pursued the enemy to their new positions. The Germans took considerable care in destroying road and rail systems, burning and destroying buildings, cutting down trees and poisoning water supplies. In addition, hundreds of mines and booby traps were put in place to hinder the Allied advance. Even dead bodies were 'wired' up with deadly devices for any person who tried to move or bury a corpse. As a result of their retreat to this new line, the Germans reduced their front line by 25 miles and released fourteen extra divisions. Possibly, and of most importance, the new tactic upset the Allies' own plans and caused confusion to the High Command.

While General Nivelle was planning his 'breakthrough' on the Aisne, the British and Canadians were to move eastwards from Arras in early April and capture Hill 145, better known as Vimy Ridge. The Third Army under General

Allenby was to attack the German lines to the east of Arras, which would involve penetrating part of the newly constructed Hindenburg Line. General Sir Henry Horne's First Army, which included the Canadian Corps, was to take Vimy Ridge. Forty-eight tanks as well as 2,800 guns were to be used in the attack. To the south, the German vacation of the Bapaume Salient led to problems for the British artillery, which now had to move across an area devastated by the departing German army.

The battle was delayed by one day and began on 9 April – Easter Monday. Weather conditions could not have been worse and included snow, sleet and sheer cold. Despite this, the initial progress of the Allied Army was successful. In the centre of the battlefield the 12th and 15th Divisions managed to advance up to 2 miles. To the left the Canadian Corps had secured Vimy Ridge, their main objective, and they now had observation over the German-held plain of Douai. It was a magnificent achievement and one which has been written about in countless books. To the right of the line the fortified village of Neuville-Vitasse also fell to the Allies.

At Bullecourt, though, things had gone desperately wrong and General Gough's late decision to use tanks to break down the German wire, without adequate preparation or rehearsal, turned out to be a major blunder. One feels that after Bullecourt, which was basically an Australian affair, General Gough would not be trusted again. Men had been needlessly sacrificed owing to sheer incompetence.

On 11 April, two days after the attack began, the British managed to capture the strategically important hill village of Monchy-le-Preux, a major achievement. Nevertheless, the German Army was recovering, and gaps were being plugged and reinforcements brought up. Using hindsight, it might well have been sensible to have stopped the advance there and then. However, Haig was committed to supporting the Nivelle Offensive and really had little choice; the attack had to continue. Unfortunately, the Nivelle Offensive on the Aisne turned out to be a disaster, caused largely by the French general's over-optimism. He promised to deliver a victory and he did not succeed. French casualties numbered 187,000 compared to a German total of 163,000. As a result of this defeat Nivelle was replaced by General Pétain, and General Foch was appointed Chief of General Staff.

In the Arras sector Haig learnt of the failure of the French offensive and decided to 'draw breath' and take stock. Consequently, a new offensive was planned for 23–24 April; named the Second Battle of the Scarpe, this was to be carried out to the north and south of the river of that name. This time the attack was to be on a 9 mile front, following the line Gavrelle–Roeux–Guémappe–Fontaine-lès-Croisilles. The German Army, under the command of Col. F. Lossberg (CGS First Army), had learnt how to use the Hindenburg Line to the best advantage. The British artillery was still finding it difficult to provide adequate support over the soft and devastated ground. The fortified village of Roeux proved to be a very difficult place to take, but the British did manage to capture Gavrelle and Guémappe.

On 3 May a third battle of the Scarpe was launched, with the use of British divisions that were already in the area. Bullecourt and Roeux were both finally taken by the British. On the minus side, the Germans managed to re-take the village of Fresnoy.

After the second battle of Bullecourt in the first half of May, the campaign shifted northwards to the Franco-Belgian border. For some time a plan had been formulated to capture the high ground of Messines Ridge. This battle began with high hopes on 7 June, but despite initial success the gains were not fully exploited. As at Arras, and at Cambrai later in the year, it appears that the Allies were so unused to a successful advance that they were unable to capitalize upon it when one occurred.

The present book in the 'VCs of the First World War' series is chronologically the follow-up to the volume on the Somme battle of 1916. The last man to be written about in that book was Lt-Col. B.C. Freyberg, who won his VC in November during the capture of the village of Beaucourt. The first member of the British Army on the Western Front to win the coveted medal in 1917 was Sgt E.J. Mott on 27 January, nearly eleven weeks later. By the end of July, on the eve of the Third Battle of Ypres and Passchendaele, another forty-nine soldiers had won the VC on the Western Front.

Finally, a note about medals: most of the men written about in this book shared certain medals, although several differences and variations occur. The 1914 Star (or Mons Star) covers active military service for the period August–November 1914. The 1914–15 Star was awarded to men who served actively up to 31 December 1915 and who had not already been awarded the 1914 Star. The British War Medal was given to soldiers who served overseas in the period 1914–18. The Victory Medal was awarded to soldiers who served in an overseas theatre of war. Any VC holder mentioned in this book who survived the First World War, and was still alive in 1937, would have been entitled to a George VI Coronation Medal, and the same applied for the coronation of Queen Elizabeth II in 1953.

Gerald Gliddon, Brooke, Norfolk, January 1998

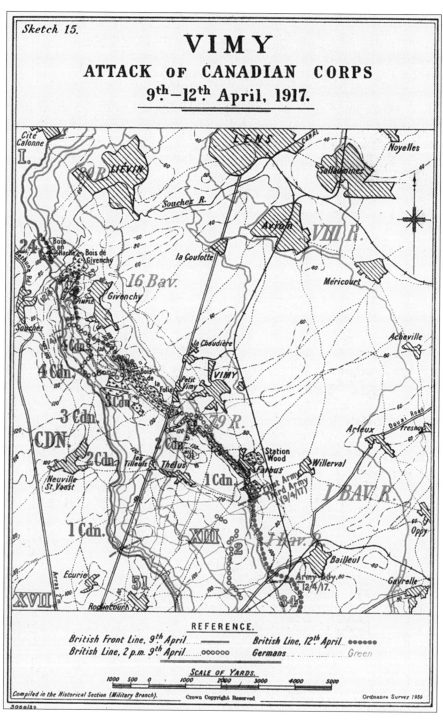

Map showing the attack on Vimy Ridge, April 1917

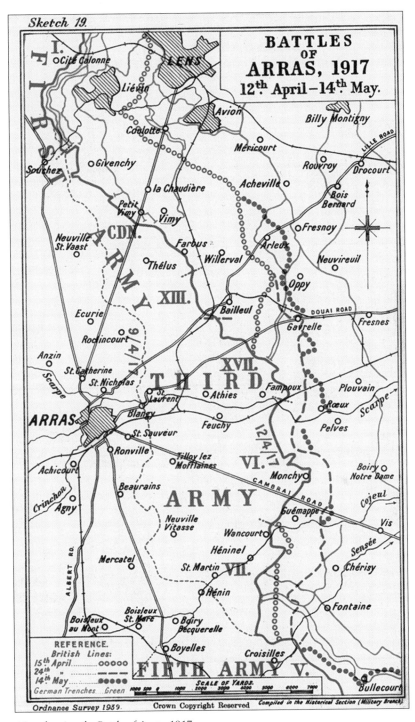

Map showing the Battle of Arras, 1917

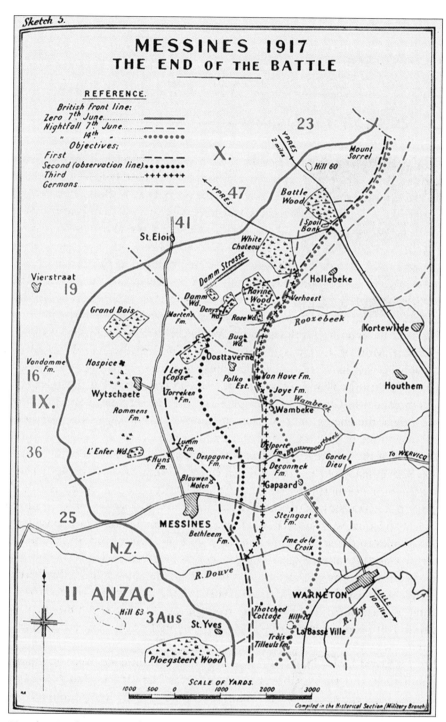

Map showing the area around Messines, 1917

E.J. MOTT

South of Le Transloy, France, 27 January

Fighting on the Western Front had virtually ended for the year in mid-November 1916 when the British captured the Somme village of Beaumont-Hamel, a success which seemed to come as a surprise to the British High Command. Several attacks were carried out in the Beaucourt valley of the Somme region during the winter months. In early January 1917 the British were requested by the French High Command to extend their line of responsibility to 5 miles south of the Oise, below Barisis.

The first VC won by a soldier on the Western Front in 1917 was awarded to Sgt Edward Mott of the 1st Border Regiment (87th Brigade, 29th Division). The operation he was involved in was described as a minor one and was one of a series carried out by Gen. Rawlinson under the instructions of Sir Douglas Haig, the Commander-in-Chief. The main purpose of these secondary operations was to encourage the enemy to think that the Somme operations of the year before were to continue now that the new year had begun.

The first of the secondary operations was planned to take place on 27 January by the 87th Brigade of the 29th Division on the front of XIV Corps. It was to be launched in a northerly direction and would be 750 yards wide, astride the Frégicourt–Le Transloy road; the German name for the position was Landwehr Trench. Frégicourt was about a mile to the east of Combles and Le Transloy was about 3 miles to the south-east of the German-held town of Bapaume. The final objective was 400 yards distant from the centre of this frontage.

In the early morning, the first of two British barrages fell on the German front line and lasted for five minutes. The second, overlapping the first by one minute, fell just in front of the enemy front line and then the two lifted off to a position 100 yards northwards. Australian artillery also assisted the British barrage.

The 1st Royal Inniskilling Fusiliers, also of the 87th Brigade, were on the right of the attack and the 1st Borders on the left. The attack, which began at 5.30 a.m., took the enemy by considerable surprise and the frosty ground helped the attackers to move forward quickly. The Germans surrendered without putting up much of a fight, although a machine-gun in a strongpoint offered opposition. It was at this point that Mott, although wounded in the eye, worked round the flank and rushed forward. In a hand-to-hand struggle he overcame the gun crew. The trench map reference for the strongpoint was N36d 3 2 N36 c 6 0. All objectives were taken and there was a considerable haul of prisoners – 368 were captured and taken back to Antelope Trench where the headquarters of the operation was positioned. Mott was awarded the VC for his bravery; it was the thirteenth VC won by the 29th Division.

His VC was gazetted on 10 March 1917:

> For conspicuous gallantry and initiative when in an attack the company to which he belonged was held up at a strongpoint by machine-gun fire. Although severely wounded in the eye, Sgt Mott made a rush for the gun, and after a fierce struggle seized the gunner and took him prisoner, capturing the gun. It was due to the dash and initiative of this non-commissioned officer that the left flank attack succeeded.

After their involvement in this successful attack, the 1st Borders marched back to the village of Carnoy where they were thanked by the Divisional Commander for their excellent work on the 27th. For most of the next two months the battalion remained in the training area around the village of Bussy.

Edward John Mott was born at Drayton near Abingdon in Berkshire on 4 July 1893. He was the son of a labourer, John Mott, and attended the local council school in Abingdon. When he was only seventeen years old he enlisted in the 1st Border Regiment; his service number was 9887. He took part in the Dardanelles landing in April 1915, and on the 28th of that month he won the DCM (*London Gazette*, 3 July 1915), which he subsequently received from the hands of the King in Liverpool. He was evacuated to Egypt from the Gallipoli peninsula and left for service in France in March 1916. On 4 April 1917 he received his VC at Buckingham Palace.

After the war Mott became a commissionaire at Selfridges in Oxford Street, London, then in 1926 he returned to Berkshire, his home county. At some time he became a warden at an RAF depot, a position which he left in October 1940. During his life Mott regularly attended VC functions, including the 1920 VC garden party at Buckingham Palace and the VC centenary in Hyde Park in 1956. In 1962 he was among the 151 VC holders who attended a garden party at Buckingham Palace; he was accompanied by his daughter, Edna, and his granddaughter, Jennifer Stone. From 1959 he had lived with his wife, Evelyn, at 38 New Yatt Road, Witney, which was the home of Mrs Rona Stone, another daughter. In 1964 Mott was Guest of Honour at the ABC cinema in Oxford for a

No. 38 New Yatt Road, Witney

showing of the film *Zulu*, being the story of the battle at Rorke's Drift in 1879 in which no fewer than eleven VCs were won.

The Mott family ran a building firm which employed Bernard Mott and his father Edward who owned the firm.

Edward Mott died on 20 October 1967, leaving a widow, four sons and four daughters. His body was cremated. The original house in Witney where Mott died had been built as a home for foremen who were employed at the local blanket factory. It was formerly named Pendennis.

Mott's medals, which were displayed in Witney during his lifetime, included the VC, DCM, 1914–15 Star, VM, WM, George VI Coronation Medal and Queen Elizabeth II Coronation Medal. During the 1930s his VC was stolen and subsequently a copy was made. His regiment bought his medals for £1,950 from Glendinings in March 1976.

H.W. MURRAY

Stormy Trench, France, 4/5 February

At the end of January 1917 the 4th Australian Brigade (4th Australian Division) was ordered to capture an enemy position called Stormy Trench, north-east of Gueudecourt, towards the village of Le Transloy, in what was another minor operation. It was a position of great tactical importance around 1,000 yards from Gueudecourt village and from it one had a view that stretched for miles. At the beginning of February the 15th Australian Battalion attacked it and although they were partially successful on the left flank they were held up on the right. The attack was a failure and the men of the 15th Battalion fell back to Shine and Grease Trenches where the 13th Battalion relieved them. The knowledge gained from the raid helped the 13th Battalion to capture the position a few days later, on the night of 4/5 February.

In preparation for the second attack, Capt. Henry Murray of the 13th Battalion and his scouts crawled out into no-man's-land in order to examine the terrain over which they were to attack; especially, of course, they needed to find out about the condition of the German wire. Within a couple of days Murray had a very accurate knowledge of the position that they were ordered to capture. The greatest worry was how to hold on to the position against counter-attacks once they had taken it. There was to be no shortage of armament: 20,000 Mills bombs and 1,000 rifle grenades were requested, along with artillery support. To the south of Shine Trench was a position called the Chalk Pit where much of this material was initially dumped; the pit was also the advance position of Col. Durrant, who was in charge of the operation. In order to keep

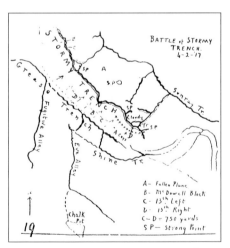

Map showing the battle for Stormy Trench, 4 February 1917

4

the enemy in ignorance it was decided not to send men up to the advance positions until after dark. Murray's A Company was to the right of the proposed attack with the other companies to their left. The forward positions occupied by the Australians were, in effect, a maze of old saps. It was extremely cold and the Australians wrapped their feet in sandbags to prevent the sound of tramping on the frozen ground alerting the enemy.

Murray's A Company was one of four companies which went into the attack preceded by a fierce artillery barrage at about 10.00 p.m. The company began with 140 men. They made good progress, moving quickly over the hard ground, but they were held up on the right as the 15th Battalion had previously been. The Germans were very much on the alert, although some of them were slow to emerge from their dug-outs. They sent over showers of hundreds of 'eggs' (grenades) and 'potato-mashers'. This impeded the Australians' progress and Murray sent an SOS to the artillery which brought a quick response. Despite this, the German counter-attack continued and a group of bombers under Murray and Pte Robinson managed to push the Germans back towards their original positions. In the small hours the firing died down, but at 3.00 a.m. the enemy made one more attempt to turn the Australians out of their positions and fierce hand-to-hand fighting took place before the Germans decided that they had had enough for one night. After twenty-four hours Murray's A Company was reduced to 58 men and they sought relief, which was supplied by members of the 16th Battalion who took over from their victorious colleagues in the 13th Battalion.

Not only had Murray's fighting ability and planning been outstanding, but Col. Durrant had been an inspired commander. He visited the captured Stormy Trench soon after it was taken and went backwards and forwards over the surrounding ground in order to align the new positions and communication trenches. Many of the men who fought were taking part in battle for the very first time. On 22 February the 4th Australian Brigade moved back over snow-covered roads to Ribemont. Although it had been cold for most of February, at the start of March the weather turned even colder. At this time rumours were circulating that the Germans were about to leave their Somme positions and retreat to the newly built Hindenburg Line. Open warfare training was subsequently carried out during the month of March.

There was great rejoicing in the 13th Battalion when Murray's VC was announced on 12 March. It was gazetted on 10 March:

For most conspicuous bravery when in command of the right flank company in attack. He led his company to the assault with great skill and courage, and the position was quickly captured. Fighting of a very severe nature followed, and three heavy counter-attacks were beaten back, these successes being due to Capt. Murray's wonderful work. Throughout the night his company suffered heavy casualties through concentrated enemy shell fire, and on one occasion gave ground for a short way. This gallant officer rallied his command and saved the situation by sheer valour. He made his presence felt throughout the line, encouraging his men, heading bombing parties, leading bayonet charges, and carrying wounded to places of safety. His magnificent example inspired his men throughout.

Henry William Murray was the son of Edward Kennedy Murray, a farmer, and his wife Clarissa Murray, née Littler. He was born on 30 December 1884 at Evandale, Launceston, Tasmania. His father died when Murray was still quite young, and on leaving the local state school at Evandale he helped to run the family farm.

Murray's connection with the Army began when he joined the Australian Field Artillery (militia) at Launceston, with whom he trained for six years. At the end of his teens he moved to Western Australia and worked in the goldfields as a mail courier. His method of transport was either bicycle or horseback.

Two months after the war began Murray enlisted as a private in the Australian Imperial Forces, giving his occupation as 'bushman'. He had employed men to cut timber for use in the railways in the south-west of the state. At the time of his entering the Army, Murray was said to be a tall, well-built man with dark hair, and a natural leader of men. He was sent to Blackboy Hill Camp close to Perth, where the 16th Battalion was being formed and which he joined. During his training period Murray teamed up with a man called Percy Black and they were destined to become great friends.

When the 16th Battalion landed at Gallipoli on 25 April 1915 Murray was a member of one of its machine-gun crews. His friend L/Cpl Black was serving with him. The day after the landing the two gun crews were on the rear side of Pope's Hill, sniping at Turkish soldiers who were moving on to Russell's Top. Later, both men, although wounded, refused to leave their posts during the following week's fighting. On 13 May Murray won the DCM (as did Black) for 'exceptional courage' in the period 9–13 May and was also promoted to lance corporal. Murray was wounded again on 30 May and was evacuated, but was back on the peninsula on 3 July. On 8 August he was wounded yet again when his machine-gun section was covering the withdrawal after the attack on Hill 971. Five days later he was made up to sergeant, and was subsequently commissioned as a second lieutenant and transferred to the 13th AIF.

The story behind this rapid success was that the commander of the 13th Battalion, Col. L.E. Tilney, was short of a machine-gun officer and Gen. Monash agreed to Murray's speedy promotion. After leaving the peninsula, Murray was promoted to lieutenant on 20 January 1916 while in Egypt, and then to captain on 1 March. In that same month the 13th Battalion moved to France.

Murray was involved in most of the fighting that his battalion encountered; in addition to the operations at Stormy Trench in February 1917, Mouquet Farm, Pozières and Bullecourt all featured in his military career. In particular, in August 1916 Murray stormed the ruins of Mouquet Farm on the Somme with fewer than a hundred men. After seeing off the German counter-attackers four times he ordered his group to withdraw. Eventually the farm was recaptured by a force of 3,000 men. Murray was rewarded with the DSO (*London Gazette*, 14 November 1916):

> For conspicuous gallantry in action. Although twice wounded, he commanded his company with the greatest courage and initiative, beating off four enemy counter-attacks. Later, when an enemy bullet started a man's equipment exploding, he tore the man's equipment off at great personal risk. He set a splendid example throughout.

Murray rejoined his battalion on 19 October, once his wounds had healed.

After the recapture of Stormy Trench in February 1917, at the end of the following month the 13th Battalion moved to Fricourt, Méaulte, Bazentin and Warlencourt, and then to dug-outs between Favreuil and Biefvillers. From 3 April the unit was at Favreuil during a period of sleeting wind, and worked for a week at road-making and cable-burying and carrying. The Hindenburg Line was studied from high ground close to Noreuil and on 8 April the Australian Brigade was planning an attack against the Hindenburg Line which would take place on the 10th. The 13th Battalion was to move up to Noreuil and there it would join the rest of the brigade. The Hindenburg Line was to be broken through with the use of tanks and infantry only; artillery was not to be used. Scouts advised against the wisdom of this plan, but it was seemingly too late to halt or change it.

In the fighting that followed, Murray's unit was supporting the 16th Battalion. He could see the men ahead being held up by wire and cut down by machine-gun fire. The tanks which were supposed to deal with the wire were soon knocked out and the artillery cover was non-existent. In this fighting Black was killed. Despite the conditions a small group of 4th Brigade men managed to squeeze through the enemy wire and into the first two lines of German trench lines. At 7.15 a.m. Murray sent back for more grenades and ammunition which were vital if they were to have any chance of holding their positions. However, communication was inadequate and conflicting reports led to the artillery not firing, enabling the Germans to take advantage of the situation. The follow-up British reinforcements were wiped out and a heavy German barrage began. In addition, enemy small-arms fire swept the Australian positions on three sides. By 8.00 a.m. communications were completely cut off. The few survivors had no choice but to try to struggle back to their original lines, taking cover in the shell holes on the way back. It was a question of 'every man for himself'.

Murray played a leading role in getting his men out of a very dangerous situation. It was the last time that he was to lead as a company commander in an offensive action, and it seems that his experience at Bullecourt deeply distressed him. He must have been appalled at the idea of trying to capture a section of the Hindenburg Line without the use of artillery.

Murray won a bar to his DSO for his role at Bullecourt:

> For conspicuous gallantry and devotion to duty. He gallantly led his company over 1,200 yards of fire-swept ground. Later, he went along the whole frontage, organizing the defence, encouraging the men of all units by his cheerfulness and bravery, and always moving to the points of danger. He is not only brave and daring, but a skilful soldier, possessing tactical instinct of the highest order.

Murray was subsequently promoted to temporary major on 11 April, a position confirmed on 12 July and he was now in temporary command of the 13th Battalion. In March 1918 he was promoted to lieutenant colonel and given the command of the 4th Machine-Gun Battalion, a role that he played until the end of the war a few months later. He was described as being 'cool, determined and confident'. He believed strongly in discipline, but also cared very much for the welfare of the troops under his command.

Murray received his VC along with the two DSOs from the King in Hyde Park on 2 June 1917. In January 1918 he was awarded the French Croix de Guerre and in May 1919 he was made a Companion of the Order of St Michael and St George. During the period from 1917 to 1919 he was Mentioned in Despatches on four occasions.

While waiting to return to Australia at the end of the war Murray, along with another holder of the VC, W.D. Joynt, was in charge of various men who were aspiring farmers, and they studied agricultural methods both in the United Kingdom and in Denmark before leaving for Australia. Once in Australia Murray began to look for a sheep farming property.

On 9 March 1920 his association with the AIF ended when he was discharged in Tasmania. He then moved to Queensland and became a grazier at Blairmack, Muckadilla. He married Constance Sophia Cameron, an estate agent, on 13 October 1921 at Bollon. They lived in the town for four years and were then separated when Murray moved to New Zealand. Their marriage was dissolved on 11 November 1927 and nine days later he married Ellen Purdon Cameron at the Auckland Register Office. Murray returned to Queensland with his new wife and purchased a 74,000 acre property called Glenlyon Station near Richmond. He was to live there for the next thirty-eight years. During this time he occasionally wrote articles about his experiences in Gallipoli and France during the First World War which were published in *Reveille*.

During the Second World War, when there was a real risk of a Japanese invasion of North Australia, Murray returned to the Active List and commanded the 26th Battalion (the Logan and Albert Regiment) in North Queensland until February 1942. His troops were known as 'Murray's Cowboys' and they used to scour the country of North Queensland until the threat of invasion was passed. Murray later became the lieutenant colonel of his local battalion of the Volunteer Defence Corps. Nearly two years later he retired from military service, on 8 February 1944.

Murray was a member of the Australian VC contingent to London in 1956. He lived on at Glenlyon for nearly ten more years and died of heart failure in the Miles District Hospital, Brisbane, on 7 January 1966, after a car accident the previous day. He was a passenger in a car which had had a puncture, skidded and overturned. Known during the First World War as 'the man the enemy could not kill', it was ironic that such a warrior should die as a result of a car accident. His body was cremated at Mount Thompson after a funeral service with full military honours at St Andrews Presbyterian Church, Ann Street, Brisbane, on 14 January. At the funeral his medals were carried behind the coffin by Maj. D. Kayler Thomson and dozens of wreaths were sent to the service along with sheaves of flowers. The Last Post and Reveille were sounded at the cremation by members of the 18th Field Squadron. Murray left a widow and a son and daughter. His portrait by George Bell is in the Australian War Memorial in Canberra. His medals, which are not publicly held, include the VC, CMG (1918), DSO and bar, DCM, Croix de Guerre and George VI Coronation Medal. Murray was the most decorated Australian soldier of the First World War and his name is frequently mentioned in C.E.W. Bean's *Official History of Australia in the War*.

F.W. PALMER

North of Courcelette, France, 16/17 February

On 28 January 1917 the 22nd Royal Fusiliers (99th Brigade, 2nd Division) moved into Wolfe Huts on the Albert–Bapaume road. They were in support of the 23rd Royal Fusiliers of the same brigade and A Company was based in Courcelette at the Red Château. The area in which the battalion found itself was part of the battlefield that had been taken from the enemy during the battle of the Somme, the previous year. According to the regimental historian, Christopher Stone, the landscape was 'desolate, treeless, a mass of mine craters, shell holes and wire entanglements, with a few repaired roads and beaten tracks to link up with the front area. The trenches in front of Courcelette were isolated fragments of old battered trenches reclaimed . . .'. It was extremely cold throughout February and 'trench foot' was combated by a plea for extra socks to be sent from the regimental depot in Middlesex.

On 17 February the 22nd and 23rd Royal Fusiliers of the 99th Brigade were both involved in the fighting. With headquarters established in West Miraumont dug-out, the 22nd Battalion assembled in positions between East and West Miraumont Roads. A and B Companies began the attack at 5.45 a.m. while D Company formed a defensive flank stretching from the former British line to the final objective, south of Miraumont. When moving forward, D Company advanced along the right side of East Miraumont Road but soon came under heavy machine-gun fire from the right. The enemy were alert, having had an early warning of the attack as they had been given the information by deserters.

It was at this point that Sgt Frederick Palmer took a hand as all the officers in his company had become casualties, including Maj. Walsh who had been with the 22nd for two years. Against point-blank machine-gun fire, Palmer managed to cut through the wire entanglements and, together with six men, rushed the enemy machine-gun post which had been holding up the advance, and then established a block. His group was able to repel at least seven determined enemy counter-attacks, which were accompanied by a continuous barrage of bombs and grenades. At one point, when Palmer left the position in order to collect some more bombs from headquarters, he returned to find that the enemy had managed to drive a wedge into his position which threatened the whole flank. Exhausted though he was, Palmer managed to rally his men and they forced the enemy back.

Meanwhile, A and C Companies found that the wire in front of them was uncut and one platoon on the left side of West Miraumont Road was captured. However, the troops reached South Miraumont Road, although an outflanking movement on the right forced them to fall back to their first objective. The enemy was prevented from emerging on the East Miraumont Road, but at a cost: the battalion casualties were eighty-five killed. A week later the enemy retired in this area anyway, to new and stronger positions in the new Hindenburg Line.

On 4 April the news came through to the battalion that Sgt Palmer, the bombing sergeant with A Company on 17 February, had won the VC; the other survivors of his attacking party won either DCMs or MMs.

Palmer's citation was gazetted on 3 April:

> For most conspicuous bravery, control and determination. During the progress of certain operations, all the officers of his company having been shot down, Sergt. Palmer assumed command, and, having cut his way, under point-blank machine-gun fire, through the wire entanglements, he rushed the enemy's trench with six of his men, dislodged the hostile machine-gun which had been hampering our advance, and established a block. He then collected men detached from other regiments, and held the barricade for nearly three hours against seven determined counter-attacks, under an incessant barrage of bombs and rifle grenades from his flank and front. During his temporary absence in search of more bombs an eighth counter-attack was delivered by the enemy, who succeeded in driving in his party and threatened the defences of the whole flank. At this critical moment, although he had been blown off his feet by a bomb, and was greatly exhausted, he rallied his men, drove back the enemy and maintained his position. The very conspicuous bravery displayed by this non-commissioned officer cannot be over-stated, and his splendid determination and devotion to duty undoubtedly averted what might have proved a serious disaster in this sector of the line.

By 3 May Sgt Palmer had become 2nd Lt Palmer, still of the 22nd Royal Fusiliers, and to quote Christopher Stone again:

> A second attack was launched at 03.45 on 3rd May, over ground to the north of Oppy Wood. So weak was the Division that it was reorganized as a composite brigade under the command of General Kellett with four composite battalions: A, B, C and D. One hundred men – all that was left of 22nd Royal Fusiliers – formed a company under the command of 2nd Lieutenant Palmer VC, which was allocated to D Battalion under Major Stafford of 1st KRRC. Initially the Brigade made some progress, particularly on the left where the

Canadians were again successful, but heavy counter-attacks forced them back on the right, the attack of 31st Division (further to their right) having failed. The 22nd's contingent suffered a further 24 casualties.

Two-and-a-half months later Palmer was asked to attend a Special Meeting of the Council of the Metropolitan Borough of Hammersmith, held in the Council Chamber of Hammersmith Town Hall. The date was 18 July and the time 6.15 p.m. The meeting was called in order to ask Palmer whether he would inscribe his name on the Roll of Honour of the Borough; the previous person to sign the Roll had been Queen Mary. At the meeting Palmer's citation for the VC was read out. It was then moved by the mayor that in view of Palmer's distinguished service he should be invited to sign the Roll of Honour, which had been instituted in March 1907.

When Palmer entered the council chamber he was welcomed with cheers, and his reply to the mayor's address was greeted with further cheers and applause. Palmer said he felt very nervous indeed and that having a VC had disadvantages as well as advantages. He also drew attention to the impossibility of people at home fully comprehending what life was like in France and Belgium for the British troops. He expressed a wish that members of the audience would write

Lt F.W. Palmer signing the 'Golden Book'

regularly to someone at the front at least once a week as the news from home would cheer them up; a regular parcel would also be most welcome.

Frederick William Palmer was born on 11 November 1891 in Hammersmith, London, and was working for a publisher at the outbreak of war. He enlisted in the Royal Fusiliers. In 1916 he won the MM in Gallipoli and was mentioned in despatches. He won the VC on 16/17 February 1917 when a lance sergeant and received the MM and the VC together from the King on 2 June 1917 in Hyde Park, London. Soon after winning the VC he was commissioned in his regiment and later transferred to the RAF with the rank of Lieutenant in 1919.

After demobilization he lived in Singapore and became a director of Kyle, Palmer & Co. Ltd, and other companies. In 1942 the family home was destroyed when Singapore fell to the Japanese; his Chinese wife, a magistrate's daughter who had worked as a nurse in Singapore, and the Palmers' two young children were driven north and placed in a refugee camp for four years. During this time Palmer had no news of them, but when the war was over the family was reunited and they moved to Hordle in Hampshire. In November 1940 he had been awarded a commission in the RAFVR as a pilot officer (Administrative Special Duties Branch) and he served in the ground defence forces of the RAF; he was later promoted to wing commander.

Palmer died in Lymington Hospital, Hampshire, on 10 September 1955 at the age of sixty-three and was buried in St Michael's churchyard, Hordle. He left a widow, three sons and a daughter.

His medals are not publicly held.

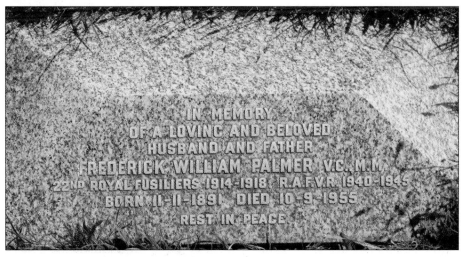

Palmer's grave in St Michael's churchyard, Hordle, Hants. (Photo: Donald Jennings)

G.E. CATES

East of Bouchavesnes, France, 8 March

In early March 1917 the 24th and 25th Brigades of the 8th Division were in the formerly French-occupied area around the village of Bouchavesnes, about 1½ miles south of Rancourt and 3 miles to the north of Péronne.

On 4 March the two brigades attacked the German first and second lines on a front stretching a mile from a point about 500 yards to the south of the Bouchavesnes–Moislains road northwards. The 2nd Rifle Brigade (25th Brigade) acted as reserve in that part of the attack made by the 2nd Royal Berkshires and was actively involved in supporting the attack.

The operation achieved its main object, which was to deny the enemy observation of British positions. The British could now see the German lines and gun positions in the Moislains valley. However, the Germans retreated to a new defensive line called R1 a few days later.

On 8 March, when in charge of a working party engaged in deepening a captured German trench, 2nd Lt George Cates of the 2nd Rifle Brigade gained a VC which was gazetted on 11 May 1917:

> For most conspicuous gallantry and self-sacrifice. When engaged with some other men in deepening a captured trench, this officer struck with his spade a buried bomb, which immediately started to burn. Cates, in order to save the lives of his comrades, placed his foot on the bomb, which immediately exploded. He showed the most conspicuous gallantry and devotion to duty in performing the act which cost him his life but saved the lives of others.

Cates succumbed to his injuries the next day and was buried in Hem Farm Military Cemetery, which lies on the north bank of the River Somme, adjacent to a large farm on the south-west outskirts of the village of Hem-Monacu. The cemetery was begun by the British in January 1917, being used for the next two months. It was used again in September 1918. Cates's grave is in Plot 1, Row G15. His posthumous VC was presented to his father in Hyde Park on 2 June 1917.

Cates is also commemorated on a tablet in the war memorial of the parish church of St Mary the Virgin in Wimbledon, together with two of his brothers, 2nd Lt Geoffrey Cates of the 10th Durham Light Infantry and William Frederick Cates of the Canadian Army Medical Corps.

Geoffrey Edward Cates was the seventh child of George and Alice Ann Cates and was born at 86 Hartfield Road in Wimbledon, Surrey, on 8 May 1892. Cates attended Rutlish School, Merton, Surrey, and later King's College, Worple Road, Wimbledon. He became assistant scoutmaster with the 2nd Wimbledon Troop.

Cates's grave in Hem Farm Military Cemetery (Photo: Donald Jennings)

Cates enlisted in the Artists Rifles, 28th London Regiment, and was given the number 3035; subsequently all of his platoon were commissioned. He was a signaller from 8 December 1914, and went to France on 15 June 1915. He was commissioned in the Rifle Brigade and joined their second battalion. At the time of his death in 1917 the family home was at 39 Compton Road, Wimbledon. After his death there was some discussion as to whether there should be a Court of Inquiry, but it came to nothing. His medals were sent to his sister, Ethel Cates. Later, his personal effects were sent back to his family, and included a cigarette case, a pipe, a comb, a broken pen, a pocket knife, a gold ring, a key chain, a whistle and strap, a collar stud, a pocket book, a tobacco pouch and some small coins.

His medals included the 1914–15 Star, BWM and VM. His VC, a replacement of the original which was destroyed by fire in 1951, is in the collection of the Royal Green Jackets in Winchester.

C.A. COX

Achiet-le-Grand, France, 13–17 March

The German defensive line known to the enemy as the R1 Line and to the British as the Loupart Line ran roughly from Bucquoy to Le Transloy in a south-easterly direction. It bypassed the villages of Achiet-le-Petit and Achiet-le-Grand as well as Grévillers; near the last named stood Loupart Wood.

The German retreat to their new defensive line, the Hindenburg Line, was planned to take place in several stages. The village of Irles, to the south of Achiet-le-Petit, had been occupied by the British on 10 March and soon afterwards patrols found that the enemy had deserted Loupart Wood in front of the village of Grévillers. The Germans were having to adapt their plans; they needed to decide whether to stand and fight, become involved in a general engagement or take the remaining option, which was to break away and retreat to their new line as quickly as possible. In the end, in the area of Achiet-le-Grand, the enemy chose the middle course and fought a controlled rearguard action.

The 18th Division had moved up from the Ancre valley and the 7th Bedfords (54th Brigade) were to occupy the village of Achiet-le-Grand when the enemy had withdrawn. On 13 March the 54th Brigade moved into the Loupart Line; at the time the Germans were still in Achiet-le-Petit and were strongly holding Achiet-le-Grand and Bihucourt, the village to the east. Both villages fell to the 54th Brigade on the 17th. The fighting in this period took place over open ground and the enemy conducted these actions with their usual great tenacity. It was during the fighting in front of Achiet-le-Grand that Pte Christopher Cox (13908) of the 7th Bedfords (B Company) won his VC, while acting as a stretcher-bearer between 13 and 17 March. His citation, gazetted on 11 May 1917, described his actions:

During the attack of his battalion (the 7th Bedfordshire Regiment) the front wave was checked by the severity of the enemy artillery and machine-gun fire, and the whole line had to take cover in shell holes to avoid annihilation. Private Cox, utterly regardless of personal safety, went out into the open over fire-swept ground and single-handed rescued four men. Having collected the wounded of his own battalion, he then assisted to bring in the wounded of an adjoining battalion. On the two subsequent days he carried out similar rescue work with the same disregard of his own safety. He has on all occasions displayed the same high example of unselfishness and valour.

He continued to rescue the wounded on 16 and 17 March, with complete disregard of his own personal safety.

An Army form dated 29 March 1917 included the following remarks about Cox:

This private soldier has been in every engagement in which his battalion has taken part since July 1916 and he has on all occasions displayed the same high example of unselfishness and personal courage. I consider him worthy of the highest decoration that can be bestowed.

Cox was recommended by Lt-Col. G.F. Mills, Commanding Officer of the 7th Bedfords, Lt-Col. C.C. Carr, CO of the 54th Brigade, and Maj.-Gen. R.P. Lee, in command of the 18th Division.

We are fortunate that several eyewitness accounts of Cox's gallantry have survived and that copies of these were sent to his family after his death. Together they illustrate the various steps that have to be followed for a VC to be awarded. The first account was written by Sgt F. Bayford of No. 5 Platoon, B Company:

On the 15/3/17 while the attack was held up by heavy machine-gun and shell fire, he proceeded to the front line, bandaging and dressing wounded men, bringing them in, regardless of danger, upon his back. Whilst making one of these journeys, a wounded man he was carrying received another wound. After tending all the men of the Beds Regt he could find, he again went forward, still under heavy fire, and did good work among the Middx Regt (12th Bn). After attending and bringing in Machine Gunners, he returned for their drums of Amo [sic], returning them safely to the guns. This is not the only occasion that his zeal and devotion to duty under very adverse circumstances has been noticed and praised by men witnessing same.

Then from Sgt B.W. Eakins:

Going out to the furthest Point and bringing in a wounded man on his back under a terrific machine-gun fire.

Also attending to other wounded under heavy fire.

After salvaging machine gun drums and taking them on to another team when the first team got knocked out. Also marking out gaps in the barbed wire with tapes.

He was still carrying on with the good work when we were digging in.

From Cpl W.V. Simmonds:

Cox went forward quite alone and picked up four men who were wounded and brought them safely back. Whilst carrying one of the Middlesex on his back the wounded man got shot again but Cox kept on, also while assisting a Corporal on a stretcher the corporal got wounded again but Cox kept on with his work; he also marked where the barbed wire was cut so we could rush through.

From 2nd Lt S.R. Chapman, acting OC of B Company:

On the 13th March I saw Pte Cox carrying back wounded from the Loupart Line through a heavy barrage of machine-gun fire and heavy calibre shells to the dressing station; in spite of the heavy bombardment he never hesitated to take back a second case having just returned from taking one.

On the morning of the 15th I saw him wandering about in front of Hill 130 in the front wave attending to the wounded. He showed absolute contempt of the volume of machine-gun fire, and heavy bombardment, although M.G. opened on single targets. I previously saw him carry back a man on three different occasions, and on withdrawing my Company I found he had treated six others, two of whom were wounded a second time while he was carrying them.

On the morning of the 17th I again saw Pte Cox go forward to the assistance of the Company ahead of us; on passing through the extremely thick barbed wire he marked passages with white bandage and went on again to the front wave, where he carried back several cases through the bombardment.

All the other evidence I put in my previous report was collected from NCOs and men in the Company, none of whom can speak too highly of his conduct, emphasizing always his complete disregard of personal danger and contempt of enemy M.G. fire. All are unanimous in their desire to see him rewarded with the coveted honour VC.

From 2nd Lt F.E. Dealer of the 7th Bedfords:

On the 13th March I saw Pte Cox on several occasions in and about the Loupart Line, always either vigorously searching for wounded or carrying cases quite oblivious to the heavy bombardment.

On the morning of the 15th March 'B' Coy was advancing over Hill 130 in support of the leading companies facing the Bihucourt Line. I saw Cox come over the Hill in rear of me undisturbed by the fact that he was being fired at as an individual target. He told me he had just bound up five men and asked where he could find more work. He did not wait to be told but went straight forward.

Subsequently, I saw him carrying a wounded man near the Star Cross Roads (to the south of Achiet-le-Grand) where fire from both Artillery and M.G. was very heavy. The wounded man made a violent spasmodic movement and brought Cox to his knees. (I was told subsequently) that this was owing to the fact that he was hit again by M.G. Cox got up and carried on.

Subsequently, after his own Company had withdrawn from the front line, I saw him go up again towards the front line through M.G. fire though I believe all the wounded of his Company were already back.

He did not rejoin the Company till about 12 hours after and although a very powerful man, whom I have never seen tired before, he was thoroughly exhausted.

The troops are unanimous in their enthusiasm on his behalf to see him rewarded by an honourable decoration.

Finally, from 2nd Lt R.J. Clarke:

On March 14th 'A' Coy received orders to hold a line of shell holes on the hill directly in front of Loupart Line. Previous to their advancing, the stretcher-bearers had gone back to the dressing station with two wounded men.

On arrival at their position, the 'A' Coy again had severe casualties caused mostly by H.H. shrapnel and most of these cases were dangerous. We were without stretcher-bearers but B Coy who were then in Reserve lent us theirs and among these was Pte Cox.

It was impossible for them to take the case down at once owing to the fact that the hill was swept by M.G. fire and shells were dropping everywhere.

Heedless of the fire Pte Cox went from shell hole to shell hole and bound the wounded up and after he had finished them started back with another man, with the most severe case. For the first 200 yards he was under M.G. fire, but without hesitating once he completed his journey and I saw him come back for a second load a few hours later.

Pte Cox saved many lives that day by risking his own and I certainly think he deserved the coveted honour.

Cox's VC was presented to him by the King in the forecourt of Buckingham Palace on 21 July 1917. He was discharged in 1919.

Christopher Augustus Cox was born in King's Langley, Hertfordshire, on Christmas Day in 1889. He was educated at King's Langley Church of England School and later worked as a farm hand. On 5 October 1912 he married Maud May Swan and they had a family of four boys and four girls. After Cox enlisted he left for France on 26 July 1915. After being demobilized he attended the VC garden party at Buckingham Palace in 1920 and in 1932 he attended the annual service of remembrance at the Cenotaph where he was photographed with two other holders of the VC, T.R. Adlam and Daniel Laidlaw, who was accompanied by his famous pipes.

During the Second World War Cox served in the Home Guard and three of his sons were in the armed forces. He took part in the 1946 Victory Parade on 8 June. In 1948 he was living at Blackwall Lane, King's Langley, and later at 81 Coniston Road, King's Langley. He died on 24 August 1959 at Hill End Hospital, King's Langley, and was buried in King's Langley cemetery.

Cox's medals, which include the 1914–15 Star, BWM and VM, are still held by his family.

Cox's grave in King's Langley churchyard, Herts.
(Photo: Donald Jennings)

P.H. CHERRY

Lagnicourt, France, 26 March

Lt-Gen. Birdwood, commander of the Australian forces in France, decided to make an attempt to breach the German line on 26 March with the 2nd Australian Division and to capture the village of Lagnicourt, lying to the south-east of Noreuil. Lagnicourt was to be bombarded and additional artillery was to be with the left advanced guard. The 7th Brigade was to take the village, having relieved the 6th Brigade which had been recently ejected from Noreuil by the enemy.

The Germans had other ideas and were intending to hang on to the village as they did not want the Australians to come any closer to the Hindenburg Line. The barrage opened at 5.15 a.m. against the outskirts of Lagnicourt and continued for twenty minutes, allowing the infantry to close up to it. The Australians then began to advance. The middle company of the 26th Battalion (7th Brigade), advancing from the direction of Beugny under Capt. Percy Cherry, first overcame the enemy who were occupying the buildings of a large farm and who put up a strong resistance on the edge of the village. The company then met with stern resistance as it moved down the main street, and it was fired on from the houses on either side. A fierce fight developed in a stable yard, but the enemy later surrendered. Moving on to the centre of the village, Cherry's group came across a very large chalky crater at the crossroads, which the Germans were heavily defending from its rim. This slowed Cherry's advance and he sent a messenger back for more Stokes mortars.

Becoming impatient at the delay, after half an hour Cherry decided to rush the position under the cover of a Lewis gun and rifle grenades. He succeeded and all the German defenders were killed. Capturing the crater allowed Cherry's party to win through and they passed through the village, which had been held by about 250 Germans, and met up with the companies which had bypassed the village and who were already established to the north and east of the village. Another fierce battle had taken place with some Germans who were in dug-outs at the side of the road before Cherry was able to join up with his colleagues on the outskirts of the village at about 6.30 a.m.

Cherry's orders were to fall back into reserve, but he disregarded them because he assumed that a counter-attack was forthcoming. He was particularly anxious at the corner of the road leading towards Doignies, because by then contact should have been made with the 5th Australian Division. Soon after Lagnicourt was taken by the Australians it was put in a state of readiness for the expected counter-attack. At about 9.00 a.m. the enemy launched a very strong counter-attack under heavy artillery fire. The fighting for the possession of the village continued all day before the enemy gave up their attempts to retake it. In C.E.W. Bean's *Official History of Australia in the War*, vol. IV, there is a picture of the destroyed village.

Having been primarily responsible for the capture of Lagnicourt, Cherry was killed on 27 March by a shell bursting in a sunken road to the east of the village. He was buried in Quéant Road Cemetery, Plot VIII, Row C, Grave 10. The Australian casualties, including those of the left 15th Brigade, totalled 19 officers and 358 other ranks.

Following Cherry's death Gen. Birdwood wrote to his parents; after expressing his sympathy, he added:

as you will have heard, he was awarded the Military Cross for his fine work on the 1st March, when he led his company with such dash and courage in an attack on a trench near the village of Warlencourt. The wire where he led his men was not well cut, when he at once ran along the edge of the entanglements until he found an opening, through which he took his men. He met with fierce opposition from the Germans on entering a trench, but rallying his men he cleared it, and by his gallant and inspiring conduct ensured success. Even though wounded, he refused to leave his men, and later captured two hostile machine-guns, which he turned on the enemy . . . His battalion formed part of a force which captured the village of Lagnicourt, and when other senior officers became casualties in his company he carried on the fighting in face of the most determined opposition, and cleared the village. Having done this he took hold of the situation, and beat off a most resolute and heavy counter-attack made by the enemy. I am sorry to say he was wounded early in the morning, but refused to leave his post, where he remained encouraging (his men) all round him until towards evening he was, to the great regret of us all, killed by a German shell.

Cherry's parents received many letters about their son after his death and one correspondent described him 'as the bravest man he had ever met'. His commanding officer regarded him as the best company commander the battalion had ever had. 'When he first took over his company he was rather unpopular, for he was a little martinet on parade, and it speaks well for his character that at the finish they simply adored him, and would have followed him anywhere.'

In mid-April the Germans made a serious attempt to wrest the village from the hands of the Australians but, despite initial progress, they were driven back to the Hindenburg Line.

Cherry's VC was gazetted on 26 March 1917 as follows:

For most conspicuous bravery, determination and leadership when in command of a company detailed to storm and clear a village. After all the officers of this company had become casualties he carried on with care and determination in the face of fierce opposition, and cleared the village of the enemy. He sent frequent reports of progress made, and when held up for some time by an enemy strongpoint, he organized machine-gun and bomb parties and captured the position. His leadership, coolness and bravery set a wonderful example to his men. Having cleared the village, he took charge of the situation and beat off the most resolute and heavy counter-attacks made by the enemy. Wounded about 6.30 a.m., he refused to leave his post, and there remained, encouraging all to hold out at all costs, until, about 4.30 p.m., this very gallant officer was killed by an enemy shell.

His medal was presented to his father by Sir Francis Newdigate, the Governor of Tasmania, in Hobart in October 1917. In 1932 a photograph of Cherry was unveiled at the headquarters of the 26th AIF at Dinnerley, Brisbane.

Percy Herbert Cherry was born in Murradoc, Drysdale, Victoria, Australia, on 4 June 1895. He was the son of Elizabeth and John G. Cherry. When he was seven years old the family moved to Tasmania and took over an apple orchard, and young Cherry became an expert apple picker along the way. On one occasion he won a competition by filling thirty-five cases of apples in only an hour, and at a fruit show in Launceston he won a championship which had not been bettered by the time of his death in March 1917. Cherry attended Cradoc State School, near Hobart, where he remained until 1908 when his education was continued by private tuition. He later became a complete all-rounder. He was a keen cadet, joining up in 1908, becoming a sergeant and later a second lieutenant; he used to drill cadets in four different districts. He was also a good shot: at the age of sixteen he won the President's Trophy, Gold Medal, for being the best shot at the rifle range at Franklin. He rowed with the Franklin rowing club, played cornet in the Franklin brass band and sang in the school choir; he was a multi-talented young man and was always willing to help in a good cause.

On the outbreak of war he entered Claremont Camp and quickly took up duties as drill instructor. On 5 March 1915 Cherry enlisted in the Australian

Imperial Forces and was posted to the 26th AIF Battalion. He qualified as an infantry officer but was still considered too young. His commanding officer at Claremont wrote in glowing terms of Cherry's devotion to duty, honesty and truthfulness. Cherry became QMS and left Tasmania for Gallipoli, where he served from September 1915 until he was wounded on 1 December. He was evacuated to Egypt and, owing to a shortage of officers, he was commissioned as a second lieutenant on 9 December the same year. By March he had completed a machine-gun course and was posted to the 7th Machine-Gun Company. He served with the company in France and on 5 August 1916 he was badly wounded at Pozières. He had been sniping at a German officer and at one point the two men fired simultaneously and were both wounded, the German fatally. Cherry went up to him and the German asked Cherry to arrange for some letters to be censored and posted. Cherry readily agreed. He was Mentioned in Despatches at around this time and was also promoted to lieutenant. On recovering from his wounds he was appointed as an adjutant to a camp at Wareham, but managed to be transferred to his battalion in France as a captain with C Company, 26th AIF, in December 1916.

The battalion was involved in the fighting around the village of Warlencourt in March 1917 and took part in an attack on the German lines known as Malt Trench. The wire had not been adequately cut by the artillery, but Cherry managed to find a small break in it. Once through the gap he charged two enemy machine-guns and managed to capture both of them, turning one of them on the enemy. Cherry was wounded by this time. The enemy found themselves caught between Cherry's party and the company on the left. In the end the Germans left the trench positions and fled to the rear. It was this action that gained Cherry an

MC, which was announced on the same day as his VC, though he would not have known about either award. His medals are with the Australian War Memorial in Canberra.

Cherry's grave at Quéant Road Cemetery
(Photo: Donald Jennings)

F.M.W. HARVEY

Guyencourt, France, 27 March

Harvey, a drawing by Francis M.L. Barthropp

The Canadian Expeditionary Force went to Europe in 1915 and fought in the trenches during the autumn and winter of 1915/16. The Canadian brigade to which Lt Frederick Harvey belonged was withdrawn from the line for training and in March 1917 the Lord Strathcona's Horse were serving with XV Corps north of Péronne on the Somme. Other cavalry units in the brigade included the Royal Canadian Dragoons, the Fort Garry Horse and the Royal Canadian Horse Artillery, along with a machine-gun squadron and a field ambulance.[*]

On 24 March the brigade was ordered to form a front that was to extend for 12 miles with Nurlu in its centre. This village (on today's D917 road) is east of the Canal du Nord and south of Equancourt. The orders were for the cavalry to advance beyond the British infantry positions. By evening the Dragoons were occupying former enemy positions, including the woods to the south-west of Liéramont. The Fort Garry Horse had captured the villages of Etricourt and Ytres to the north-west. In the afternoon of the next day the Fort Garrys captured two more woods and launched an attack on a third and more strongly held wood. This clearance was carried out at the gallop and had the effect of emptying the wood of the enemy. This was the first time in two years of warfare that the cavalry had ridden successfully at a position strongly held by rifles and machine-guns.

On the following day the Lord Strathconas were ordered to capture a wood south of Equancourt and the village itself, to the north and south of the railway line. The wood was taken and the enemy were driven back into the village. The Lord Strathconas dismounted, advanced on foot and captured the village at the point of the bayonet. At the same time the Fort Garry Horse, attacking from a northerly direction, captured their objectives, despite machine-gun fire.

[*] The writer is indebted to the book *Thirty Canadian VCs* for much of the following information.

During the evening of 26 March and the morning of the 27th the Dragoons occupied Longavesnes and Liéramont; they then handed the defence of the former over to the infantry, while remaining themselves in Liéramont. The next targets were the village of Guyencourt and Saulcourt. The Fort Garrys and the Lord Strathconas attacked in the evening of the 27th, but a heavy snow-storm delayed the beginning of the attack until 5.15 p.m. Visibility was adequate and the Fort Garrys galloped forwards to Hill 140; there they established two machine-guns in commanding positions. They then went around the hill to Grebaussart Wood, Jean Copse and Chauffeurs Wood, and managed to post three more machine-guns. Other squadrons from the brigade rode straight at the village of Saulcourt and reached its outskirts. Canadian machine-gunners caught the retiring German infantry. The Lord Strathconas moved on to a ridge on the left side of Guyencourt and, on reaching the north-west corner of the village, they were able to take some shelter in the lee of its walls.

It was at this point that Harvey won his VC. He was in command of the leading troop (Second Troop, C Squadron) and rode well to the front of his men. His citation, gazetted on 8 June 1917, tells what happened:

During an attack by his regiment on a village, a party of the enemy ran forward to a wired trench just in front of the village, and opened rapid fire and machine-gun fire at a very close range, causing heavy casualties in the leading troop. At this critical moment, when the enemy showed no intention whatever of retiring, and fire was still intense, Lt Harvey, who was in command of the leading troops, ran forward well ahead of his men and dashed at the trench, skilfully manned, jumped the wire, shot the machine-gunner and captured the gun. His most courageous act undoubtedly had a decisive effect on the success of the operations.

Not surprisingly, the German machine-gunner was overwhelmed with the speed of events and did not live long. The trench was captured and the village of Guyencourt fell to the Lord Strathconas.

Harvey was at first awarded a DSO by Sir Douglas Haig and for two weeks wore the ribbon. Then he received the news that it had been made up to the nation's highest honour and he was decorated with the VC by the King at Buckingham Palace on 21 July. About a year later Harvey again distinguished himself when Brig.-Gen. Seely of the Canadian Cavalry Brigade instructed him to reconnoitre Fontaine-sous-Montdidier. In a brilliant manoeuvre he attacked and captured the village, a few miles to the south of Moreuil. Shortly afterwards, on 30 March 1918, he won the MC when involved with Lt Gordon Flowerdew, also of Lord Strathcona's Horse, at the Bois de Moreuil. Flowerdew was mortally wounded in a cavalry charge and died the next day. Flowerdew's VC citation reads as follows:

In the attack, by his fearless leading, he overcame the resistance of the enemy, although the latter were in greatly superior numbers. He engaged many of the enemy single-handed and, although wounded and suffering from considerable loss of blood, continued to fight his way forward until he effected a junction with another mounted party, thus contributing in a great degree to the success of the attack . . .

Harvey was awarded his MC on 10 July 1919 by the King.

Frederick Maurice Watson Harvey was born in Athboy, Co. Meath in Ireland, on 1 September 1888. He was one of seven brothers born to the Revd and Mrs Alfred Harvey. He attended the Portora Royal School at Enniskillen and Ellesmere College. As a young man he excelled as a rugby footballer, and was also proficient in boxing and athletics. At one time he lived for a short period in Dublin at 8 Woodstock Gardens, and played rugby for the Dublin team called the Wanderers, and also for Ireland. Other VC holders who played for the Wanderers team included Robert Johnston and Thomas Crean.

Harvey moved to Canada in 1908 and lived for three years in Fort Macleod, Alberta. He enlisted in the Canadian Mounted Rifles at Fort Macleod in 1915, was commissioned in 1916 and went overseas with the Rifles. Soon he was transferred to the Lord Strathcona's Horse. This regiment had been raised during the Boer War and originally consisted mainly of recruits from the Royal Northwest Mounted Police. The regiment distinguished itself during the South African War and afterwards became a permanent part of the Canadian Militia.

Harvey married Winifred Lillian Patterson in 1914. She was a daughter of Superintendent Patterson of the Royal Northwest Mounted Police and had been born on the family farm. She went to England during the First World War, following her husband there, and worked in an ammunition factory. When the war was over Harvey trained for a time as a physical education instructor and in 1927 was sent to Kingston, Ontario. In 1938 he was made a lieutenant-colonel and took command of the Lord Strathcona's Horse; as commanding officer he was responsible for A Squadron at Winnipeg and B Squadron in Calgary. During this pre-war period he went to England for a six-month course for senior officers at Sheerness. Soon after the Second World War began he was promoted to brigadier and on 5 November 1940 he was appointed District Officer commanding Military District Number 13, one of the most important Canadian military commands. During this time his wife lived again in Britain, helping with the wounded.

It was in 1943 that Harvey 'blotted his copybook' and upset a great number of people when he was quoted in the press as being severely critical of teaching methods, Canadian home life and of boys themselves. The young men they had grown into were seemingly 'selfish and lacking in Canadian ideals'. With hindsight, Harvey may have been correct with his criticism but, nevertheless, it seemed to be an inappropriate time to state such views. In 1944 Harvey went to Britain for a two-and-a-half month tour of the Canadian Army and returned to Canada with many ideas for training, which he used in his command at Currie Barracks. In 1945 Harvey's only son, Lt. Dennis Harvey, was killed in action in northern Europe. In December Harvey retired from the Army and a large dinner dance was organized as a tribute to the popular officer. In 1956 he was a member of the Canadian contingent to the VC review at Hyde Park. Harvey was Honorary Colonel of the Lord Strathcona's Horse from 1958 to 1966. In 1968 he led a contingent of 109 men to Ottawa for a wreath-laying ceremony on Remembrance Day.

Harvey was described by Lt-Col. Ian McNabb of the Lord Strathcona's Horse in the following way:

> He came here an immigrant, married locally, went to war and came back a hero. He has really been the father of the regiment. He was an excellent example of officer-like qualities, had a tremendous sense of humour and loyalty to the military.

Harvey was a tall man, quiet but also very determined, and always seeking perfection in his command. Being a soldier was his career, but horses were his hobby and he often served as a judge of hunter and jumper divisions. His wife, too, shared his love of horses. After he retired from the Army Harvey travelled to Australia, New Zealand and Ireland, as well as to Britain, attending various horse shows or races.

Harvey died on 24 August 1980 at the age of ninety-one and a service was held at St Stephen's (Anglican) Church on 25 August followed by burial at Union Cemetery, Fort Macleod, Alberta. He had lived in Calgary for a very long time, the home of the Lord Strathcona's Horse, and for the last eighteen months of his life he lived at Trinity Lodge, llll Glenmore Trail, Calgary. A service of full military honours was held at St Stephen's on 13 September and at the parade ground at Sarcee Barracks a service was held in driving rain in front of 150 people. The service included a riderless horse with a pair of riding boots reversed in the stirrups to symbolize a fallen soldier and alongside marched a troop of brass-helmeted soldiers dressed in scarlet tunics with lances at their sides. Other soldiers carried the colours of the regiment. The pipes and drums of the Calgary Highlanders were on parade and an eleven-gun salute was fired. Harvey's wife Winifred, who was born two years after her husband, lived until 9 August 1989.

Frederick Harvey's grave

Harvey's name is commemorated in Calgary where a barracks is named after him. His medals, including the CBE and Croix de Guerre (French), are not publicly held.

J.C. JENSEN
Noreuil, France, 2 April

Noreuil was one of seven villages that Gen. Gough of the Fifth Army directed to be captured on 2 April 1917. Noreuil was one of the outpost villages and about 1½ miles to the north-east was the German-held Drocourt–Quéant Line, which was a continuation of the Hindenburg Line. Although the planned Battle of Arras was only a week away, the only outpost village defending the Hindenburg Line that had fallen to the Allies so far was the village of Lagnicourt. Until these outpost villages were captured it would be difficult for the Allies to make a proper assault on the new German defence line.

The attack on Noreuil was planned for 2 April and was to begin at 5.15 a.m. The 13th Brigade of the 4th Australian Division was to capture the village by surrounding it. The 50th (South Australia) Battalion was to move up from the south-east and the 51st (Western Australia) Battalion was to move past the village to the north. The middle flanks of the two battalions would then rest on two converging roads. On reaching the village the 50th Battalion would swing round and move forwards on the flank of the 51st Battalion to a point between 800 yards and 1,000 yards to the east of the village, on the road to Bullecourt. Noreuil was also to be 'mopped up'.

When the attack began the 50th Battalion began to advance from Lagnicourt towards Noreuil along a road that went downhill; the barrage that accompanied them was poor and was later described as 'too thin and rather slow'. The enemy had established well-defended barricades on the sunken roads that led down to the village which the Australians proceeded to bypass as these positions were later to be dealt with by Stokes mortars and bombers. However, when the Australians reached the German cemetery at the south-west corner of the village a German platoon behind a barricade began to cause many casualties. A bombing party was assigned to deal with it.

To the right the advance was also being checked on the Noreuil–Lagnicourt road. Thus a gap began to open up between the right and central companies. Stokes mortars and grenades were not achieving their objective and at one point it looked as though the right company might have to leave pockets of German defenders unattended to in its rear. The plan to surround the village was always likely to be a bit of a gamble – success would depend entirely on the total annihilation of the German defenders. However, it was at this point that Sgt J. Wilson DCM, in charge of the central company, detached his bombers to deal with the rear pockets. Pte Jorgan Jensen was in charge of this bombing party and won the VC when, with five comrades, he:

> attacked a barricade behind which were about 45 of the enemy and a machine-gun. One of his party shot the gunner, and Private Jensen, single-handed, rushed the post and threw in a bomb. He had still a bomb in one hand, but taking another from his pocket with the other hand, he drew the pin with his teeth, and by threatening the enemy with two bombs and by telling them that they were surrounded, he induced them to surrender. Private Jensen then sent one of his prisoners to order a neighbouring enemy party to surrender, which they did. The latter party were then fired on in ignorance of their surrender by another party of our troops, whereupon Private Jensen, utterly regardless of personal danger, stood on the barricade and waved his helmet, causing firing to cease, and sent his prisoners back to our lines. Private Jensen's conduct throughout was marked by extraordinary bravery and determination. (*London Gazette*, 8 June 1917)

Most members of the 50th Battalion had managed to swing past and the dangerous gap between the two companies was closed up by Lewis gunners who were firing from the hip as they advanced and therefore managed to keep the Germans' heads down.

On balance, the 51st Battalion had an easier role to play and went to ground in a newly dug shallow trench 250 yards short of the Lagnicourt–Bullecourt road. The men who had been ordered to 'mop up' in Noreuil were far too few and many of them became casualties or were taken prisoner. Confused fighting continued. However, the Germans were not planning to hold on to the village and during the night the Lagnicourt–Bullecourt road was abandoned, enabling the Australians to take over the remaining enemy positions immediately and later the village. The price for the capture of Noreuil was high: the 13th Brigade had casualties of 600 men, more than twice as many of those of the enemy, who were members of the 119th Reserve Regiment.

Jorgan Christian Jensen was born on 15 January 1891 at Løgstør, Ålborg, Denmark. He became a sailor and, though Danish by birth, he took Australian citizenship in 1914. When first in Adelaide he worked as a labourer and was at one time employed on a River Murray steamer.

He enlisted on 23 March 1915 with the service number 2389. He was posted to the 10th (South Australia) Battalion as one of its reinforcements. He was sent to Gallipoli and joined his battalion there on 28 September. After the evacuation from the Gallipoli Peninsula various new units were made from the survivors of the units which served there. In February 1916 some 500 men from the 10th Battalion were transferred to help form the 50th Battalion. Although Jensen served in France with the 10th Battalion and was wounded in August, he was transferred to the 50th Battalion in January 1917. The 50th Battalion left the area of Eaucourt l'Abbaye on 27 March and went through Bapaume to the front line south of Vaulx, arriving on the 28th. After the fighting at Noreuil the battalion went back to Vaulx in reserve, where it acted as a support battalion.

Jensen was promoted to the rank of lance corporal on 4 April 1917 and three months later he was made a corporal. He was decorated by the King in the Buckingham Palace forecourt on 21 July 1917. On 5 November 1917 he was made up to sergeant. He was severely wounded on one occasion during a patrol near Villers-Bretonneux on 5 May 1918. He spent a long time in hospital and eventually returned to Australia for demobilization in Adelaide on 12 December 1918. He died on 31 May 1922 at the age of thirty-one in St Peter's, Adelaide, where he had lived since his demobilization. He was still troubled by his war injuries. He left a widow, Katey, who later remarried. His VC passed into the ownership of Mrs L.M. Winger of Largsbay, South Africa, who was his stepdaughter.

In February 1987 Jensen's VC was handed over to the Australian War Memorial in Canberra at a special ceremony attended by Queen Margrethe II of Denmark. Jensen's decoration, along with his other medals, was later displayed in the Australian War Memorial's Hall of Valour.

F.W. LUMSDEN
Francilly, France, 3/4 April

In early April 1917 the Anglo-French boundary lay south-west of the German-held town of St Quentin. There was not only a strong defence line on the town's western side, but also, immediately behind the town on the eastern side, there was a second line of defence and a couple of miles further east was the Hindenburg Line itself.

On 2 April the 14th Brigade (32nd Division) was involved in action in front of St Quentin in the region of the villages of Holnon and Selency, east of Holnon Wood. Owing to fading light it was decided to change the brigade orders to allow it to move up during the night to a position between Savy and Savy Wood. The wood was to the north-east of the village and was close to a railway line.

The attack was made from these positions next morning at 5.00 a.m. and it was directed almost due northwards with its left on the Savy–Holnon road. The attack succeeded. On the right, to the south-east of Francilly-Selency, a village between Savy and Holnon, the 2nd Manchesters (14th Brigade) had managed to capture six enemy guns which had been firing over open sights. They had lost fifty men as a result of enemy fire from a quarry which they also captured. (This quarry was part of Manchester Redoubt which became famous in March 1918 when the 16th Manchesters made a stand there and their commanding officer, Lt-Col. Wilfrith Elstob, won the VC.)

In very quick time the villages of Francilly-Selency, Selency and Holnon were captured and contact with the 61st Division was made to the north of Holnon Wood. The wood was large, being a mile wide from west to east and 2 miles from north to south. It had been surrounded rather than taken by a frontal attack, but the Germans did manage to evacuate it and all the guns except for one captured battery.

The retrieval of the guns was the task allotted to Maj. Frederick Lumsden of the Royal Marine Artillery. He was put in charge of a party from the 15th Highland Light Infantry (32nd Division) and ordered to bring in the six German field guns that had been captured and had been left dug-in. The guns were in fact

around 300 yards in advance of the British troops and as a result of this the enemy kept their lost guns under very heavy fire. Lumsden set out to try to bring them into British lines and somehow he managed to lead four artillery teams and a party of infantry through the German barrage. One of these teams was knocked out and Lumsden left the remaining three teams in covered positions. He then led the infantry through extremely heavy rifle, machine-gun and shrapnel fire to the captured guns. By his inspiring example he succeeded in sending back two teams with guns before going back through the barrage with the team for the third gun. He returned to the remaining guns to wait for further teams and despite fierce rifle fire took two more guns to safety. The German infantry then stormed through the British infantry and managed to blow up the breach of the remaining gun, thus disabling it. Lumsden then went back, drove the enemy off, hooked the wrecked gun to a team and took it back to safety.

Lumsden was decorated by the King at Buckingham Palace on 21 July 1917 (*London Gazette*, 8 June 1917) with his VC and the DSO, together with three bars to the DSO. At the same public investiture about twenty other men were awarded their VCs. The *Daily Sketch* wrote of the event: 'Such a galaxy of heroes has not assembled before.'

The citation of his VC was as follows:

For most conspicuous bravery, determination and devotion to duty. Six enemy field guns having been captured, it was necessary to leave them in dug-in positions, 300 yards in advance of the position held by our troops. The enemy kept the captured guns under heavy fire. Major Lumsden undertook the duty of bringing the guns into our lines. In order to effect this, he personally led four artillery teams and a party of infantry through the hostile barrage. As one of these teams sustained casualties, he left the remaining teams in a covered position, and through very heavy rifle, machine-gun and shrapnel fire, led the infantry to the guns. By force of example and inspiring energy he succeeded in sending back two teams with guns, going through the barrage with the teams for the third gun. He then returned to the guns to await further teams, and these he succeeded in attaching to two of the three remaining guns, despite rifle fire, which had become intense at short range, and removed the guns to safety. By this time the enemy, in considerable strength, had driven through the infantry covering points, and blown up the breach of the remaining gun. Major Lumsden then returned, drove off the enemy, attached the gun to a team and got it away.

On 2 August 1917 Lumsden was wounded when commanding the 14th Infantry Brigade; however, he did not leave his post for long. On 25 October 1917 he was promoted to lieutenant-colonel. On 1 June 1918 he was appointed CB, but it is possible that he never knew of the award as he was killed two days later at Blairville, a village a few miles south of Arras, during the night of 3 June 1918. A fellow officer wrote this account of Lumsden's death:

He was up in the front line trenches of his brigade when there was an alarm of an attack. Instantly the general, 'in his usual fearless manner', walked up to see for himself where the trouble was. He exposed himself without regard to his own safety, thinking only of that of his men, and in doing so he was shot through the head by a rifle bullet and killed instantly. He was without exception the finest leader I have ever met. I have worked with him now for a year and a half, and we all feel his loss to the division is irreparable. All the honours he gained during the last year even, in every case were won over and over again, as there was hardly a day when he did not expose himself to danger in a way which was an example to all. His brigade became the finest in the division, solely owing to his fine influence and example. I can't express to you how much every soldier in this division admired him, and how much we all feel his loss.

Lumsden was buried in Berles New Military Cemetery, Plot III, Row D, Grave 1. The cemetery is in the north-west part of the village where the La Cauchie Road joins with the Bailleulmont Road.

Lumsden's grave in Berles New Military Cemetery (Photo: Donald Jennings)

35

Frederick William Lumsden was born in Fyzabad, India, on 14 December 1872. He was a son of John James Foote Lumsden (Indian Civil Service) and his wife, Marguerite. As a boy he was sent to England and was educated at Bristol Grammar School in Gloucestershire, where he was a boarder in Mr Browne's House with his two brothers. He left for Sandhurst in 1888. He was commissioned as a second lieutenant in the Royal Marine Artillery on 1 September 1890 and he became a lieutenant ten months later on 1 July 1891. On 17 December 1894 he embarked in the battleship HMS *Nile* and served in the Mediterranean and on Malta, where the ship was recommissioned. On 20 January 1896 he joined the garrison on Ascension Island where he served for four years. He was promoted to captain on 16 June 1897. He then served on the battleship HMS *Resolution* in the Channel Squadron in June 1900. On 10 October in the following year he transferred to HMS *Formidable* and served in the Mediterranean for a second time. At Hythe he distinguished himself in a musketry course when he passed out second among 120 officers. Lumsden also specialized in signalling and gunnery. He graduated at Staff College in 1907 and then studied German for six months, gaining a first class interpreter's certificate in the language. On 4 June 1910 he was appointed GSO 2 in Singapore, a position that he held for four years. He was given the brevet of major on 1 September 1911 and was promoted to major in the RMA on 10 June 1913, before returning to England on 3 June 1914.

Lumsden married the second daughter of the late Lt.-Gen. Harward RA and Mary Harward. He began his service in the First World War when he went to France in command of No. 1 Howitzer Battery RMA on 15 February 1915 and proceeded to St Omer. The brigade set up their 15 inch howitzer at Locre from where it fired its first round on 6 March. For the first part of April the gun went through an experimental stage. On the 19th Lumsden was appointed Commander of the Royal Marine Artillery Howitzer Brigade, now with four guns. During his command Nos 1, 2 and 4 guns all saw action, No. 2 at Fezenberg Ridge on 8–13 May and Nos 1 and 4 at Aubers Ridge on 9 May and also at Festubert on 15–25 May. Lumsden was then given a staff appointment, becoming GSO 3 on 27 July 1915 with HQ First Army. He was made brigade major on 21 November 1915, Staff Officer Canadian Corps Troops from 27 November to 26 January 1916, and GSO 2 V Corps on 27 January 1916; later on he served with the headquarters staff of 32nd Division. He was made brevet lieutenant-colonel on 1 January 1917, when he was temporary CO of the 17th Highland Light Infantry (3rd Glasgow Battalion) from 5 April until 12 April. Lumsden was promoted to brigadier-general of 14th Brigade, 32nd Division, on 12 April 1917. His first DSO was gazetted on 1 January 1917. The citation in the *London Gazette* on 11 May said of his bar:

He made a reconnaissance of the enemy's position, moving over open ground under very heavy fire and bringing back most valuable information. He rendered invaluable services throughout the operations.

A second bar, also dated 11 May, stated:

For conspicuous gallantry and devotion to duty when in charge of a strong reconnaissance party. He carried out the task allotted to him with conspicuous success and skilfully withdrew his party at a critical time. His conduct, rapid decision and good judgement saved many casualties.

The *London Gazette Supplement* of 22 April 1918 wrote of the award of his third bar:

During a large raid on the enemy's lines, in which a portion of his brigade formed the left of the attack, he first superintended the assembly in our advanced line, and then advanced to two successive objectives, encouraging the men. At the first objective, where, owing to heavy machine-gun and rifle fire and the exhaustion of the troops, there was some slight hesitation, he led the assault on a group of seven 'pill-boxes', and after their capture made a valuable reconnaissance of the enemy's position. He then supervised the withdrawal, forming a covering party, with which he himself withdrew, being the last to leave the enemy's position. Such coolness, determination to succeed, and absolute disregard of danger not only ensured the success of the operation but afforded a magnificent example to all ranks, the value of which can hardly be exaggerated.

He thus had gained four DSOs in the First World War and he was also Mentioned in Despatches four times. By the time he was killed, at the age of forty-five, Lumsden was certainly one of the most highly decorated soldiers in the British Army. His decorations included the VC, CB, DSO and 3 Bars, and the Croix de Guerre (Belgian). He was also awarded the 1914–15 Star. He is commemorated at the Old Garrison Church in Eastney, Portsmouth, Hampshire. His portrait hangs on the wall of the Great Hall at his former school, Bristol Grammar, and his name appears on the school memorial board. Angell James VC attended the same school.

Lumsden's wife Mary lived on until 25 January 1933 when she died in Rustington, Sussex. She was normally a resident of Hampton Court Palace but died at the home of her daughter Violet and son-in-law, Maj. A.K. North. After Maj. North, Violet's first husband, died Violet married Capt. C.A. Fowke MC, who was also a member of the Ox & Bucks Regiment as North had been. North had been blinded during the Battle of the Somme. Violet died on 23 December 1948 near Southampton, leaving a son who followed the military tradition of the family; he was Frederick Lumsden North, a former major who lived in Hove.

Lumsden's medals are held by the Royal Marines. On 23 July 1920 a memorial was dedicated at St Andrew's Church, Eastney Barracks, Hampshire. After the service the congregation moved to the parade ground where a memorial to Brig.-Gen. F.W. Lumsden was unveiled: a bust of Lumsden in bronze relief. Two sides of the memorial show his awards and his appointments as Howitzer Brigade Commander; the other two depict him as a member of the Staff and finally as commander of a brigade of infantry.

The Lumsden memorial in its original position at Eastney Barracks

W. GOSLING

Near Arras, France, 5 April

On 5 April 1917 645112 Sgt William Gosling, who had previously joined the 3rd Wessex Brigade, RFA (Territorial Force), won his VC when he was serving in a trench mortar battery attached to the 51st Highland Division near Arras. Acting as Battery Sergeant, he was in charge of a heavy trench mortar.

When a faulty cartridge fell only 10 yards from the mortar Sgt Gosling leapt out of his trench and lifted the nose of the bomb, which had already sunk into the ground. He quickly unscrewed the fuse and threw it to the ground, where it exploded. This prompt action saved the lives of the detachment.

In the *Daily Sketch* of 13 July 1964 an article was published under the name of Charles Fowler of Sevenoaks, with the heading 'A VC is won on the toss of a coin'. Although the event had occurred forty-seven years before, Fowler claimed to remember it as if it had happened the day before.

> It was then that I learned that the heroism for which men win medals is not always the act of a split-second impulse which galvanises the spirit and the body into some frenzy of daring.
>
> There were six of us, forming what the men called 'The Suicide Club'. Our job in that particular sector of the front line near Arras was to set up our heavy mortar in front of our trench – some ten yards out into 'no-man's-land.'
>
> Now and then Jerry fired off a brilliant white flare or two. Then you ducked. For at the slightest hint of movement Jerry would open up with heavy machine-guns.
>
> And Jerry was only 300 yards away.
>
> Our task was to remind him with our sixty-pound 'Flying Pigs' from our mortar that we were uncomfortably close too.
>
> But it was fair game for both sides. The flash of our mortar in the night pinpointed our firing position. That's how we collected our tag 'The Suicide Club'.
>
> That night we had fired off four 'pigs'. Tip 'em from the shoulder and scatter – that was the drill. Boom! And off went 60lb of best bacon for Fritz.

Then it happened.

The fifth 'pig' was faulty. It landed no more than ten yards from where we had flung ourselves down. We waited to be blasted by our own hand.

But the shell just stuck there – big, black, menacing in the churned-up mud.

We were saved – for the moment – by a faulty fuse.

But there could be no more firing from our position while the shell sat there, liable to go up in a blinding blast at the smallest vibration.

So we had to dismantle the gun, camouflage it and get it back to the trench.

Tomorrow would be another night.

And that was to be when Sergeant Bill Gosling, 3rd Wessex Brigade, Royal Field Artillery, Territorial Force, came up with his 'ammo' carrying lads.

'No use bringing that up,' said my sergeant as they arrived. 'We've dropped a "short" there.'

'Then you'll have to do something about it, mate,' answered Sergeant Gosling.

'Not me, mate,' said my sergeant. 'It can stay there as far as I'm concerned.'

And then, as if it were just a matter of who should stand the drinks at the local back in Blighty, I remember Gosling's words: 'Come on, let's toss for it.'

He tossed the coin. And he lost. Coolly and calmly Gosling went over the top.

Gone – into the night. Into the no-man's-land of mud and the dead.

And that night, only yards from where the rest of us huddled, Sergeant Gosling won his dice with death.

'Where have you been?' asked an officer who had joined us, when five minutes later Sergeant Gosling's face reappeared from the no-man's-land side of the parapet.

'Sir!' said Gosling. And he gave an account of himself.

The citation for Sergeant Gosling's Victoria Cross speaks for itself . . .

Sergeant Gosling lived until February 12, 1945. Today, I salute the memory of a comrade who saved my life and the lives of our detachment.

A coin was tossed. And a medal was won. For valour.

Gosling's VC was gazetted on 14 June 1917 with the following citation:

For most conspicuous bravery when in charge of a heavy trench mortar. Owing to a faulty cartridge the bomb, after discharge, fell 10 yards from the mortar. Sgt Gosling sprang out, lifted the nose of the bomb, which had sunk into the ground, where it immediately exploded. This very gallant and prompt action undoubtedly saved the lives of the whole detachment.

❖❖❖

William Gosling was born on 15 August 1892 at Wanborough, a village near Swindon in Wiltshire. However, he was to spend most of his life in the small town of Wroughton, a few miles to the south-west of his birthplace. Like many of his generation, he went abroad to Canada as a young man. He stayed with an uncle in Winnipeg. He worked on grain silos, for a short time was a fireman on the Canadian Pacific Railway and then became a lumberjack. He returned at the outbreak of war, having given up a good job and paid for his return ticket. On his return home he joined the Swindon detachment of the Wessex Brigade.

After Gosling's VC was gazetted, a special meeting of Wroughton Parish Council took place in order to discuss appointing a committee to arrange a welcome home and presentation. He was thus presented with a cheque for £130 5s 6d and a silver salver by the Mayor of Swindon in Swindon Town Hall in August. Later in the year he was also presented with an illuminated address.

After the war Gosling was discharged in 1919 and took a job as a tractor driver in Essex. In 1920 he attended the garden party at Buckingham Palace for holders of the VC. He was also invited to the unveiling of the Cenotaph on 11 November 1920 and the service of the burial of the Unknown Soldier at Westminster Abbey.

While working in Essex he met his wife to be, Martha, and after their marriage they had two children: a boy and a girl. Gosling was given a tip-off from his brother Bert about the tenancy of Wharf Farm in Wroughton; he applied for the tenancy and was successful. He began farming at Summerhouse Farm in 1920, where he remained until his death. His son is still living in Wroughton at the time of writing (1997). William Gosling was vice-president of the Wroughton branch of the British Legion until 1933 and between the First and Second World Wars he also ran a shop in the town. During the Second World War he was a major in the Home Guard; he was also a parish councillor and a Freemason for the last few years of his life. He died on 12 February 1945 as a result of very high blood pressure, nearly three

Summerhouse Farm, Wroughton

Gosling's shop in the High Street, Wroughton, c. 1935

Wroughton British Legion Air Rifle and Darts Club, 1948/9. Gosling is on the left of the front row

months before the Second World War ended. He was fifty-two and had been ill for about a year and was confined to bed for the last six weeks of his life. The farm no longer exists and the land was sold. A home for the elderly now occupies the position that was formerly Gosling's home. He is buried in Wroughton Cemetery which is adjacent to the parish church of St John the Baptist and St Helen at the top of a hill with spectacular views of Wiltshire. When the author visited it last, in 1997, the grave had no flowers on it and the lettering had weathered badly. Rather surprisingly, there is no plaque to his memory in the church.

Gosling's medals are not publicly held.

Gosling's grave in St John the Baptist's churchyard, Wroughton (Photo: Donald Jennings)

J.E. NEWLAND

Near Bapaume, France, 7/9 and 15 April

In early April 1917 three villages stood between the southern section of the 1st Anzac Corps and the German Hindenburg Line to which the enemy had been gradually moving back since 25 February.

The 1st Australian Division was given the task of capturing these villages, which were still in enemy hands. Hermies was the objective of the 1st Brigade and Boursies, a village close to Louverval on the Bapaume–Cambrai road, was the objective of the 12th Battalion of the 3rd Brigade. Capt. John Newland, in command of A Company and also of a platoon of B Company, was allotted the task of capturing Boursies. He was to win the VC for his actions at Boursies, around Bullecourt and at the village of Lagnicourt over the next eight days.

The left company advanced at 4.00 a.m. on 7 April down the valley between the Louverval and Boursies spurs and came under heavy fire. Newland's right company was gathered at a position which was north of the Bapaume–Boursies–Cambrai road and north-east of Lagnicourt; they were protected by a bank in the valley. As the Australians made their way towards Boursies, Newland organized an attack on a ruined mill – an important objective on the north side of the road which was around 400 yards from the village. He led a bombing attack against this mill and his company came under heavy shell fire. As his men neared the outskirts of Boursies the German machine-guns began to take their toll and the Australians suffered heavy casualties. Despite this, however, Newland managed to rally his men and was himself one of the first to reach the mill and secure a foothold. During the next night his company, which had occupied German positions, was holding a commanding position when it was heavily counter-attacked. Newland, together with Sgt John Whittle, succeeded in breaking up the enemy and recapturing the position with the judicious use of reserves. On 10 April the exhausted 12th Battalion was relieved by the 11th Battalion. The capture of Boursies had cost 240 casualties, including 70 killed or missing.

On the eve of 14 April the 12th Battalion relieved the 9th Battalion at Lagnicourt, where at around dawn the next day the Germans launched a very strong counter-attack against the front of the 1st Australian Division. Newland phoned battalion headquarters and informed them that the Germans were attacking his left (in the direction of Noreuil) and at the same time the enemy was also attacking the front of his own company. As if that weren't enough, the enemy was also attacking from the rear and the Australians were heavily outnumbered. Newland managed once more to drive off the attack that was coming from two directions by falling back to a sunken road where his men took up positions and fought back. At this time Sgt Whittle attacked and captured a German machine-gun with which the enemy was about to enfilade the whole position. Battalion headquaters sent up every spare man as reinforcements; indeed, troops from the 9th Battalion came up to assist at the double. Newland continued to fend off the attackers and soon the reinforcements themselves counter-attacked, restoring the threatened line. It was Newland's bravery, which set such an example, that encouraged his men to hold out and to fight back against a determined foe. During the fighting the 12th Battalion suffered 125 casualties with 66 killed or missing.

Newland's VC was gazetted on 8 June 1917 and he was decorated by the King at Buckingham Palace on 21 July 1917, one of five Australians decorated that day. He was thirty-six when he won the VC, which was considered quite old at the time. His citation for the deeds he performed were gazetted as follows:

For most conspicuous bravery and devotion to duty in the face of heavy odds on three separate occasions. On the first occasion he organized an attack by his company on a most important objective, and led personally, under heavy fire, a bombing attack. He then rallied his company, which had suffered heavy casualties, and he was one of the first to reach the objective. On the following night his company, holding the captured position, was heavily counter-attacked. By personal exertion, utter disregard of fire and judicious use of reserves, he succeeded in dispersing the enemy and regaining the position. On a subsequent occasion, when the company on his left was overpowered and his own company attacked from the rear, he drove off a combined attack which had developed from these directions. These attacks were renewed three or four times, and it was Capt. Newland's tenacity and disregard for his own safety that encouraged the men to hold out. The stand made by this officer was of the greatest importance, and produced far-reaching results.

In 1918 Newland returned to Australia. He continued to serve as an officer of the permanent forces, and was in the Army in one capacity or another for almost the rest of his life.

John Ernest Newland was born in Highton, Geelong, Victoria, Australia, on 22 August 1881. He entered the Army in 1899 and served throughout the Boer War. Between the South African War and the First World War Newland served in the artillery, first in Victoria and then in Tasmania. He became a permanent member of the Instructional Staff of the Commonwealth Military Forces. He was based in Tasmania for some years before joining the Australian Imperial Forces on 22 August 1914. He joined the 12th AIF (South Australia, Western Australia and Tasmania) Battalion, nicknamed 'The Blue and Whites', where he was regimental quartermaster sergeant. On 10 December the battalion arrived in Egypt and later sailed for the Gallipoli Peninsula, where it received its baptism of fire on 25 April 1915 at Anzac Cove. In the days after the Gallipoli landings, Newland was wounded but not before his organizational skills were noticed, and he was given a commission as a second lieutenant on 22 May. On 15 October he was promoted to full lieutenant. After the evacuation from the Gallipoli Peninsula, Newland served in Egypt as transport officer.

Newland's battalion left for France where it arrived in early April and he was then promoted to captain and made adjutant. The battalion was originally based in the Fleurbaix sector, then in July it moved to the Somme and in August Newland was Mentioned in Despatches for conspicuous courage and powers of leadership at Pozières during the Battle of the Somme, where the battalion lost 375 casualties in helping to capture this important village.

The battalion was also in action at Mouquet Farm. On 8 August Newland ceased to be the adjutant and became the commander of A Company. The battalion moved to Albert and then to Sausage Valley in preparation for the attack on Mouquet Farm, a ruined complex around 600 yards in front of their front line. The farm was a large building with extensive cellars, which were connected to enemy strongpoints and were part of the defences of the village of Thiepval. The position was finally taken in the period 26–27 September 1916 by the British 11th (Northern) Division. Newland's battalion lost heavily in the fighting and was relieved before being sent northwards to Hill 60 in the Ypres Salient. After moving to several camps they found themselves back on the Somme at the end of October at Bernafay Wood, where they lived in 'extreme discomfort'.

After the Germans began to withdraw to the Hindenburg Line in the region of Le Barque on 25 February 1917 the 12th and 9th Australian Battalions were ordered to attack the village of Le Barque on the 26th. Newland was put in charge of A Company, which was connected with the drive on Bapaume. On 26 February he was wounded for a second time but was fit enough to rejoin the battalion shortly before the April fighting. In May he was involved in the Bullecourt fighting, but was wounded again.

Newland served in the Army between the First and Second World Wars and was attached to the Australian Instructional Corps from 1 May 1930, holding various appointments including adjutant and quartermaster to the 8th, 4th and 12th Battalions, area officer and recruiting officer. In 1935 he was awarded the Meritorious Service Medal. When Newland left the permanent military forces he was made assistant commissioner of the Red Cross in the Northern Territories. In the early part of the Second World War he was seconded for duties at the headquarters of the 4th Division where he served as quartermaster instructor. In May 1940 Newland took his final appointment as quartermaster at A Branch Army Headquarters in Melbourne. After giving up his position with the Red Cross he had been living in retirement. He was placed on the Retired List on 22 August 1941 with the honorary rank of lieutenant-colonel.

Newland died after a seizure at 54 Brigg Street, Caulfield, Victoria, on 19 March 1949 and his funeral took place with full military honours at Bathurst's Chapel, Glenhuntly Road, Elsternwick, before burial at East Brighton Cemetery on 21 March. His gravestone is of the type used by the Commonwealth War Graves Commission. He was survived by his wife, Vivienne Heather, who lived on for another twenty-eight years, and a daughter, Dawn Robinson, who was living in Melbourne in 1984. Originally she owned her father's medals, but they are now in the Australian War Memorial Collection at Canberra.

Newland's grave at Brighton General Cemetery, Melbourne, Australia (Photo: Bob Archer)

T. BRYAN

Near Arras, France, 9 April

L/Cpl Thomas Bryan won the VC when serving with the 25th Battalion (2nd Tyneside Irish) Northumberland Fusiliers (34th Division) on 9 April 1917, the first day of the Battle of Arras. Six divisions were involved in an ambitious plan to reach the town of Cambrai and subsequently to roll up the rear of the German Army in this sector.

To the north of Arras and the River Scarpe were the 9th, 34th and 51st (Highland) Divisions of XVII Corps. The 34th Division was in front of the village of Roclincourt and its 103rd Brigade was to keep in touch with its neighbouring unit the 51st (Highland) Division. The two battalions leading the 103rd (Tyneside Irish) Brigade's advance were the 24th and the 25th Battalions of the Northumberland Fusiliers. They ran into trouble as soon as they reached the German front line. Heavy machine-gun fire held up their advance and the commander of the 24th Battalion was killed.

Capt. Huntly and L/Cpl Bryan went forward to see what they could do and when Huntly was killed Bryan went on alone. He virtually saved the day when he knocked out a troublesome German machine-gun crew, allowing the division to move forward in relative safety towards the German second line. Bryan's actions had far-reaching consequences. The machine-gun had enjoyed an excellent field of fire and caught the advance as the soldiers came over a ridge around 300 yards to its front.

Bryan's VC was presented to him by the King at the ground of Newcastle United Football Club, St James's Park, Newcastle, on 17 June 1917 when the King and Queen were on a visit to the north of England. The event received a lot of press coverage and *The Times* of 18 June wrote a report under the banner headline 'Heroes of the North':

The informality of the visit of the King and Queen to the North was broken to-day by a simple and moving ceremony at St James's Park, the ground of Newcastle United Football Club. The King held an open-air investiture at which more than a hundred soldiers received awards for valour in the field. The scene was impressive as it was picturesque. Behind the men in uniform spread a small irregular band of women and men who were in mourning, widows and fathers of dead heroes. This thin black line had the effect of a band of crepe drawn across a stirring picture, but the picture did not lose its power by the reminder that gallantry is often linked with death. Ranged around the green grass were 50,000 people gathered to see the ceremony.

The Royal party arrived on the ground at half-past twelve after attending service at the Cathedral. The King wore the uniform of a field-marshal and the Queen was dressed in light grey. They were greeted with deep and prolonged cheering as they walked to the platform . . . then came a mighty cheer as Lance-Corporal Thomas Bryan of the Northumberland Fusiliers, stepped on to the platform. . . .

L/Cpl Bryan receiving his VC from the King

The *Newcastle Daily Chronicle* of 18 June takes up the story:

Lance-Corporal Bryan stood erect and faced his Sovereign as the brave action which had won him such fame was recited in ringing tones by Major-General Montgomery. This was the only instance in which the gallantry of a man was fully told, and their Majesties were as interested as others on and about the dais. Lance-Corporal Bryan had the Victoria Cross pinned upon his breast, and the King engaged in conversation with him, and then cordially shook him by the hand. The gallant non-commissioned officer saluted and left the Royal presence wreathed in smiles and to the accompaniment of renewed thunderous applause.

However, only a couple of weeks later, at the end of June, and despite attending the ceremonies in Newcastle in mid-June, Bryan was in hospital at Alnwick in Northumberland. He had been badly wounded in the right arm when winning his VC, but was said to be making progress. While in the hospital he spoke of his deed in the following way:

On this great day, our lads were held up by a machine-gun, which was so well hidden that we couldn't check its deadly work. I therefore made up my mind to put a stop to its activities, so creeping over the top, I went from shell hole to shell hole in 'no-man's-land'. I crept into a communication trench, which was held by the enemy, where I came across three Germans. This was at six o'clock in the morning. These men were so surprised that they surrendered without showing any fight, and two of them presented me with their watches. I thereupon sent them down to the base with some of my men. I then went forward again, along with Sgt-Maj. Foster of the Fifth and ran across a German officer, who also seemed delighted. Not many minutes afterwards I surprised another Hun, who gave up his arms as meekly as a lamb. An hour later I was still prowling round, trying to fix the German machine-gun team, but was unable to spot it. Whilst working my way along, I was spotted by one of the enemy, who, letting drive, caught me in the right arm.

Following this bit of hard luck, I decided to try rapid fire on the place where I thought the machine-gun was placed, and on this being carried out, we found to our glee that the gun which had been spitting forth its fire of death barked no more. Two of the gun team tried to get away under our rapid fire, but I shot both of them.

I stayed with my comrades until half-past one mid-day, after which I left to have my wound dressed. With the machine-gun and its gunners destroyed, it was now an easy matter for our boys to advance.

His citation was gazetted on 8 June 1917 and was as follows:

For most conspicuous bravery during an attack. Although wounded, this Non-commissioned Officer went forward alone, with a view to silencing a machine-gun which was inflicting much damage. He worked up most skilfully along a communication trench, approached the gun from behind, disabled it and killed two of the team as they were abandoning the gun. As this machine-gun had been a serious obstacle in the advance to the second objective, the results obtained by L/Cpl Bryan's gallant action were very far-reaching.

Together with Pte Sykes of the 27th (S) Northumberland Fusiliers Bryan was given a civic reception in the city of Newcastle on 27 July 1917. They were both met by the Lord Mayor and were presented with war loans to the value of £100, a clock and a wallet of treasury notes. This reception took place at the Empire Theatre and the two men also signed the City's Visitors' Book in the Town Hall.

Thomas Bryan was born on 21 January 1882 at Lye in Worcestershire. His home was at Castleford, about 10 miles south-east of Leeds in Yorkshire. He was a miner and a good rugby player, and was a member of the Castleford Northern Union team. In 1903 he married Sarah and they had four children: two sons and two daughters. Bryan enlisted at Castleford on 11 April 1915 and joined the Reserve Battalion of the Northumberland Fusiliers in the same month. Eight months later he was drafted to a service battalion in France, the 25th (2nd Tyneside Irish) Northumberland Fusiliers. In April the following year he fractured his ankle and was sent home to recuperate. He was promoted to lance corporal on 26 March 1917 and nearly eighteen months later, on 16 September 1918, he was discharged. In 1920 he attended the garden party at Buckingham Palace for winners of the VC, and on 11 November 1920 he attended the dedication ceremony at the Cenotaph in Whitehall and the burial of the Unknown Soldier in Westminster Abbey.

He had returned to mining at Castleford and in 1926 he moved to Norton near Doncaster. From 1929 his home address was 11 Fairfield Villas, Norton, but in 1934 Bryan moved again, this time to Doncaster to work at the Arksey Colliery. At some point he had to give up his job as a miner because his war wounds, together with the effects of being gassed, were taking their toll on his health. He subsequently spent six weeks at a sanatorium. In all he had been wounded three times during the war, and 'his life after the war had become one of great hardship and struggle'.

Bryan died at 44 Askearn Road, Bentley, near Doncaster, on 13 October 1945 and was buried in the local cemetery four days later after a funeral service at St Peter's Church with full military honours. His first commanding officer in Newcastle, Lt-Col. Elwyn Jones, attended the funeral. Members of the local branch of the British Legion, of which Bryan was a member, provided bearers and the Gordon Highlanders provided a firing party. His gravestone is of the standard Commonwealth War Graves type. He left a widow, two married daughters and two sons.

Bryan's medals were sold at Christie's on 25 July 1989 for £9,800 and are not publicly held. In addition to the VC, they include the 1914–15 Star, BWM, VM and George VI Coronation Medal.

Bryan's grave at Arksey Cemetery, Doncaster (Photo: Donald Jennings)

H. CATOR
Near Arras, France, 9 April

The 7th East Surreys were part of the 37th Brigade of the 12th Division of the Third Army; their objective on 9 April 1917 was the strongly held village of Monchy-le-Preux. At the opening of the Battle of Arras the 12th Division had the 3rd Division on its right and the 15th on its left. At 5.30 a.m. the battalion moved out from St Sauveur in front of Arras towards the German first line, code-named Black Line by the British. The advance took place about 500 yards to the north of the Arras–Cambrai road. The battalion was then to support the Royal West Kents in their attack on the Blue Line. However, the enemy defences were made up of a series of small redoubts, and machine-guns and snipers were firing heavily from the direction of the Blue Line.

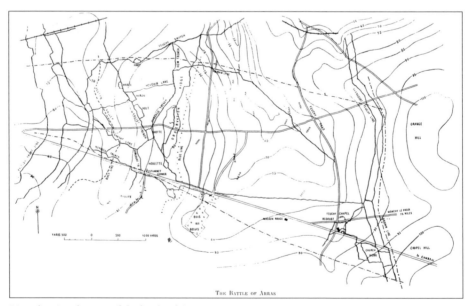

Map showing the area of the battle of Arras

This was when G/8/5190 Sgt Harry Cator took a hand and moved up towards Hangest Trench (between the Black and Blue Lines) accompanied by a colleague; they became a target for almost every German soldier in the vicinity and after a very short time, Cator's colleague was shot dead. Cator picked up a Lewis gun and some drums of ammunition on the way and continued to the German trench. He reached the German parapet where he rested his gun and enfiladed the German machine-gunners occupying a small redoubt; some fell dead and others quickly surrendered. Cator then covered the advance of the battalion bombers, who were able to clear the trench and to take 100 men prisoner and capture five machine-guns.

Three days later Cator's luck ran out when a shell burst close to him and shattered his jaw, and he was sent home for surgery. When he heard that he had won the VC he was in the Beaufort Hospital in Bristol, where he underwent several serious operations. However, when he died nearly fifty years later he still had shell fragments in his shoulder.

Cator's VC was gazetted on 8 June 1917:

For most conspicuous bravery and devotion to duty. Whilst consolidating the first-line captured system his platoon suffered severe casualties from hostile machine-gun and rifle fire. In full view of the enemy and under heavy fire, Sgt Cator with one man advanced across the open to attack the hostile machine-gun. The man accompanying him was killed after going a short distance, but Sgt Cator continued on, and picking up a Lewis gun and some drums on his way, succeeded in reaching the northern end of the hostile trench. Meanwhile, one of our bombing parties was seen to be held up by a machine-gun. Sgt Cator took up a position from which he sighted this gun, and killed the entire team and the officer, whose papers he brought in. He continued to hold that end of the trench with the Lewis gun with such effect that the bombing squad was enabled to work along, the result being that 100 prisoners and five machine-guns were captured.

Cator was presented with his VC on 21 July 1917 by the King at Buckingham Palace. Among the congratulatory letters that Cator received was the following, which was anonymous:

Allow me to offer you my heartiest congratulations in winning the most coveted honour it is possible to win. I am certain no one in the Army has been more entitled to the Victoria Cross than yourself. Every time you have been in the line you have always inspired the men by your personal bravery, and when you were with me in B and C Company, I always knew things were all right when you were about. I was extremely sorry to hear you were wounded, and trust that it is not of a serious nature. I must conclude now, trusting you are going on very nicely and sincerely hoping you will be spared to come through safely and live long to enjoy the proud distinction of the Victoria Cross.

Another extract reads:

. . . tells me you are giving Sgt Cator, VC, a welcome home and presenting him with a watch to commemorate his earning the Victoria Cross. Sgt Cator is a man who has done persistent good work throughout the war, and all of us in the Brigade are justly proud of him. In offering him your congratulations, will you add mine and the whole of my brigade. The act for which he was awarded the Victoria Cross was magnificent. It is only deeds of simply colossal heroism which get the Victoria Cross, so you can imagine how proud and delighted [we were] when Sgt Cator was awarded the most coveted honour.

The *Surrey Comet* also wrote up the deeds of the Great Yarmouth man:

The gallant East Surreys have covered themselves with glory in this war, and have a record for the highest honours of which any regiment might be proud, and which few, if any, can rival. To its proud Honours' Roll there is added now a fifth Victoria Cross, won by Sgt Harry Cator, for the performance of deeds of gallantry which will fill everyone who reads of them with admiration. Sgt Cator is a New Army man and his home is in Great Yarmouth. . . . This is indeed a glorious episode, for which the name and fame of Sgt Harry of the East Surreys will be enshrined for ever in the hearts of his countrymen and in the annals of the regiment, which is proud of him. Performed in contempt of death and of great odds, such deeds are as if inspired. Was ever the Victoria Cross bestowed more worthily?

Cator was welcomed back to Drayton, Norwich, in March 1918 and he and his wife were met off the train at Drayton by a four-wheeled wagon with a Union Jack wrapped round its front. The wagon was drawn by a team of 'lusty human horses' to the village green, where Cator was presented with the Military Medal and Croix de Guerre by the mayor.

Harry Cator, the son of Robert and Laura Cator, was born in Drayton, Norwich, on 24 January 1894. He was educated at Drayton School. He began his working life with the Midland & Great Northern Railway and at one time he was a railway porter at the station at Thursford, near Fakenham, Norfolk. Cator married Rose Alice, only daughter of W.J. Morriss of Great Yarmouth on 2 September 1914. The ceremony took place at St Nicholas' Church in Yarmouth and the day after the wedding Cator promptly enlisted and joined the East Surrey Regiment at Great Yarmouth. He was posted to the 7th (Service) Battalion. In 1915 he went to France and became a Sergeant, and he won the Military Medal on 3 July 1916 for his 'fine work' during the battle of Albert, when he helped to rescue from no-man's-land thirty-six men who had become caught up in German barbed wire. He subsequently declined the offer of a commission. After the war Cator worked for a time as a Norwich postman from February 1929 and was later with the Unemployment Assistance Board.

When the Second World War began Cator joined up and became a captain quartermaster to the 6th Battalion Norfolk Home Guard in 1942; he was later posted to a transit camp at Newhaven as quartermaster. Subsequently, he was commandant of a prisoner-of-war camp at Cranwich. He learnt to speak German and he must have been well liked by some of the German prisoners in his camp as after the war some of them kept in touch with him by letter. To quote just one of these letters:

It took a long time before I realized that you taught us a lesson worth remembering. In a world full of passion you demonstrated an independent unanimity. You showed all understanding of the former emergency that we, the prisoners of Hostel Cranwich, have all reason to be thankful to you. I think you gave us an example how our attitude should be. This letter is to give you our sincere thanks.

After the war Cator returned to his civilian job and joined the Territorial Army, something that he had wanted to do before the war. In January 1951 he retired from the 284th (1st East Anglian) HAA Regiment, RA (TA).

Cator was a keen gardener and was very fond of birds; he was also a mountaineer and he and his wife used to follow this hobby until he was well into his fifties. He was a prominent member of the local British Legion and used to act as standard-bearer at the annual ceremonies in Drayton. He also attended meetings of the Old Comrades' Association as well as very many of the VC/GC Association functions.

In 1964 Cator and his wife celebrated their golden wedding anniversary. They lived at 36 Allen's Lane, Sprowston, in a house since demolished. Harry died of pneumonia in Norfolk and Norwich Hospital on 7 April 1966. His funeral took place six days later at the parish church of St Mary's and St Margaret's, Sprowston. The service was taken by Revd A.A. Coldwells and a bugler sounded the Last Post and Reveille at the graveside. Five officers from the Queen's (the regiment that had absorbed the East Surreys and other regiments) attended the service, as did Col. H.B.L. Smith. The Freemasons were also represented, as Cator had once been a past master and provincial

Harry Cator in his postman's uniform, with his wife and son

No. 36 Allens Lane, Sprowston (now demolished)

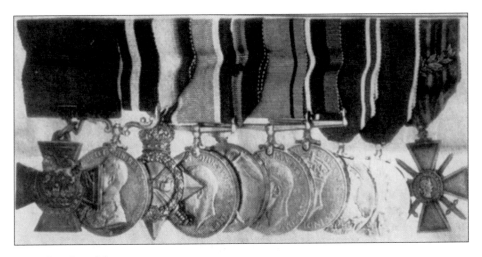

Harry Cator's medals

sword-bearer. His wife Rose and a son outlived him, and Rose died on 20 January 1969. Cator also left two grandsons and one granddaughter.

In his will Cator left £2,990 13s gross and £2,895 13s net. His medals were sold, possibly a bit too hurriedly, in order to pay for a home for Rose. On 6 June 1985 Cator's medals, which included the Croix de Guerre with bronze palm, 1914–15 Star, BWM, VM with a Mention in Despatches emblem, DM, 1939–45 War Medal, George VI Coronation Medal and Queen Elizabeth II Coronation Medal, were sold at Spinks, together with two photographs and some newspaper cuttings, and the lot fetched £10,500. Eleven years later, the collection was sold by Spinks again and this time they fetched £28,500. The medals are not publicly held.

Cator's grave at Sprowston (Photo: John Bolton)

T.J.B. KENNY

Hermies, France, 9 April

Before 9 April 1917 the German front line curved in a south-easterly direction from Lagnicourt towards the Canal du Nord and Havrincourt Wood. One of the outpost villages that the line took in was the village of Hermies to the south of the Bapaume–Cambrai road.

The 2nd and 3rd Australian Battalions of the 1st Brigade (1st Division) were ordered to capture Hermies, despite the fact that the village of Boursies to the north had not been taken the day before according to the original plan. The 2nd Battalion was to attack from the north-west, while the 3rd Battalion was to approach from the south-west, from the direction of Haplincourt. The operation to capture Hermies turned out to be a very successful one for the 1st Brigade, as the Australian soldiers literally left no one alive; the Germans were either killed or taken prisoner.

The attack began at 4.15 a.m. on 9 April – prematurely, owing to a flare that created a small fire in some straw and alerted the enemy. The west side of the village saw fierce fighting, but by 6.00 a.m. the village was in Australian hands and by this time 200 prisoners had already been taken. However, a rumour that the adjoining village of Demicourt, to the north-east, had already been vacated by the enemy turned out to be false and as a result the attacking force suffered heavy losses caused by German machine-gun fire. By midday Demicourt, along with Boursies, had fallen to the Australians. By the end of the day Australian casualties totalled 649.

It was during this fighting that Pte Thomas Kenny won his VC as a member of No. 15 Platoon of D Company. His platoon had been ordered to go around the village to reach a sunken road beyond it, in the direction of Demicourt. Once there, they were to dig in under the shelter of a ridge. As at Lagnicourt, the Australians were to engage the enemy as they were driven out of the village. However, the platoon suffered casualties on the way to their objective, and by the time they considered that they had reached their objective they were down to eight or nine men. For about twenty minutes they were able to shoot down the enemy as they retreated from Hermies and during a brief respite they moved to a nearby chalk pit; the move proved with disastrous, as they were then sprayed with machine-gun fire while they attempted to dig in. The Australians were pinned down and their situation became desperate. Their colleagues, emerging from Hermies, were unaware of the trap that they were entering and suffered severely from machine-gun fire from the strongpoint.

This was when Kenny decided to take direct action and, asking for covering fire from two of his mates, he leapt up from his position in the chalk pit and rushed towards the enemy post, throwing bombs as he went. His first bomb fell short of the strongpoint, but the second bomb fell close to the enemy position which was in a pit. His third bomb was on target and his platoon colleagues crawled forward in support. On reaching the position they found Kenny already in charge and the Germans who remained alive were taken prisoner. Soon after, Kenny's company established a ring of defence posts with the assistance of other companies emerging from the village and thus Hermies was sealed off and the enemy could no longer escape towards Demicourt. Altogether the fighting lasted for about an hour. By the end of this day the Australians had captured not only Hermies but also had Demicourt and Boursies.

Kenny was immediately promoted to lance corporal and repatriated to England as he was suffering severely from trench foot. According to *Reveille* of October 1930, this is how Kenny learnt that he had won the VC:

After getting out of hospital and obtaining leave, he was on a bus in Victoria Street, reading a copy of the *Daily Mail* when he remarked to a cobber: 'Why, here is the name of my old school pal, killed in action, and in the next column is someone with the same name as mine who has been awarded the VC!' He did not realise then that the name of the VC winner was his own. Near Victoria Station he was stopped by an Australian military policeman, who examined his pass in the usual way, and on ascertaining his name, told him he was wanted at Australian Headquarters, Horseferry Road.

Kenny thought his leave was going to be cancelled for some reason, and as he had completed plans for a trip to Ireland, he cleared out of London to Richmond, where he met Lt Benson, of the 54th Battalion, who had enlisted with him in 1915. Benson nearly shook his hand off, and made even his large frame shake with the pats he gave Kenny on the back. Next morning Benson and the now enlightened Kenny reported at Horseferry Road where, between congratulations, he collected £20 on a badly over-drawn paybook.

Kenny's VC was gazetted on 8 June 1917 and he received his medal from the King at Buckingham Palace on 21 July. The citation was as follows:

For most conspicuous bravery and devotion to duty when his platoon was held up by an enemy strongpoint and severe casualties prevented progress.

Private Kenny, under very heavy fire at close range, dashed alone towards the enemy's position, killed one man in advance of the strongpoint who endeavoured to bar his way. He then bombed the position, captured the gun crew, all of whom he had wounded, killed an officer who showed fight, and seized the gun. Private Kenny's gallant action enabled his platoon to occupy the position, which was of great local importance.

Kenny rejoined the 2nd Battalion a year later at Hazebrouck on 26 July 1918. He was wounded a month later on 26 August near the town of Méteren. A few weeks later he was invalided to Australia with the new rank of corporal. His wounds were obviously quite serious. On 9 October he arrived home to a hero's welcome and turned down the offer of joining the Military Police, but for a while did help out with recruiting. He was discharged two months later on 12 December.

Thomas James Bede Kenny was born in Paddington, Sydney, New South Wales, Australia, on 29 September 1896. He was the son of a butcher, Austin James Kenny, from Auckland, New Zealand, and his wife, Mary Christina. Bede Kenny was educated at the Christian Brothers' College in Waverley. His first job was as a chemist's assistant, but three months later, on 23 August 1915, he enlisted in the Australian Army; his number was 4195. This was during the Gallipoli campaign and Kenny went overseas with the 13th Reinforcements, 2nd Battalion. After arriving in Egypt he served with the 54th Battalion before joining the 2nd Battalion on 27 February 1916. The following month saw him in France, where he took part in the fight for the village of Pozières on the Somme in July 1916 as a member of the battalion bombing platoon. However, after the fight for Pozières, this bombing group ceased to exist as a separate entity and Kenny joined D Company under Lt G.N. Mann MC, with whom he was at Hermies in April 1917.

When the war was over Kenny was discharged with the rank of sergeant in 1918 and he then trained to be a travelling representative for the firm of Clifford Love & Co. of New South Wales. However, he left that job and joined the *Sunday Times* in Sydney, but shortly afterwards he joined Penfolds Wines Ltd as a traveller. On 29 September 1927 he married Kathleen Dorothy Buckley, a florist, at St Mary's Cathedral, and they had three children. Like many of his Army colleagues, Kenny suffered throughout his life from the effects of trench foot and in addition the war had left him partially deaf. He lost two of his children to rheumatic fever, his eldest daughter dying in 1943 at the age of thirteen.

Kenny always turned out for Anzac Day marches in April; he used to present a striking figure as he was at least 6 ft 4 in tall and weighed 20 stone! He died at Concord Repatriation Hospital in Sydney on 15 April 1943, aged fifty-five, and was buried in Botany Bay Cemetery, Sydney, where there is a plaque to his memory in the garden of remembrance. His pall-bearers were military policemen, which was ironic as he had no liking for the breed. He had always been a devout Catholic and was a man of great character and often took part in pranks. He left a widow and a daughter, who both attended the VC review in Hyde Park in 1956. In 1957 the Bede Kenny Memorial Ward was opened at Wentworth Private Hospital in Randwick, which was intended to provide beds for ex-serviceman. According to *They Dared Mightily*:

> This unusual memorial was conceived by the Eastern Metropolitan District Council of Sub-branches of the R.S.S. & A.I.L.A., which several years earlier had established the Roy McDonald Hospital Trust, designed to ensure that old soldiers in the council's area of Sydney would not be denied proper hospitalisation, if ineligible for repatriation treatment and down on their luck financially.

Kenny's wife lived on until 23 March 1970.

In 1985 Kenny's family put his medals up for sale with a reserve price of 40,000 Australian dollars and they fetched 46,000 Australian dollars at Spinks in Australia on 24 November 1985. At present they are in the collection of the Australian War Memorial in Canberra.

Thomas Kenny's memorial, Eastern Suburbs Memorial Park, Sydney, Australia (Photo: Harold O'Keefe)

T.W. MACDOWELL

Vimy Ridge, France, 9 April

Despite the Canadian Army's eventual success in capturing Vimy Ridge in April 1917, the fighting did not initially go according to plan in all parts of the operation. For example, the 4th Canadian Division, on the extreme left of the line, had the shortest distance to cover but the hardest task to accomplish. Indeed, the high ground known as the 'Pimple' to the north of Hill 145 and south of the Souchez River did not fall to the Canadians until the 12th.

Capt. Thain MacDowell was OC B Company of the 38th (Ottawa) Battalion, which had been reorganized after the Somme battle of 1916 and had moved up to the Vimy Trenches soon after Christmas Day. Thus the battalion was positioned in front of the Ridge for three months before April 1917. On the 9th, and with two runners, Ptes Hay and Kebus, MacDowell was looking for a suitable place for use as a command post. Ahead of them were some German machine-guns and MacDowell promptly knocked out one of the machine-gunners by throwing a bomb which killed him. The German's colleague decided to make himself scarce and disappeared into a hole in the ground. The Canadians quickly followed up the vanishing German and discovered that they had come across a major enemy fortification.

MacDowell called on the 'unseen' to surrender and there was no reply, so with his two runners posted at the two entrances, he began to investigate. He descended a stairway. After fifty-two steps he rounded a corner into the main room of the underground fortress and was suddenly confronted by a large group of the enemy. He quickly decided on a course of action and called back up the steps using a voice full of great authority to 'supposed' colleagues waiting at the head of the tunnel. The Germans were seemingly convinced and immediately raised their hands in a gesture of mass surrender; they even piled arms in the centre of the room when ordered to do so. MacDowell was then able to send them out of the tunnel in small groups of about ten at a time.

Very soon the process stopped and MacDowell later found out that his runners had shot the first ten men to emerge as they did not know that they were not armed. MacDowell sternly commanded the remaining Germans to move out of the tunnel and they did so in groups of twelve. At one point things looked bad for MacDowell when a German snatched up a rifle, but he did not have time to use it. It turned out that the men were mainly Prussian Guardsmen, and the final total came to seventy-seven prisoners.

Although he was wounded in the hand, MacDowell continued to hold the position for five days and had to endure some heavy shellfire. Eventually he was relieved by his battalion.

MacDowell received his VC, together with an earlier-won DSO, during the investiture in the forecourt of Buckingham Palace on 21 July 1917. The King was accompanied by Field Marshal the Duke of Connaught and Admiral the Marquess of Milford Haven. The parade was witnessed by the Queen, along with Princess Mary, from the balcony in front of the palace. All told, twenty-three men received the VC at this investiture and eight families received the medal as the recipient's next of kin.

In the *War Diary* for the 38th Canadian Infantry Battalion of 9 April are four reports that were written by MacDowell; three of them are reproduced below. He gave his location as 'Dug-out approximately Junction of Cyrus and Clutch' and the first report was timed at 8.00 a.m. The reports were addressed to the Commanding Officer of the 38th Battalion.

Objective reached but I am afraid is not fully consolidated. The mud is very bad and our machine-guns are filled with mud. I have about 15 men near here and can see others around and am getting them in hand slowly. Could D Company come up in support if they have stopped in the front line? The runner with your message for A Company has just come in and says he cannot find any of A Company officers. I don't know where my officers and men are but I am getting them together. There is not an NCO here. I have one machine-gunner here but he has lost his cocking piece off the gun and the gun is covered with mud. The men's rifles are a mess of mud and they are cleaning them. My three runners and I came to what I had selected previously as my company headquarters. We chucked a few bombs down and then came down. The dug-out is 75 feet down and is very large. We explored it and sent out 75 prisoners and two officers. This is not exaggerated as I counted them myself. We had to send them out in batches of 12 so they would not see how few men we were. I am afraid that a few of them got back as I caught one man shooting one of our men after he had given himself up. He did not last long, and I am afraid we could not take any back except a few who were good dodgers as the men chased them back with rifle shots. The dug-out is a very large one and will hold a couple of hundred. The men were 11th Regiment R.I.R. I cannot give you an estimate of our casualties but believe they are severe. Will send one back as soon as possible.

There is a field of fire of 400 yards or more and if there were a couple of brigade machine-guns we could keep them back easily as the ground is almost impassable – horrible mess. There are lots of dead Bosche, and he evidently held well. I can see 72nd men on our left. The 78th have gone through after we reached here. The barrage was good, but men did not keep close to it enough and held back. There are no shovels found yet so we will just get our rifles ready. No wire is here and cannot spare men to send out. The line is obliterated. Nothing but shell holes, so wire couldn't be of much use. Men are pretty well under pressure. There is no artillery officer left here. His fire is very weak and suppose he is going back. This is all I can think of at present. Please excuse writing.

The next report was at 10.30 a.m.:

Have been along the line. The dug-out we occupy is at the corner of Cyrus and Baby. It has three entrances well distant from each other and will hold easily 250 men at the very least. The tunnel leads down towards our line which I did not explore. It has a winch and cable for hoisting. There are only 15 men with me of whom two are stretcher-bearers. The rifles are one mass of mud. I have two Lewis guns and only four pans. Both guns are out of action on account of the mud. We have a very few bombs as we had to bomb several dug-outs.

The 78th I have no trace of but there are two German machine-guns just in front of us. They are firing constantly. Snipers are also busy. We cannot locate them as yet. The 72nd are on the left and seem to be spread along fairly well. The ground is practicably impassable. His aeroplanes came over and saw a few of my men at the dug-out entrance and now we are getting his heavies from our right on his left.

I have no subalterns or NCOs and unless I get a few more men with serviceable rifles I have to admit it, we may be driven out. Three of my men are wounded as it is so I might as well tell you the facts of the case.

The runner has just come in with your message. We are in BABY trench slightly to the right of Cyrus. I was wrong in my other message as to my location. I had just arrived. I will try to get in touch with Major Howland D Coy. 38th but don't like to leave here as I mentioned above have not an officer or NCO. There are a lot of wounded out of here as I can see by the rifles standing up. The heavy battery from the right is working very well at present.

Then at 2.45 p.m.:

While exploring this dug-out Kelty and I discovered a large store of what we believe to be explosives in a room. There is also an old sap leading away down underground in the direction of No. 7 Crater. This was explored down to a car but no further as it may be wired. Would you get in touch with brigade as quickly as possible and ask that a party of either 176th or 182nd Tunnelling Company come up and explore these. We have cut all wires for fear of possible destructive posts. The dug-out has three entries and will accommodate easily 250 or 300 men with the sap to spare. It is 75 feet underground and very comfortable. The cigars are very choice and my supply of Perrier water is very large.

If I might I would suggest that you take it up with the brigade that this place be occupied in strength as there is a great field of fire to the north and west as well as to the east. This you see makes it a very strong supporting post to our left flank and I would strongly recommend that it ought to be occupied by brigade machine-guns. I cannot locate them. I have no NCOs to leave in charge here to look out for them myself.

It is quite all right for any one to come up here. They are firing at us all the time with their heavy guns from the south-east but I have no casualties to report since coming in here except being half scared to death myself by a 'big brute'.

I cannot impress upon you too much the strength of the position and the value of it as a strong supporting point to the left flank by which they will undoubtedly make their counter-attack. Observation is good here on the side of Lens and other villages and battery positions can be seen. We have taken two machine-guns that I know of and a third and possibly a fourth will be taken to-night. This post was a machine-gun post and held by a machine-gun company. I believe they are Prussian Guards. All big strong men who came in last night. They had plenty of rations but we had a great time taking them prisoner.

It is a great story. My two runners Kebus and Hay did invaluable work in getting me out of the dug-out as we had to conceal the fact we were only three in number. I don't think they all got back though.

Please have these Engineers sent up at once to examine wire further as this is a great dug-out and should not be destroyed. I believe the sap runs into No. 7 Crater and might help in being an underground CT.

There are a large number of wounded in front of here, as I can see by the rifles stuck in the ground. We are using German rifles as ours are out of business. I now have three Lewis guns but only about 15 pans of ammunition. Kelty is here with me. I have no NCOs. Please point out the value of this as a supporting point on our left flank.

I cannot think of anything further. Tell Ken to come up for tea to-morrow if it is quiet. Sorry to hear of the CO and Hill and the others.

MacDowell's citation for his VC was gazetted on 8 June 1917 as follows:

For most conspicuous bravery and indomitable resolution in face of heavy machine-gun and shell fire. By his initiative and courage this officer, with the assistance of two runners, was enabled, in the face of great difficulties, to capture two machine-guns, besides two officers and seventy-five men. Although wounded in the hand, he continued for five days to hold the position gained, in spite of heavy shell fire, until eventually relieved by his battalion. By his bravery and prompt action he undoubtedly succeeded in rounding up a very strong enemy machine-gun post.

Thain Wendell MacDowell was born in Lachute, Quebec, Canada, on 16 September 1890. His parents were living at Carp, Ontario, but his mother went to her grandparents' home in Lachute for Thain's birth. His father was the Revd J.V. MacDowell and soon the family moved to Lyn, Ontario, where his father served as a Methodist minister until his death in 1894. The family consisted of four boys and one girl. After Mrs MacDowell remarried, the family moved into the home of her new husband in Maitland, Ontario. Thain grew up in the Brockville area and was educated at Maitland Public School, Brockville Collegiate Institute and Victoria College, University of Toronto, where he received his BA early on in the First World War. Soon after graduation he enlisted and was commissioned on 7 September 1914 in the 48th Battalion, but he transferred on 9 January 1915 to the 38th Battalion of the Canadian Expeditionary Force. After intensive training in London, Ontario, he was made up to captain on 1 August 1915 and embarked for Bermuda a week later. He trained in England for three months and arrived in France on 3 August 1916. On 18 November 1916 he won a DSO on the Somme near Petit Miraumont in an attack against Desire Trench and Desire Support Trench. 'He led his B Coy against the German trenches and, advancing to within throwing distance, he bombed three German machine-guns which had been holding up the advance. After severe hand-to-hand fighting he captured three officers and fifty men.' The following day he was wounded in action and returned to England.

By January 1917 he had recovered; he returned to his battalion and was promoted to major on 28 February. After winning his VC at Vimy Ridge in April he was invalided to England in July 1917 and received permission to return to Canada on sick leave. On 1 March 1918 he returned to England and worked until the end of the war at Headquarters, Overseas Military Forces of Canada, and the Canadian Training School. He was struck off the strength of the CEF on 14 October 1919 and in the same year he received an Hon. MA at the University of Toronto as the member of the university who had won the highest military honour during the war.

On 1 May 1920 he became lieutenant and brevet major with the Ottawa Regiment (the Duke of Cornwall's Own), and seven years later he was transferred to the Reserve of Officers. For five years, between 1923 and 1928, he acted as private secretary to the Minister of National Defence at Ottawa. Later he became interested in mining and worked as a director with a number of mining companies, making his base in Toronto where he lived. In 1921 he attended the VC Dinner in London and the similar dinner which took place in the House of Lords in 1929. In 1933 he was appointed Honorary Lieutenant Colonel, Frontenac Regiment. He also attended the 1956 VC/GC review in Hyde Park.

In 1937 and 1938 MacDowell had an impostor (not unusual for the holder of a VC), who paraded under 'false colours' in Sydney, Australia with a miniature medal of the VC. MacDowell himself has been described as a 'big burly Canadian' who later wore rimless spectacles. He was proficient at golf and during the Second World War he gave lectures to the Canadian Army.

MacDowell died at Nassau in the Bahamas on 28 March 1960 and was buried at Oakland Cemetery, Brockville, Ontario, Canada. On 2 September 1970 a plaque to his memory was unveiled by MacDowell's widow at the intersection of Maitland Road and Highway 2, Maitland. It was one of a series of plaques being erected by the Ontario Department of Public Records and Archives. It was dedicated by the Revd Vernon Macpherson, padre of the Brockville Rifles. This particular ceremony was sponsored and arranged by the Brockville Rifles, and Lt-Col. W.S. Watson acted as programme chairman. Various dignitaries attended the ceremony.

MacDowell's VC is owned by the University of Toronto Memorial Trust.

MacDowell's grave in Oakland Cemetery, Brockville, Ontario, Canada (Photo: Donald Jennings)

W.J. MILNE

Near Thélus, France, 9 April

Milne, a drawing by Francis M.L. Barthropp

By April 1917 Vimy Ridge had been in German hands for three years and during this time they had turned it into a seemingly impregnable position. In 1915 there was an attempt by the French to take the ridge which failed at a cost of 130,000 casualties, and a year later the British also made an unsuccessful assault. However, in the spring of 1917 a new attack was planned by the Allies to capture the important ridge, and extremely careful and elaborate plans were drawn up. These included an extension to the tunnels that ran towards the ridge which would give considerable protection to the attackers as they moved up to the front line. The Canadian Corps was assigned the task of taking the ridge.

On 9 April 1917, Easter Monday, the assault began at 5.30 a.m. in appalling conditions of sleet and snow. The advance began after a bombardment that had lasted for five days – representing a gun for every 8 yards over a 12 mile front. In front of Vimy, from right to left, were the four Canadian divisions numbered from 1 to 4, and we are concerned here with the role of the 16th Battalion of the 1st Division in the initial fighting.

The division's first objective was the German line known as Zwolle Graben (Black Line), which was close to the Arras–Lens road; it was also the last trench belonging to the German front line system. Once taken, the Canadians were to remain there for 40 minutes. The second line was the Zwischen Stellung (Red Line), where they were to remain for up to 3¼ hours before moving on to the third or Blue Line; here they were to stay for 1 hour 36 minutes. The fourth and final line to be captured was the Brown Line, which lay to the east of the main ridge and had belts of wire. Here, the barrage was to continue for 12 minutes, giving time for the Canadians to catch up with it. The next enemy position after the village of Thélus was Farbus, in front of which was a wood where the enemy had a considerable number of gun positions.

As it happened, the 1st Division was extremely successful and reached its final objective, the Brown Line, at about 1.10 p.m. or nearly 7¾ hours after the attack began. It became quite clear that the effort put into the very detailed planning of the attack had paid off. The Canadians were well prepared and knew the ground. In addition, once the final objective was reached, it was clear that the enemy guns in Farbus Wood would be out of action.

No. 1 Company of the 16th Battalion had assembled and the men were able to complete their journey to the start line by use of the Bentata Tunnel, which was shellproof and thus allowed the troops considerable protection as they moved up towards the front line. By 4.20 a.m. on the 9th, at dawn, all companies were in position and 40 minutes later their flanking units were also in place, namely the 14th Battalion to the right and the 18th Battalion to the left. When the barrage ceased, the Canadians went forward over land which was full of mine craters blown by the French during their efforts to capture Vimy Ridge in 1915, as well as by the British and Germans in 1916. These craters were as much as 20 ft deep and had steep or greasy chalk sides down to 6 or 7 ft of slimy water. To add to this hazard, the enemy, who had been taking shelter from the Canadian barrage, now emerged and machine-gunners were waiting on the far lips of these craters. The attackers dashed forward in small groups, taking on some of these craters and quickly overcoming a few of them. However, other enemy machine-guns were also placed in zigzag positions and the Canadians were fired on from both the front and the flanks, and men kept falling. In addition, one German line had escaped the attention of the Canadian barrage and the Germans put up a stiff resistance before succumbing to the bayonet.

The right-hand company of the battalion became held up after the Visener Graben Line was taken, and from a position to their half-left an enemy machine-gun was causing many casualties. The dead from the 16th Battalion lay in front of this strongpoint and then a series of explosions could be heard in the direction of the enemy machine-gun position. This was the result of the actions of Pte William Milne, who had leapt from a shell hole close to the position while signalling his comrades to advance. He crawled on his hands and knees to within bombing distance of the machine-gun crew and with hand-grenades put the whole position out of action. Later he did the same for another enemy machine-gun point between the Black and Red Lines; concealed in a haystack near Terry Trench, this position was also holding up the advance. Sadly Milne was killed before the day's end.

The Black Line fell as planned and after a pause the advance continued towards the Red Line. It was at the Red Line that the enemy's morale began to give way despite the protection of deep dug-outs, and many of them turned and ran, a number being shot down as they did so. Once the Canadians had reached the Red Line they could see both to left and right just how successful the day had been and they moved forward over the previously impregnable ground as if they were on manoeuvres.

The men of the 16th Battalion were spectators for the rest of the day as they had reached their objective; their colleagues continued their advance and the 1st Brigade passed through them. By the end of the day the 1st Brigade had even reached the far side of Farbus village, a tremendous achievement.

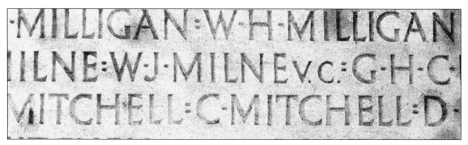

Milne's name on the Vimy Memorial to the Missing (Photo: Donald Jennings)

Milne was awarded a posthumous VC and his name is listed on the Vimy Memorial. His citation was gazetted on 8 June 1917:

For most conspicuous bravery and devotion to duty in attack. On approaching the first objective, Private Milne observed an enemy machine-gun firing on our advancing troops. Crawling on hands and knees, he succeeded in reaching the gun, killing the crew with bombs, and capturing the gun. On the line reforming, he again located a machine-gun in the support line, and stalking this second gun as he had done the first, he succeeded in putting the crew out of action and capturing the gun. His wonderful bravery and resource on these two occasions undoubtedly saved the lives of many of his comrades. Private Milne was killed shortly after capturing the second gun.

William Johnstone Milne was born at 8 Anderson Street in Cambusnethan, Lanark, in Scotland. In 1910 he emigrated to Canada and worked on the land in Saskatchewan. He enlisted (No. 427586) in Moose Jaw in September 1915 and embarked for England on 16 June 1916. He joined the 16th Battalion (Canadian Scottish) the next day in the trenches in the Ypres Salient. In August 1916 the 16th Battalion took over from the 1st Anzac Corps and became responsible for 3,000 yards of front line trench along Pozières Ridge. Milne's battalion took part in a joint attack with the 52nd and 49th Battalion on the Fabeck Graben Line on 4 September and a few weeks later they also took part in an attack on Regina Trench. This was the occasion when Piper Richardson won his VC. In late October the 16th Battalion, as part of the 1st Canadian Division, was relieved and went north to take over in the Vimy sector to the north of Arras.

Milne's medals became the property of his sister, Ellen Milne, who lived in Wishaw. They were later sold to a Scottish medal collector and subsequently purchased by a Canadian collector, Jack Stenabach. In July 1989 the medals, which included the VC, VM and WM together with the next-of-kin bronze plaque, were sold for 94,000 Canadian dollars.

E.W. SIFTON

Near Neuville-St-Vaast, France, 9 April

On 9 April 1917 the 18th (Western Ontario) Canadian Battalion of the 4th Brigade of the 2nd Canadian Division was opposite Hill 135 and the village of Thélus, which were their objectives for the day. On their right was the 16th Battalion and to their left was the 19th Battalion. At the beginning of the long-planned attack to capture Vimy Ridge the weather was very cold with a mixture of snow, sleet and driving rain. When the Canadian artillery barrage moved forward from the German first line, the 18th Battalion began their attack with a three-platoon frontage in four waves at 5.30 a.m. They had to face the tenacious Germans who in many cases had been sheltering in strong concrete dug-outs or underground fortresses, some of which were large enough to contain a whole unit.

L/Sgt Ellis W. Sifton was a member of C Company of the 18th Battalion on the right of the 4th Brigade. The German first line was quickly taken with very few casualties, but the Canadians were held up in the fight for possession of the second line. As they advanced, German machine-gunners enfiladed them and they began to suffer casualties. Two machine-guns in particular began to take a toll of the Canadians and several of Sifton's colleagues became casualties. He was the first to spot the position of one of these machine-gun nests and he leapt up and rushed the trench, quickly overcoming the enemy position. He used his bayonet, killing the crew and knocking over their gun; they were simply overwhelmed by the speed and ferocity of his attack. His colleagues quickly came to his aid and together they took on another party of Germans who were rapidly advancing down a trench. Sifton even resorted to using his rifle as a club. However, one wounded German who had survived took careful aim at Sifton and shot him dead.

Sifton was awarded a posthumous VC which was presented to his father Mr S.J. Sifton in Canada by the Governor-General, His Excellency the Duke of Devonshire, in 1917. His citation was gazetted on 8 June 1917 as follows:

For most conspicuous bravery and devotion to duty. During the attack on enemy trenches, Sgt Sifton's company was held up by machine-gun fire, which

Lichfield Crater Military Cemetery (Photo: Peter Batchelor)

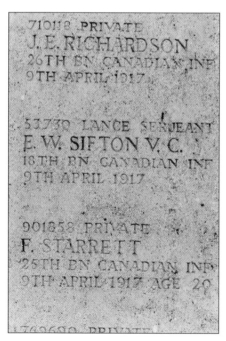

Sifton's name on the Lichfield Crater Memorial to the Missing (Photo: Donald Jennings)

inflicted many casualties. Having located the gun, he charged it single-handed, killing all the crew. A small enemy party advanced down the trench, but he succeeded in keeping these off till our troops had gained the position. In carrying out this gallant act he was killed, but his conspicuous valour undoubtedly saved many lives and contributed largely to the success of the operation.

Sifton had made a major contribution to the capture of this part of the German defences of the supposedly impregnable Vimy Ridge, most of which was captured by the end of the day.

Sifton is buried in the Lichfield Crater Cemetery, whose original name was CB 2 and which is situated close to the N17 Arras–Lens road, about ½ mile to the east of Neuville-St-Vaast. The cemetery is enclosed by a circular rubble and flint wall; fifty-eight men (mainly Canadians) are buried there. Together with the nearby Zivy Crater, it is a very moving place to visit; the names of the dead are listed on panels.

Ellis Welwood Sifton was born in the settlement of Wallacetown, Ontario, in Canada on 12 October 1891. He enlisted in the 18th Battalion of the Canadian Expeditionary Force in October 1914, and after training he left for France and became an excellent soldier. He was made a lance sergeant.

His family used to worship at St Peter's Church, Tyrconnell, and on 21 May 1961 a provincial historical plaque commemorating Sifton's life and career was unveiled there. The church is south-east of Wallacetown on County Road 15, near the John E. Pearce Provincial Park. Tyrconnell is a hamlet by Lake Erie and the church is the burial place of many members of the Sifton family. The plaque itself was commissioned by the Ontario Department of Travel and Publicity with the help of the Archaeological and Historic Sites Board, also of Ontario. The ceremony of unveiling was sponsored by the London Branch of the 18th Battalion Association and was carried out by two of Sifton's sisters, Miss Ella and Miss Lila. The president of the Battalion Branch acted as programme chairman and the plaque was dedicated by the Revd John Graham, recorder of St Peter's. Around a hundred members of the former 18th Battalion attended the ceremony, together with their families and around a thousand spectators.

Sifton's medals are held at Elgin County Pioneer Museum, Canada.

E. SYKES

Near Arras, France, 9 April

Pte Ernest Sykes of the 27th (4th Tyneside Irish) (S) Battalion of the Northumberland Fusiliers won his VC on 9 April 1917, the same day as L/Cpl Thomas Bryan of the 25th (2nd Tyneside Irish) Northumberland Fusiliers, and so the service histories of the two men are not surprisingly similar.

On 9 April the 34th Division was in position east of the village of Roclincourt, nearly 3 miles north of Arras. To the right was the 9th Division and on the left was the 51st (Highland) Division with whom the 34th was to keep close contact throughout the day. The two leading battalions of the 103rd (Tyneside Irish) Brigade of the 34th Division were the 24th and 25th Northumberland Fusiliers and they reached the enemy front or Black Line without too much opposition. Later on the companies formed up behind the barrage for their attack on the German second line, the British-named Blue Line. However, by this time the officers from C and D Companies were all casualties. When A and B Companies advanced behind the barrage, with A to the right and C in support, they were fortunate as the ground gave them a certain amount of cover in their approach to the Blue Line. Later, the men of B Company, who were on the left, began to suffer greatly from enemy machine-gun fire from their left. Men coming up on the left of the 152nd Brigade (51st Highland) Division were also held up by the same machine-guns and veered to the right into the 34th Division area. The 26th Northumberland Fusiliers also came up and added to the confusion.

However, after causing many casualties, the machine-gun was dealt with by L/Cpl Bryan, and the 27th Northumberland Fusiliers were ordered up to occupy and consolidate the Blue Line with their sister battalion, the 26th. The two battalions also occupied positions to the east of the line and made connections with the 102nd (Tyneside Scottish) Brigade to their right in the Gavrelle Weg, and with the 152nd Brigade on their left. It was during the above fight to capture the Blue Line that Pte Sykes won his VC when his battalion was held up by intense fire from the front and flank. Despite these dangerous conditions, Sykes went forward and recovered four wounded men. He made a fifth journey out and then proceeded to bandage all those men who were too badly wounded to be moved.

Sykes received his medal from the King in the forecourt of Buckingham Palace on 21 July 1917. Like Bryan's, Sykes's VC had been gazetted on 8 June 1917; the citation read as follows:

For most conspicuous bravery and devotion to duty when his battalion in attack was held up about 350 yards in advance of our lines by intense fire from front and flank, and suffered heavy casualties. Private Sykes, despite this heavy fire, went forward and brought back four wounded – he made a fifth journey and remained out under conditions which appeared to be certain death, until he had bandaged all those who were too badly wounded to be moved. These gallant actions, performed under incessant machine-gun and rifle fire, showed an utter contempt of danger.

After he won the VC, Sykes went home on leave and on 13 July 1917 he and his wife Alice, along with their two sons Harold and Percy, were greeted by the Mayor of Newcastle. Together with Pte Bryan, Sykes was given a civic reception at Newcastle on 27 July and they were both formally presented to the Lord Mayor at the Empire Theatre, where they were given war bonds valued at £100, a timepiece and bronzes, as well as a wallet of treasury notes and silver. They also signed the Visitors' Book at the Town Hall. In addition, the officers from his battalion presented Sykes with a silver tea service.

Ernest Sykes was born at Quick View, Mossley, Saddleworth, Yorkshire, on 4 April 1885. After leaving school at St Georges, Stalybridge, he worked on the railways as a platelayer at Micklehurst station with the London & North-Western Railway.

He enlisted in Halifax on 31 August 1914 in the West Riding Regiment with the number 13425. In Gallipoli he was seriously wounded in the foot and evacuated to Egypt where he was told that his foot would have to be amputated. However, he refused permission for the operation and was sent back to England, where he was sent to a hospital in London. Several operations were performed on his foot which allowed him to get about with the aid of a stick although he still limped. He was then ordered to appear before a medical board and was passed for home service. Be that as it may, he ended up in France on active service. He had been transferred to the Northumberland Fusiliers and in 1916 he moved from the 25th (2nd Tyneside Irish) (S) Northumberland Fusiliers to the 27th (4th Tyneside Irish) (S) Northumberland Fusiliers and was given the new service number 40989. Presumably his wounds caught up with him, as he was discharged early owing to sickness on 26 May 1918 and returned to the railways, this time as a guard.

*Sykes's grave in Woodfield
Cemetery, Lockwood, Yorkshire
(Photo: Donald Jennings)*

After the war Sykes attended the garden party for VC holders in 1920. Towards the end of the 1920s he unveiled the war memorial to the employees of the LNWR at Euston which still stands in the forecourt of the station. During the Second World War he served with the Home Guard 25th Battalion (West Riding). After a year of ill health he died on 3 August 1949, aged sixty-four, at 17 Thornfield Avenue, Lockwood, Huddersfield. He left three children by Alice, his first wife, and a widow from his second marriage, Gladys Clough. When he died he was about to retire after working for thirty-eight years on the railways. He was buried at Lockwood Cemetery, Section F, Number 227 on 6 August. He had a railway engine of the LMS named after him, 'Claughton' Class 4–6–0 no. 2035 (LMS no. 5976), and later his name was transferred to a 'Patriot' Class 4–6–0 with the number 45537. The latter was built in Crewe in 1933 and was in service for twenty-nine years until 9 June 1962. The nameplate was presented to the Museum of the Royal Northumberland Fusiliers at Alnwick, Northumberland, on 20 September 1967. His son Harold and grandson Stephen both attended the presentation. Harold had also worked for the railways at Mossley as a porter.

In addition to his VC, Sykes's medals included the 1914–15 Star, BWM, VM and George VI Coronation Medal. His VC is at present in the collection of the Royal Northumberland Fusiliers at Alnwick, but his remaining medals are in Canada and are not publicly held.

J.W. WHITTLE

Near Boursies, 9 April and Lagnicourt, France, 15 April

In early April there remained three uncaptured outpost villages between the area to the south of 1st Anzac Corps and the Hindenburg Line. The 12th (South Australia) Battalion (3rd Brigade, 1st Division) was given the task of capturing the village of Boursies, and this was to be a diversion from an attempt of the 1st Brigade to capture the village of Hermies. Capt. John Newland was in charge of A Company and 2902 Sgt John Whittle was responsible for the left platoon. After assaulting and capturing a derelict mill, Whittle took up a position beyond it. At around 10.00 a.m. on the 9th, after a barrage of 'pineapple' grenades, the Germans made a determined counter-attack in order to recapture the mill. The enemy, advancing down the main road, captured the forward posts close to the mill. It was at this point that Whittle acted, according to his citation, gazetted on 8 June 1917:

> For conspicuous bravery and devotion to duty on two occasions. When in command of a platoon, the enemy, under cover of an intense artillery barrage, attacked the small trench he was holding. Owing to weight of numbers, the enemy succeeded in entering the trench, and it was owing to Sgt Whittle personally collecting all available men and charging the enemy that the position was regained. . . .

When Capt. Newland arrived on the scene the two men worked together until the position was re-established.

A few days later, on 15 April, Newland and Whittle were again in action in tandem at Lagnicourt when the enemy was penetrating the D Company line in a counter-attack. The Germans had worked around the back of both D and A Companies. Newland, under attack from three sides, decided to withdraw to a sunken road which led to Doignies and then defend the banks of the road with his depleted company. When this movement was completed Whittle saw a group of the enemy setting up a machine-gun that was clearly able to enfilade both the sunken road and its banks. Whittle leapt up and, despite heavy fire from several directions, moved against the German post and completely wiped it out using bombs. He then took a further dangerous risk when he picked up the gun and carried it back to A Company's positions. The action undoubtedly 'saved the day'; Newland's defence plan ultimately worked and all the lost positions were recaptured when the 9th Battalion showed up and a counter-attack was organized.

The second part of Whittle's citation describes the events:

On a second occasion when the enemy broke through the left of our line, Sgt Whittle's own splendid example was the means of keeping the men well in hand. His platoon were suffering heavy casualties, and the enemy endeavoured to bring up a machine-gun to enfilade the position. Grasping the situation, he rushed alone across the fire-swept ground and attacked the hostile gun crew with bombs before the gun could be got into action. He succeeded in killing the whole crew, and in bringing back the machine-gun to our position.

Whittle was decorated by the King in the forecourt of Buckingham Palace with his VC and DCM on 21 July 1917. The DCM had been won in February 1917.

He was wounded twice, first during the German assault of March 1918 and again at the end of July, and took no further active part in the war. After his discharge from hospital he returned to Australia where he assisted with recruiting during the last weeks of the war.

John Woods Whittle was born on Huon Island, in the Port Cygnet district of Tasmania, on 3 August 1883. He spent most of his early life in Hobart, the capital of the island. When the South African war began Australia contributed men for service in the campaign; Whittle enlisted in the 2nd Imperial Bushmen and spent a year on active service. On returning to Australia he joined the Navy, serving for five years as a stoker, and his ships included the *Challenger* and *Pioneer*, both on the Australia Station.

After his time in the Navy, Whittle returned to the Army and served for three-and-a-half years in the Army Service Corps until 1905. He then moved on to the artillery and saw service with the 31st Battery and later spent five years with the Tasmanian Rifle Regiment. On 6 August 1915 he joined the Australian Imperial Forces from Launceston. He sailed for Egypt as a reinforcement for the 26th Battalion, but on reaching Egypt he was reallocated to the 12th Battalion. He joined the strength on 1 March during a period of divisional reorganization prior to the battalion's embarkation for France. On 13 April Whittle was made lance sergeant. Soon after, the unit was involved in fighting and he was wounded on 18 June 1916. He was promoted to sergeant on 14 October.

In February 1917 Whittle and Capt. J.E. Newland were involved in the 12th Battalion's attempts to capture the town of Bapaume and in the assault on the villages of Le Barque and Ligny-Thilloy just to the south-west. At Bark Trench, on the north side of the centre of Le Barque, Whittle entered the German-held position throwing bombs and chased the occupants out of the position. The Germans fled down Misty Trench, which led to the main Albert–Bapaume road. For his part in this fighting he was awarded the DCM.

After his discharge on 15 December 1918 in Tasmania, Whittle decided to move to the mainland and spent the rest of his life in Sydney, New South Wales. He attended the VC dinner in Sydney on Armistice Day in 1929.

For some years he acted as an inspector on the staff of a large insurance company. He later worked at other jobs, including a spell at Tooth's Brewery in Sydney, and in 1930 he re-enlisted with the 4th AIF for a short period.

In 1934 Whittle showed that he had not lost his gallantry. He was walking across University Park one day when he was accosted by a small boy who blurted out that his small brother had fallen into the lake. Whittle dived into the weed-choked lake and after groping around in the weeds he found the boy's body, brought him to the bank and applied artificial respiration for about half an hour. The child came round and was later taken to hospital. Whittle left the scene and went home in a taxi without leaving his name, but was later tracked down and duly presented with a Certificate of Merit by the Royal Life Saving Society. Whittle himself was ill for a fortnight from the effects of swallowing some of the foul water in the lake.

Whittle died on 2 March 1946 at his home at 27 Avenue Road, Glebe, Sydney. His wife Emily Margaret survived him, as did a son and three daughters. Another son Ivan, was killed in an aircraft accident when his Liberator bomber crashed into a marshalling yard on 7 September 1943 at Port Moresby, New Guinea. Whittle's funeral and burial were in his home town of Glebe. His medals are not publicly held.

Whittle's plaque in Rookwood Cemetery, Sydney, Australia (Photo: E.W. Bullock)

79

J.G. PATTISON
Vimy Ridge, France, 10 April

On the left of the Canadian line on 10 April 1917, the second day of the Battle of Arras, the Canadian Army was still engaged in clearing a few parts of Vimy Ridge which it had not taken the day before and, in particular, the enemy was tenaciously hanging on to an outpost line on the eastern slope of Vimy Ridge beyond Hill 145.

Maj.-Gen. Watson, commander of the 4th Division, decided that as the 11th Brigade was exhausted the battalions of the 10th Brigade should carry out the attack on the 11th Brigade's final objectives. The task was given to the 44th Battalion and the 50th Battalion, who were to start from Hill 145. Soon after midday the two battalions crossed the Zouave Valley in artillery formation and then deployed along the road near the side of the hill. After a fifteen-minute barrage, they left their positions at zero hour, 3.15 p.m. Having not been involved in the first day's fighting, the two battalions went forward with great determination; they charged down the slope and entered the German Hangstellung Trench very soon after the barrage had lifted.

At first progress was very slow and casualties mounted; the main reason for this was that the German defenders had a clear field of fire for their machine-guns. One strongpoint in particular stood in the way of the men of A Company who, with the assistance of B Company, made several attempts to take it out. It was at this stage that Pte John Pattison of the 50th Battalion moved forward alone from shell hole to shell hole, keeping as close to the ground as he could in order to avoid the fire from the machine-guns. He finally reached a position from which he could throw bombs with some degree of accuracy and lobbed three grenades on to the German position, managing to knock out the machine-guns and killing or wounding several of the crew. He then rushed the strongpoint and finished off the surviving Germans with his bayonet. Twenty minutes later all the enemy objectives had been taken and the Canadians consolidated the captured line.

The operation was a success but the 50th Battalion had nearly 240 casualties. While mopping up the enemy dug-outs the Canadians came across 150 unwounded prisoners who were subsequently released. They also claimed a number of enemy machine-guns. When the 44th Battalion moved forward to the north side of the Bois de la Folie they were able to link up with the left flank of the 3rd Division. By the next day the whole of the main section of Vimy Ridge was in Canadian hands: a front of 7,000 yards and up to 400 yards in depth.

Pattison survived the day's fighting and also remained unscathed after the next day's successful attack on the position known as The Pimple. He had been informed that he had been recommended for the VC, but he did not live to wear it. He died on 3 June 1917 during the attack on Lens electric generating station and his last hours were described in a letter from his son Henry to Canon Lummis:

> The attack proved a very heavy loss to the 50th Battalion, which required all available men to be used from Base Headquarters, where my Father was recuperating from a foot injury sustained in a previous engagement. He was sent back in the line and put on outpost duty when a direct shell-hit wiped out all those in that position. This position was taken over by the enemy and my Dad was reported missing for three months. It was not until a wooden cross, erected by the enemy, was found, that his death was confirmed. No personal possessions were ever recovered.

Pattison was killed at Callons Trench. When his body was found it was taken to La Chaudière Military Cemetery on the western side of the Lens–Arras road,

La Chaudière Military Cemetery
(Photo: Peter Batchelor)

Pattison's grave in La Chaudière Military
Cemetery (Photo: Donald Jennings)

for burial in Plot 6, Row C, Grave 14. The cemetery, which can be seen from the top of Vimy Ridge, was begun next to a house which used to contain a German gun position. Pattison's grave has the inscription '"Lest we Forget" mother, wife and family'. The cemetery contains the graves of 638 Canadians and 268 Britons. Originally it was very small; it became known as Vimy Canadian Cemetery No. 1 when other burials from small cemeteries and isolated graves near the ridge were brought into it.

Pattison's VC was gazetted on 2 August 1917:

For most conspicuous bravery in attack. When the advance of our troops was held up by an enemy machine-gun, which was inflicting severe casualties, Pte Pattison, with utter disregard of his own safety, sprang forward, and jumping from shell-hole to shell-hole, reached cover within thirty yards of the enemy gun. From this point, in face of heavy fire, he hurled bombs, killing and wounding some of the crew, then rushed forward, overcoming and bayoneting the surviving five gunners. His valour and initiative undoubtedly saved the situation and made possible the further advance to the objective.

John George Pattison was born in Woolwich, London, on 8 September 1875. He was the son of railwayman Henry Alfred Pattison and Mary Ann Pattison. He was the only child to survive from a family of three. In 1879 the Pattison family moved to New Cross, Deptford, and John attended school there at Clifton Road London County Council School.

After leaving school Pattison trained as a platelayer in the shipyards. At some point he married Sophia Louise Ann Allen and they had four children: two sons and two daughters. In June 1906 the family emigrated to Canada. At first they lived in Rapid City, Manitoba, and later they moved to Calgary, where Pattison worked in the Operation and Construction Department of the Canadian Western Natural Gas Co. in 1912. In early 1916, Pattison, at the age of forty, decided to enlist and the unit he joined was the 137th Battalion. He had already tried to join his son Henry's battalion, the 82nd, without success. Henry, however, managed to obtain a transfer to the 137th and the two men went overseas together.

John Pattison was drafted to the 50th Battalion and left England for France in January 1917. Henry was left behind as he was too young and he did not join his father's battalion until August 1917. In the following month Henry was allowed to wear a miniature VC medal and ribbon in honour of his father. Initially, Henry was to go to England for the VC presentation, but this arrangement was changed and instead the medal was presented by Lt-Gov. Brett to Henry's mother, Sophia Pattison, in Victory Park, Calgary at a public ceremony on

10 April 1918, the medal having been sent on by the War Office. However, Henry did have his moment of glory at a special ceremony at the town hall in New Cross when Deptford Borough Council presented him with an illuminated scroll telling of his father's valour.

On 3 June 1939 Mrs Sophia Pattison was introduced to King George VI during his state visit to Canada. Mrs Pattison had worked for the same department as her husband and she retired on 2 May 1940, living on until 25 March 1947. The Geographical Society of Alberta decided to name one of the peaks in the Jasper Park area after Pattison (several other peaks were named after winners of the VC). Pattison's portrait used to hang on the walls of the Canadian Western's boardroom. In 1967 a bridge over the River Elbow was also named to commemorate Pattison; he used to live in the district of the bridge and had also trained in the local barracks.

At some point Pattison's medals were acquired by the Glenbow Museum, where they remain. The museum also owns the colours of the 137th Battalion of the Canadian Expeditionary Force, raised in Calgary in 1916.

H. WALLER
South of Héninel, France, 10 April

In early April the 9th and 10th Battalions of the King's Own Yorkshire Light Infantry (KOYLI) of the 64th Brigade, 21st Division, had been practising attacks near Boisleux-au-Mont on the River Cojeul in preparation for an assault on the Hindenburg Line. On 7 April 1917 they entered the trenches from which they were to launch their attacks on the section of the Hindenburg Line which was part of the high ground from Héninel to Fontaine-lès-Croisilles. Their objective target was around 1,500 yards from their lines. On 9 April the 9th KOYLI were to the left of the brigade front and at first the sister 10th Battalion was in brigade reserve. The artillery was not efficient enough to destroy the wire completely in front of the 9th Battalion. However, the infantry assault began in mid-afternoon and the first wave struggled through the first line of wire only to be held up in the second. As gaps were frantically sought, the casualties mounted. Worst of all was the loss of leaders. An attempt to use a Stokes mortar to smash the wire failed. At 6.00 p.m. the men who survived were gathered in shell holes in front of the wire and were then withdrawn to the original first line position to the south of Héninel.

Soon after dusk fell the 10th Battalion arrived and casualties from the afternoon's fighting were gathered up as the second line was to be shelled the next day. B and C Companies had been digging trenches behind the sunken road and by 3.30 a.m. the new trench was ready for occupation by the 10th Battalion. In addition, a new communication trench was made which connected up with the new front line, formerly the German front line. The 9th Battalion was ordered to fall back to the sunken road and the 10th Battalion was in position on the extreme left flank, which was held by a bombers' block. This block had to be held at all costs, otherwise the enemy could penetrate the British front trenches.

It was at this point that Pte Horace Waller, a member of C Company, won his VC. His involvement began when the first of two strenuous counter-attacks began at 8.00 a.m. on 10 April. To quote Waller's citation (*London Gazette*, 8 June 1917), he was awarded his medal:

For most conspicuous bravery when with a bombing section forming a block in the enemy line. A very violent counter-attack was made by the enemy on this post, and although five of the garrison were killed, Pte Waller continued for more than an hour to throw bombs, and finally succeeded in repulsing the attack. In the evening the enemy again counter-attacked the post, and all the garrison became casualties except Pte Waller, who although wounded later, continued to throw bombs for another half an hour, until he was killed. Throughout these attacks he showed the utmost valour, and it was due to his determination that the attacks on this important post were repulsed.

Of Waller's bravery Brig.-Gen. H.R. Headlam, commander of 64th Brigade, wrote:

I command the brigade in which is the battalion to which he belonged, and consequently know very well the situation during which Private Waller performed his magnificent act of bravery. His fearless conduct and splendid bravery on that occasion were deciding factors at a critical period, and no man ever won the Victoria Cross more deservedly.

Waller's VC was presented to his parents at Buckingham Palace on 21 July 1917. He is buried at Cojeul British Cemetery, Row C, Grave 55. The cemetery is 1,000 yards to the south-east of St-Martin-sur-Cojeul, overlooking the River Cojeul (which is more of a stream than a river). It now lies close to the A1 autoroute. The cemetery was started by the 21st Division in April 1917 and Waller would have been one of the first men to be buried there. It was used by fighting units for the next six months.

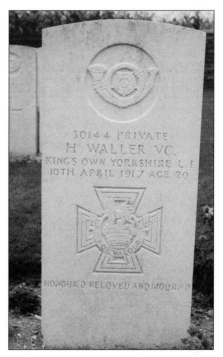
Waller's grave (Photo: Donald Jennings)

Horace Waller was born on 23 September 1897 at 11 Woodhill Terrace, Batley Carr, in the sub-district of Dewsbury, Yorkshire. He was the son of John Edward Waller, who ran a plumbing business, and his wife Esther, daughter of John Myers of

Bradford. The family home was a small terraced house, though later the Wallers moved to Upper Road, Batley Carr, and later to Healds Road, Dewsbury.

Waller was educated at Purlwell Council School and later won a free scholarship to Batley Grammar School. At the age of seventeen he had to leave the school in order to help out with the family plumbing business, which was called Strickland, Waller & Sons, but he continued his studies at the local technical college. He joined the Army as a private on 30 May 1916, having failed the medical on two occasions. In the end he scraped through as a Class C man and joined the King's Own Yorkshire Light Infantry; his service number was 30144. In December 1916 he left for France and was killed four months later. He was unmarried.

In addition to his grave in France, Waller is also commemorated on the family grave in Dewsbury where his parents are buried. Owing to a certain rivalry between Dewsbury and Batley Carr, Waller's name is listed on both war memorials. Waller and John Ormsby, another Dewsbury VC, both had roads named after them. Both were members of the KOYLI.

In February 1980, when Christie's sold Waller's VC to Messrs Spinks for an anonymous client, it was still in its original case. The lot was offered without any of Waller's other First World War medals, and it fetched £8,800.

The Waller family memorial in Dewsbury Cemetery, Yorkshire

D. MACKINTOSH

North of Fampoux, France, 11 April

By nightfall on 9 April 1917, the first day of the Battle of Arras, to the north of the River Scarpe the British had taken the first three German lines called the Black, Blue and Brown Lines. They had also already penetrated sections of the fourth (Green) line. This represented an advance of nearly 4½ miles and was a remarkable achievement. However, in the attempt to secure the fourth and fifth lines of the German defences in the area of the village of Roeux, to the north of the River Scarpe, the assault was about to go horribly wrong. There was simply no sensible plan in operation that would take advantage of the successful advance and allow for further exploitation.

Lt Donald Mackintosh, who was shortly to win a posthumous VC, was a member of the 2nd Seaforth Highlanders (10th Brigade, 4th Division) in reserve to the 9th (Scottish) Division on 9 April. The British had been unable to bring up adequate artillery owing to the soft nature of the open ground and yet, despite this, the plan was to take Roeux and its chemical works with virtually unsupported infantry. It was already known that the chemical works, as well as other sections of the village, were extremely well fortified.

The 2nd Seaforth Highlanders were informed on 10 April that they were to attack the chemical works, as well as Greenland Hill which was beyond the works, at noon next day. The Seaforth Highlanders were in positions behind the village of Fampoux and were to make their way to the sunken road leading northwards from the village towards Hyderabad Redoubt, which was a brigade headquarters. Unfortunately, the road was not sunken for its whole length and the enemy had the Seaforths in its machine-gun sights, together with the 1st Royal Irish Fusiliers who were close behind the Highlanders and who were to make the assault with them on their right. The ground over which the attackers had to move was completely open and, as if that were not enough, it was also snowing at the time of the advance, which was carried out behind the shelter of a very weak barrage. Enemy fire came from all the main buildings and positions in Roeux including the château, station, chemical works, the railway station and an embankment.

The remains of the German blockhouse at Roeux (Photo: Peter Batchelor)

The casualties of the Scottish battalion were an appalling 93 per cent from three companies, and this figure included all of their officers. At the end of the day a long line of dead Highlanders, caught by the enemy machine-guns, could be seen on the bare landscape. The total casualty figures for the abortive assault numbered over one thousand members of the 10th Brigade. It was during this fighting that Lt Mackintosh won his VC when, in the face of intense machine-gun fire, he led the initial advance. Despite being wounded in the right leg, he managed to lead his men forward and capture a German trench situated 150 yards to the west of the Roeux–Gavrelle road. Once there, he organized men from another company who were leaderless and with them he drove back a number of counter-attacks. Mackintosh was hit again and this time he could no longer move but, in spite of this, he managed to keep control of the situation. When his party was down to fifteen men they made one more charge; with great difficulty Mackintosh succeeded in climbing out of the trench, but was hit a third time and fell mortally wounded.

Three weeks after Mackintosh's death his battalion again attacked and again they suffered heavy casualties including all their officers. On 11 May the village was captured in an attack launched in the evening by the 4th Division, supported by 152nd Brigade of the 51st (Highland) Division.

Mackintosh's grave is in Brown's Copse Cemetery, Roeux, Plot II, Row C, Grave 49. The cemetery was designed by Edwin Lutyens and is around 1,000 yards to the

Brown's Copse Cemetery (Photo: Peter Batchelor)

west of Roeux and close to the River Scarpe, which in this section has been turned into a canal. The main railway line and the A1 autoroute are close by. The cemetery also stands in the former no-man's-land, across which so many troops from England, Scotland, Ireland and Australia fought in vain over a period of a month from 11 April until 11 May. There are nearly 3,000 graves in the cemetery, which supposedly takes its name from a small copse on the cemetery's eastern side that used to be called Nightingale Wood. It is possible that Mackintosh's body was first buried in an earlier burial ground at Seaforth Cemetery in the village of Roeux. A memorial to the Seaforth Highlanders is in the sunken road close to Fampoux, which overlooks the whole area where the Highlanders lost so many men. Further up the same track is the Sunken Road Cemetery.

Mackintosh's grave in Brown's Copse Cemetery (Photo: Donald Jennings)

The Seaforths memorial at the sunken road, Fampoux (Photo: Peter Batchelor)

Mackintosh's VC was published in the *London Gazette* of 8 June 1917:

For most conspicuous bravery and resolution in the face of intense machine-gun fire. During the initial advance he was shot through the right leg, but, though crippled, he continued to lead his men and captured the trench. In the captured trench Lt Mackintosh collected men of another company who had lost their leader, and drove back a counter-attack. He was again wounded, and although unable to stand, he continued, nevertheless, to control the situation. With only fifteen men left he ordered his party to be ready to advance to the final objective, and with great difficulty got out of the trench and encouraged his men to advance. He was again wounded and fell. The gallantry and devotion to duty of this officer were beyond all praise.

The medal was presented to his father and mother, Dr and Mrs D. Mackintosh, on 21 July 1917 at Buckingham Palace.

Donald Mackintosh was born in the parish of Partick near Glasgow on 7 February 1896. He was the son of Dr Donald James Mackintosh and was educated at Fettes College, Edinburgh. While still a student he enlisted into the Royal Army Medical Corps on 14 August 1914. He was 5 ft 8 in tall and weighed 11 stone 3 lb. He became an acting sergeant before his commission. On his discharge he joined the Special Reserve of Officers, Seaforth Highlanders, in February 1915 and was granted a commission with the 3rd Battalion on 20 February 1915. Almost a year later he was made a full lieutenant. He was severely wounded on 21 March 1916 and was transferred to Le Touquet Hospital on 23 March before being sent to England. By July 1916 his wounds had healed and on 15 August 1916 he joined the 3rd Battalion. He was listed as wounded and missing on 11 April 1917, and on 21 May he was officially listed as killed in action. At the time of his death his family address was Western Infirmary House, Glasgow.

Mackintosh's medals included the VC, 1914–15 Star, BWM and VM. His VC is in the keeping of the Seaforth Highlanders.

The village of Roeux has an underground system of tunnels and caves to which several entry points still exist. Although the site of the chemical works has been tidied up, a huge blockhouse still survives which is in the grounds of the former château. The entrances to the blockhouse have been sealed up quite recently.

H.S. MUGFORD

At Monchy-le-Preux, France, 11 April

By the evening of 9 April 1917 the British line to the south of the River Scarpe still fell short of the German third line, called the Brown Line by the British, which was approximately 2 miles from the outskirts of Monchy-le-Preux. To the east of this village was the German fourth or Green Line. In the late morning on 10 April the 3rd Cavalry Division sent out patrols from the 10th Hussars and the Essex Yeomanry, 8th Cavalry Brigade. Two other patrols, from the 6th Brigade, were also sent out. The patrols were able to confirm that Monchy was still in German hands and that it was also held in some strength. The cavalry suffered many casualties during these patrols, particularly among the horses. Conditions during the night were nightmarish as it was bitterly cold and there was a lack of water and fodder for the horses. In addition, desultory enemy artillery fire continued, which also caused casualties in the horse lines.

On 11 April the British infantry began an assault on the village at 5.00 a.m., and by 7.00 a.m. it was reported that the village had been taken except for its eastern side. The plan for the 3rd Cavalry Division was to advance after the infantry to the western outskirts of the village. The 6th Cavalry Brigade was to move south of Monchy and the 8th to the north on the Boiry–Notre-Dame Line. At 8.30 a.m. the Essex Yeomanry was to advance to the eastern side of Monchy and try to secure the high ground which ran from Bois des Aubépines to the mill at Pelves. The Essex Yeomanry were to be on the right and the 10th Hussars on their left. They were then to capture a small wood called Bois du Sart, which was east of Pelves. Both these regiments possessed two machine-gun subsections and they set off to the south of Orange Hill, as machine-gun fire from the direction of the River Scarpe to the north was expected to be bad. If the fire became too severe the two regiments were to change the plan and enter the village from the western side.

The cavalry regiments which had the task of advancing to the south of Monchy had a very quick success, but for their colleagues advancing northwards it was a different story. When the horses were still 1,500 yards from Monchy, as they emerged from Orange Hill they became targets for the German artillery which continued firing strongly as they advanced to the north-west of the village. As the cavalry moved across the open countryside the first two troops of the Essex Yeomanry were virtually annihilated. An account of what happened was written by Tpr Clarence Garnett of the 8th Machine-Gun Squadron; his story has been quoted in previous books, but it tells the story as well as any other account and also includes a reference to Harold Mugford VC:

I was riding a little horse called Nimrod and leading another with a pack saddle on his back loaded with boxes of machine-gun ammunition. We had not gone far when a huge shell burst to my right. Someone yelled, 'Garnett's pack-horse has broken its leg!' Our corporal, Harold Mugford, shouted at me to keep going but the pack-horse fell, and as I was holding on to him so tightly, he pulled me out of the saddle. I let go and managed to stay on Nimrod, regaining my balance, but then my saddle slipped under his stomach. I rode on, hanging on for dear life, on his bare back. All the rest of the column had left me and seeing a huge hawthorn tree, I got behind it and adjusted the saddle. I remounted and rode on alone to where the others had gone and quickly entered the village where I saw a dead pack-horse with ammunition on his back, so I dismounted and took a box. Galloping along the street I soon reached the building marked 'Château' on my map, where I was stopped by our officer who demanded my box of ammunition and told me to follow him. By now there were a few of us and the shelling had become very heavy, so the officer ordered us to lie down under the shelter of a wall. As I was lying in a gap between two cottages, I immediately got up, still holding my horse, and lay down under the wall of a cottage opposite. I had not been there long when a light shell came through the gap in the cottages and cut down the officer and most of the others. Nimrod was terrified and he reared up violently, dragging me along the street for some yards until I was forced to let go. I never saw him again after that. As it was pointless staying in that spot, I wandered along the street and into the main square which was simply covered with dead horses and men. To my horror, I saw one of our blokes cut in two at the waist. One half of him was on one side of the street, the other on the other side. Later that morning it started to rain and I swear the streets of Monchy ran red with blood.

No. 51407 Harold Mugford was a lance corporal with the 8th Machine-Gun Squadron, Machine-Gun Corps. His VC was gazetted on 26 November 1917 as follows:

For most conspicuous bravery and devotion to duty when under intense shell and machine-gun fire, L/Cpl Mugford succeeded in getting his machine-gun into a forward and very exposed position. From this point he was able to deal more effectively with the enemy, who were massing for a counter-attack. His No. 2 was killed almost immediately, and at the same moment he himself was severely wounded. He was then ordered to a new position, and told to go to a dressing station as soon as the position was occupied. He refused to go to the dressing station, but continued on duty with his gun, inflicting severe loss on the enemy. Soon after he was again wounded, a shell breaking both of his legs. He still remained with his gun, begging his comrades to leave him and to take cover. Shortly afterwards this non-commissioned officer was removed to the dressing station, where he was again wounded in the arm. The valour and initiative displayed by L/Cpl Mugford was instrumental in breaking up the impending counter-attack of the enemy.

Monchy had been an objective for 9 April, but was not taken until two days later and then in a snowstorm. The two infantry divisions most associated with its capture were the 37th and 15th, and the former has a marvellous memorial in the centre of the village adjacent to the château wall, as does the Royal Newfoundland Regiment: a caribou on a German blockhouse. Despite the

The 37th Division memorial at Monchy (Photo: Peter Batchelor)

tremendous heroism of the cavalry in their attempt to capture Monchy, it has to be admitted that they achieved little apart from clogging up the streets of the village with scores of dead horses.

Harold Sandford Mugford was born in St James's, London, on 31 August 1894. As he grew up he developed an interest in sport and became a keen cricketer.

At the beginning of the war he joined the Essex Yeomanry and was later transferred to the 8th Squadron MGC, with the number 51407. He was presented with his VC by the King in the forecourt of Buckingham Palace on 3 July 1918 and was discharged in 1919.

Mugford had been severely disabled during the war as a result of his wounds. Both his legs were paralysed and he had to use a wheelchair in order to get about for the rest of his life. His first post-war home was at Mill House, Little Waltham, and later he moved to Chelmsford where he was a familiar and cheerful figure around the town. Mugford was a keen supporter of local organizations and contributed financially to many of them. He was vice-president of the Chelmsford Amateur Operatic and Dramatic Society. He chose never to talk about the time when he won his VC.

Mugford died on 16 June 1958 in Chelmsford after a short illness. His home address was Ashburton, Chignall Road. He left a widow, Amy, but the couple had no children. At his funeral on 19 June, which took place at Chelmsford Cathedral with full military honours, a guard of honour was supplied by members of the Old Comrades Association of the Essex Yeomanry. The coffin was draped in a Union Jack and Provost Eric Gordon conducted the service. Afterwards a bugler from the Essex Yeomanry Band sounded the Last Post and Reveille. Later Mugford's body was cremated at Southend Crematorium.

Amy, his widow, lived on until 1978 and when she died she bequeathed her late husband's medal to his pre-war employers, Messrs Furness Withy, in recognition of their giving her husband an ill-health disability pension for the rest of his life. She, too, received a pension from them, after her husband's death. The firm was a little embarrassed at owning the medal and lent it to the Imperial War Museum where it remains to this day. It has been displayed in at least one exhibition organized there on the history of the VC.

J. CUNNINGHAM

Bois-en-Hache, near Barlin, France, 12 April

At the northern edge of Vimy Ridge in the area of the First Army, the 24th Division was in position with the 4th Canadian Division to its right. The 2nd Battalion The Prince of Wales's Leinster Regiment and the 9th Royal Sussex, both of the 73rd Brigade, 24th Division, were to make an assault; their objective was the Bois-en-Hache to the north-east of Souchez and the strongpoint known as the Pimple. Zero hour was 5.00 a.m. on 12 April. The wood was of irregular shape and was the eastern edge of the Lorette Ridge; if the Pimple were captured the Allies would overlook the Souchez Valley from Givenchy to Angres. The Leinsters were to carry the southern and central sections, and the Royal Sussex were to take the northern section and the slope beyond. The preceding afternoon had been a very wet one with snow in the early evening. However, when the troops began to move forwards to their front line positions, the snow ceased. The troops left their billets near Petit Sains at Fosse 10 and moved forward via Aix-Noulette and the main Arras road. The men were given a hot meal and some rum before going into their assembly positions which they reached at around 4.00 a.m. Half an hour later the battalion was ready to advance. However, shortly after, the weather deteriorated and it began to rain, which then turned to snow. The wind also picked up, blowing the snow into the attackers' faces.

At 5.00 a.m. the attack began and three companies moved off in two waves accompanied by a British barrage. Landmarks were quickly concealed by the snow and the ground became slushy. Like other parts of Vimy Ridge, the ground was made up of shell holes and craters. The Leinsters continued their advance in these very poor conditions and the enemy opened a heavy rifle and machine-gun fire on them. The right-hand company was enfiladed from Bois-de-Givenchy, across the valley of the River Souchez. Around ten minutes after they set off, the Leinsters found that the enemy wire in front of them was destroyed and they closed with their opponents in their first line. In the hand-to-hand fight which followed, the Lewis gunners, including 3916 Cpl John Cunningham who was in charge of a section, used their guns as clubs and did great damage to the enemy. Several prisoners were taken, but the rest of the enemy fled to their second line.

The leading men moved downhill towards the wooded slope and the German second line. Meanwhile, hostile enfilade fire from across the Souchez Valley continued and took its toll. Cunningham was later awarded the VC for his work on this day and his citation was gazetted on 8 June 1917:

> For most conspicuous bravery and devotion to duty when in command of a Lewis Gun Section on the most exposed flank of the attack. His section came under heavy enfilade fire and suffered severely. Although wounded he succeeded almost alone in reaching his objective (a position named Long Sap) with his gun, which he got into action in spite of much opposition. When counter-attacked by a party of twenty of the enemy, he exhausted his ammunition against them, then, standing in full view, he commenced throwing bombs. He was wounded again, and fell, but picked himself up and continued to fight single-handed with the enemy until his bombs were exhausted. He then made his way back to our lines with a fractured arm and other wounds. There is little doubt that the superb courage of this NCO cleared up a most critical situation on the left flank of the attack. Cpl Cunningham died in hospital from the effects of his wounds.

Cunningham died of his wounds in hospital four days later on 16 April at Barlin, Pas-de-Calais, and is buried in Barlin Communal Cemetery near Noeux-les-Mines in Plot 1, Row A, Grave 39. Barlin is between the Béthune–Arras and Béthune–St Pol roads, around 4 miles from Bruay. The inscription on his grave says 'Our Lady of the Sacred Heart Pray for him' and his number is given as 8916, although 3916 is listed on his citation.

Cunningham's posthumous VC was presented to his mother, Mrs Johanna Cunningham, by the King on 21 July 1917 in the forecourt of Buckingham Palace.

John Cunningham was born in Ireland at Hall Street, Thurles, Tipperary, on 22 October 1890. His name is commemorated at St Mary's Church at Thurles.

His medals are not publicly held and his regiment was disbanded in 1922.

Cunningham's grave in Barlin Communal Cemetery (Photo: Donald Jennings)

J.W. ORMSBY

Fayet, France, 14 April

By the end of March 1917 the 2nd King's Own Yorkshire Light Infantry (KOYLI) of the 97th Brigade, 32nd Division, were on the left flank of the French Army in the region of the German-occupied town of St Quentin.

On 1 April the village of Savy was taken in the early morning by the 11th Border Regiment and the 17th Highland Light Infantry, with the 2nd KOYLI in support. It was a very cold and snowy day and yet an advance of 5,000 yards was made. The 2nd KOYLI were now attached to 14th Brigade, also of the 32nd Division, and on 2 April they were ordered to assist in the taking of a large wood on the western side of the village of Holnon. Holnon itself, along with the village of Francilly-Selency, was also to be captured by 14th Brigade. In the evening the battalion left the north of Holnon Wood and marched via Holnon to Francilly, a short distance to the south-east, where they expected to come up against parties of the enemy. Instead they found that the enemy had retired from these positions. The 2nd KOYLI reached their bivouacs at about 11.30 p.m. and were then ready to support either the 14th Brigade or the 96th Brigade, if called upon. Five hours later, while a new support line was being prepared, an enemy bomber flew overhead and dropped three bombs with such accuracy that 17 men were killed and 30 wounded. The battalion moved to a railway cutting in order to seek protection from further raids and from German shelling, with St Quentin lying 2 miles to the east of their positions.

On the night of 7 April B Company from the 2nd KOYLI stormed the enemy position and drove them back towards their main defensive positions. On the 9th the battalion was given a short rest at Auroir, during which time it snowed again.

On 13 April the French made a couple of unsuccessful attacks towards St Quentin. To the north-east of Holnon was the village of Fayet, which was still in German hands, and the 97th Brigade was ordered to capture it on the 14th; the start line was to be the village of Holnon. The attack on the village began at 4.15 a.m. with the 2nd KOYLI on the left and the 16th Highland Light Infantry on the right; they also had artillery support. Of the 2nd KOYLI, their A Company was on the left of the attack and B Company was on the right. A Company advanced and within half an hour had reached the sunken road leading to Fresnoy-le-Petit, to the north. D Company followed A Company.

The village was captured by B Company and Sgt John William Ormsby was one of the company NCOs. Dug-outs were cleared and prisoners taken. Still assisted by the artillery, they then moved towards their second objective which was taken by 5.30 a.m. C Company had moved up, but soon B Company had lost contact with A and C Companies. Seizing their opportunity, the enemy made a move to turn the flank of B Company. Casualties were heavy and a new line facing eastwards was held, mainly with the use of two Lewis guns. By 9.00 a.m. B Company found themselves in the very large grounds of the village château. They were not able to advance again until other objectives were taken and when they did the time was 1.50 p.m. The artillery again provided support. Twenty-five minutes later a new line was established but, soon after, 2/Lt Pickering – the only surviving company officer – was wounded and Sgt Ormsby then took over from him. The advance was successful and all the KOYLI companies were now in line. They quickly dug in, in order to protect themselves from enemy rifle and machine-gun fire. At 9.30 p.m. the battalion advanced further.

Ormsby's citation on 8 June 1917 told the story in the following way:

For most conspicuous bravery and devotion to duty, during operations which culminated in the capture of an important position. Acting as Company Sergeant-Major, he showed throughout the attack absolute indifference to the heavy machine-gun and rifle fire, and set a fine example. After clearing the village he pushed on and drove out many snipers from localities further forward. When the only surviving officer was wounded he took command of the company and led them forward, under heavy fire, for 400 yards to a new position. He organized his new position with great skill, and held his line with determination until relieved of his command. His conduct throughout was admirable, and inspired confidence in every man under his command.

Twenty-four hours later the battalion was relieved by the 16th Lancashire Fusiliers of 96th Brigade and four days later was withdrawn to Voyennes for re-formation and training. The grounds of Fayet château have now been taken over by new housing as the village is a sort of dormitory village for St Quentin; only its long brick wall still exists. The sunken road is still there (1997), although it has been modified and now passes under the A26 autoroute.

Remains of the château wall at Fayet (Photo: Peter Batchelor)

The sunken road leading to Fayet (Photo: Peter Batchelor)

About ten days before Fayet was taken Maj. Lumsden won his VC around 1½ miles to the south-west at Francilly-Selency and he was also involved in the Fayet fighting on 14 April. A further VC connection is with CSM Edward Brooks (Ox & Bucks), who won a VC at Fayet on 28 April.

In early June the 32nd Division was in the region of Messines Ridge and on 8 June an announcement about Sgt Ormsby was read out in which it was stated that he had won the VC for his work at Fayet on 14 April. On 11 June the VC ribbon was pinned on Ormsby's chest by Maj.-Gen. the Hon. A.R. Montagu-Stuart Wortley, the acting Divisional Commander, who made a reference to the other KOYLI VC won posthumously by Pte H. Waller of 10th Battalion. Ormsby was decorated by the King at Buckingham Palace on 30 June 1917.

Ormsby remained in England for a few months before returning to the Western Front, when he wrote the following home to his wife: 'We have been over the top again – it was a big battle.'

John William Ormsby came from a humble background and was born in Dewsbury, West Yorkshire, on 11 January 1881. He attended the small Catholic school of St Joseph's, Batley Carr, but he had to leave school early, before he had learnt to read and write properly. He married Catherine and the couple had two sons. Ormsby served in the Boer War and gained the Queen's Medal with clasp. When the First World War broke out he was on the reserve and was called to the colours. He left for France in 1915 and served there with the rank of sergeant.

After his VC was announced, Ormsby was given a civic reception and fêted by the people of Dewsbury; a subscription list was opened at the same time. His other medals were the MM, the 1914–15 Star, GSM, VM, 1939–45 Defence Medal, King George V Jubilee Medal and George VI Coronation Medal. After the war he was discharged in 1919 with the rank of sergeant, and the people of Dewsbury presented him with a horse and cart together with a gift of £500. This was to enable him to start civilian life again as a greengrocer. Actually he set up in business as a 'General Carrier and Marine Store Dealer', but the enterprise was not a success. When he was not going around the streets on business he used to spend time in coaching deprived boys from the back streets of Dewsbury to box or play rugby. He began his own academy which he called 'The Ormsby Boxing Troupe' and it became a popular attraction at local events. He later worked for the local corporation for thirty years. On 31 October 1951 he was presented to the Queen at QE Barracks; she was Colonel-in-Chief of the King's Own Yorkshire Light Infantry.

Ormsby died at his home 28 Low Road, Dewsbury on 29 July 1952, aged seventy-one; he had not been very well for several months. He was a regular attender at Mass and by the time of his death had become a much respected citizen of Dewsbury. He attended many ex-servicemen's functions and parades, and his medals were usually on display on these occasions. He used to say, 'I wear them for those who never came home – the real heroes.'

After Requiem Mass at St Paulinus Church on the day of his funeral, the coffin was taken by army truck to the cemetery. He was given a full military funeral and around 600 people lined the route to Dewsbury cemetery. A firing party from the KOYLI Barracks at Strensall, near York, fired three volleys over the grave and the Last Post and Reveille were played. Members of the regiment dropped white roses on to the coffin. One of the mourners was a Mr T. Gavaghan, who served with Ormsby in France during the First World War. Others included members of the KOYLI and the Mayor of Dewsbury, together with his deputy and representatives from many other civic organizations. Ormsby's grave was not marked adequately but this was put right in 1984 when a new stone was erected.

Ormsby's VC was presented to his regiment by his son, William John, and is in the King's Own Yorkshire Light Infantry Museum in York. Ormsby's other medals are with the family.

Ormsby's grave in Dewsbury Cemetery, Yorkshire (Photo: Donald Jennings)

C. POPE

Louverval, France, 15 April

During the fighting to capture the villages which screened the Hindenburg Line three men won the VC: John Newland, John Whittle and Charles Pope.

On 15 April 1917 the section covered by the 1st Australian Brigade of the 1st Australian Division was the area to the right of the main Bapaume–Cambrai road at Louverval; the 3rd Australian Brigade was to the left of the main road. The latter brigade was to advance in the direction of the Hindenburg Line using a series of well-supported posts; this would lessen the distance until the enemy line came within attacking range. The advance of the brigade's 11th Battalion in front of Louverval was to cover a line of almost 2 miles, which was divided into sub-sectors in company order.

It seems appropriate to tell the story of what happened in the words of the commanding officer of the battalion, Maj. R.A. Rafferty:

At about 0400 an intense enemy artillery barrage was opened on the picquet line and worked back to Louverval, and beyond that to our rear. The barrage appeared to last about 15 minutes, and shells were coming from flanks and front. At this time I received reports from D Company – left flank – that enemy was attacking, and a report from A Company – right flank – that they suspected enemy attack. This was shortly after confirmed.

Some little time after this A Coy reported that the enemy had broken through the company on his left and had lodged himself in an old trench commanding A Coy's positions. I sent forward another half-company to A Company. . . . Captain Hemingway then organised a local counter-attack and drove the enemy from the position he had gained.

At this time the right company picquet posts were still holding out, but were being hard-pressed by weight of numbers. Conforming to the movements of the battalion on our right, A Company's right flank picquets withdrew gradually until it reached where it held on. Just prior to this it was seen that A Company's centre picquet was surrounded and had evidently used up all their ammunition, for with fixed bayonets the remainder of the post charged into the large body of the enemy who had surrounded them. Lieutenant Pope was in charge of this post, and our patrols since report having found his dead body.

Lt Charles Pope was a member of A Company which was engaging the enemy directly in front of their position. Unknown to them, a large group of the enemy passed between Pope's position and the adjacent one. The Germans were attacked from the support line and many men were killed. A Company was in danger of becoming surrounded and Pope sent his runner, Cpl A.G.C. Gledhill, for more ammunition. Fifteen men set off with extra ammunition to try to reach Pope's position. Unfortunately, although one runner was able to get through, it was far too difficult for a large party to succeed, and they returned to their headquarters. However, although it was a hopeless task, Pope fought on and his body was found by Australian troops at the end of the day among the bodies of his men and eighty of the enemy. Later, the gaps in the line were covered with the help of the 10th Battalion and a rough line was formed further back which connected up the remaining supports.

Losses had been high, totalling 245, of whom 180 were posted as missing. Apart from using greater numbers, the main other reason for the German superiority was their sense of timing – they attacked the scattered positions in semi-darkness and few of the sentry groups could have known what was going on at even the adjacent posts. The land around Louverval was broken down into gullies, and it became relatively simple for the Germans to mop up a sentry post or two and then continue their progress along the dead ground to the rear of the picquets. However, the enemy still did not succeed in penetrating the main Australian line owing to the doggedness of the defences. The fight on this day was part of what became the Battle of Lagnicourt.

Pope was buried in Moeuvres Communal Cemetery Extension, Plot V, Row D, Grave 22. The cemetery is a mile to the north of the Bapaume–Cambrai road, on the road to Inchy in the north-west part of the village.

Pope's posthumous VC was gazetted on 8 June 1917 and was probably sent to his wife in Perth, Western Australia. The citation was as follows:

Pope's grave in Moeuvres Communal Cemetery Extension (Photo: Donald Jennings)

For most conspicuous bravery and devotion to duty when in command of a very important picquet post in the sector held by his battalion, his orders being to hold this post at all costs. After the picquet posts had been heavily attacked, the enemy in greatly superior numbers surrounded the post. Lt Pope, finding he was running short of ammunition, sent back for further supplies. But the situation culminated before it could arrive, and in the hope of saving the position this very gallant officer was seen to charge with his picquet into a superior force, by which it was overpowered. By his sacrifice Lt Pope not only inflicted heavy loss on the enemy, but obeyed his order to hold the position to the last. His body, together with those of most of his men, was found in close proximity to eighty enemy dead – a sure proof of the gallant resistance which had been made.

Charles Pope was born in Mile End, London, on 5 March 1883, the son of Police Constable William Pope and Jane Pope, née Clark. He was educated at Navestock in Essex. In the early years of the twentieth century he emigrated to Canada and for a while was employed by the Canadian Pacific Railway. A few years later, in 1906, he decided to return to England and he joined the Chelsea Division of the Metropolitan Police Force. During this period he married Edith Mary Smith at St Luke's Anglican Church, Chelsea. In 1910 he resigned from the police force and emigrated for a second time. This time he and his wife chose Australia, and when the couple reached Perth in Western Australia Pope took a job as a furniture salesman with Blain & Co. He then moved on and joined the staff of the Temperance & General Insurance Co.

Just over a year after the First World War broke out Pope decided to enlist and he was posted to the 11th Australian Imperial Forces (18th Reinforcements). By this time his marriage had produced a son and a daughter. Pope was commissioned on 10 February 1916 and on 15 July he set sail for England on the transport *Ajana*, arriving in September. On 10 December he joined the 11th Battalion in France and was made a full lieutenant on 26 December the same year.

His medals, which include the MC, are in the Australian War Memorial in Canberra.

A. HENDERSON

Near Fontaine-lès-Croisilles, France, 23 April

The Hindenburg Line was highly fortified and had a strong second line with concrete machine-gun emplacements sited every 50 yards or so. Some of these even had two storeys. Each of these two substantial lines had a 20 yard belt of barbed wire in front of it. A comprehensive system of tunnels and dug-outs completed the German defence line.

A large-scale attack was planned for 23 April 1917. The 33rd Division was to attack the section of the Hindenburg Line that ran close to the River Sensée. The 98th Brigade of this division was in the northern sector of the divisional line and was to bomb its way southwards down the Hindenburg Line. The brigade was then to meet up with the 100th Brigade in the river valley. This brigade was to make a frontal attack against the German line simultaneously.

The 33rd Division launched its attack at 6.24 p.m. on 23 April with orders for the 98th Brigade to capture the village of Fontaine-lès-Croisilles as its first objective. The 2nd Argyll and Sutherland Highlanders (A&SH) were on the left of the attack and the 1st Middlesex were on the right. Even as the attacking battalions moved down the slope over open ground towards the River Sensée, they found that the enemy was beginning to infiltrate their lines. A company from both battalions was actually cut off and attempts to rescue the men failed. However, this group then found that they were in a position to provide enfilade fire against a part of the Hindenburg Line which had been taken by the 1st Queen's Regiment (100th Brigade).

A party from the 2nd A&SH under Capt. Arthur Henderson suffered extremely heavily from enemy fire and they found themselves being attacked from the rear as well. With mounting casualties they nevertheless managed to hold the position and also to kill large numbers of the enemy. Although his left arm was wounded, Henderson personally led a bayonet charge assisted by three men against a large body of the enemy.

At first light on 24 April the 33rd Division discovered that the enemy had moved down the slope towards the line of the Chérisy–Croisilles Road. The division moved on to the place where the Fontaine–St Martin road crossed the support trench. To the north, parties from the 2nd A&SH fought with great tenacity to reach their objective. However, according to the Divisional History, the battle had been only partially successful owing to the 98th Brigade being held up in the advance.

Few, if any, of the Scottish battalion survived the battle, but the 98th Brigade had managed to capture 240 men from the 61st German Division. No fewer than seven officers were killed in the action and six were wounded, including Lt-Col. C.B.J. Richard, the commanding officer. The battalion withdrew into support in a sunken road at map reference N26c on the Hénin-sur-Cojeul–Neuville-Vitasse road. (This road is now numbered D5.) Henderson's extreme gallantry and self-sacrifice won him a posthumous VC and the whole incident was seized on by journalists at the time who gave the

Henderson's grave in Cojeul Military Cemetery (Photo: Donald Jennings)

captain the most fulsome praise. He is buried at Cojeul British Cemetery, Row B, Grave 61; this is the same cemetery in which Pte Horace Waller VC is buried.

Henderson's citation was gazetted on 5 July 1917 as follows:

> For most conspicuous bravery, although almost immediately wounded in the left arm, he led his company through the front enemy line until he gained his final objective. He then proceeded to consolidate his position, which, owing to heavy gun and machine-gun fire, and bombing attacks, was in danger of being isolated. By his cheerful courage and coolness he was enabled to maintain the spirit of his men under most trying conditions. Capt. Henderson was killed after he had successfully accomplished his task.

The news of his death reached his parents at the beginning of May and it was a double blow for them as his brother, Pte George Henderson, had been killed in action serving with the Canadian Army on the first day of the Arras battle. The two brothers had been at home together, briefly, in November 1916.

Henderson's VC and MC were both presented to his father by the King in the forecourt of Buckingham Palace on 21 July 1917.

One of Henderson's brother officers wrote the following to his father about his son's deeds: 'His conduct and courage on the 23rd would entitle him to higher honour if that was possible. He has won imperishable fame.'

Arthur Henderson was born at 18 Greenhill Road in Paisley, Scotland, on 6 May 1893. He was the son of Baillie George Henderson, a retired builder, and Elizabeth Henderson (née Purdie) of Egnal (later No. 11) Riccartsbar Avenue, Paisley. He was educated at the John Neilson Institution, Paisley. The story of the founding of his school is of interest as it was originally gifted in 1852 by a Paisley merchant named John Neilson. After leaving school Henderson began work as an accountant and stockbroker with the firm of R. Easton & Co. in Glasgow. Before the war he became a fine cricketer and played several excellent innings for the Ferguslie Cricket Club.

In August 1914, at the age of twenty-one, Henderson enlisted as a private in the Argyll and Sutherland Highlanders; he was then commissioned into the A&SH Special Reserve Battalion. He later went to France where he was attached to the 2nd Battalion with whom he won an MC on the Somme in July 1916. This was gazetted on 10 January 1917:

> He led his company in the attack with great courage and determination, advancing our lines and consolidating the position with great skill. He had previously done fine work.

On 19 August 1916 he was made acting captain.

During the Somme battle the 2nd A&SH, as part of the 98th Brigade, were involved in an unsuccessful attack from Bazentin-le-Petit towards the village of Martinpuich. Later they took part in a similarly unsuccessful attack on High Wood and later still they were involved in attempts to capture Daisy and Dewdrop Trenches, again without success.

After Henderson's death, his name was included on a memorial which was unveiled at his former school on 30 November 1932 by the Earl of Home. The memorial was placed on the right side of the vestibule (as visitors entered the school) and consisted of a bronze plaque mounted on an Austrian oak base. In a specially lit recess there was a Book of Remembrance containing the list of the seven hundred former pupils and staff who took part in the First World War, one hundred of whom died or were killed. This memorial was joined by another after the Second World War.

In 1968 the John Neilson school was rebuilt on a new site in the town and was named the John Neilson High School. Years later it was found that the new school was too large and the student population was no longer sufficient to fill it.

It was decided to merge the school with the Castlehead High School and in June 1989 the John Neilson High School closed its doors for the last time. The War Memorial, which had followed with the change of schools, was then transferred to Paisley Abbey and the memorial plaques relating to the two wars were mounted on the abbey cloisters wall, together with a new plaque commemorating the John Neilson School, 1852–1989. Neilson, the school's founder, is buried in the abbey, and the Books of Remembrance from the school are deposited in one of the chapels in the abbey, under glass. Henderson's brother, George, also killed in the First World War, went to the John Neilson school and is therefore included in the school war memorial. The two brothers were also listed on the roll of honour at Oakshaw West United Free Church.

Henderson is also commemorated on the memorial in the clubhouse of the local Ferguslie Cricket Club at Meikleriggs, Corsebar Road, Paisley. Until around 1987 a portrait of Henderson used to hang in the club together with his VC ribbon; later the picture was presented to the A&SH at Stirling Castle for safe-keeping. Altogether, fourteen former members of the club were killed or died during the war. Another place where Henderson was remembered was in the tearoom of a drapers called Robert Cochran & Sons, now owned by the House of Fraser. The tearoom used to be run by two relatives of Henderson. These two ladies later sold Henderson's medals which then became the property of a member of the Scottish Military Collections Society. Christie's sold Henderson's medals on 4 July 1978 for £8,200 and twelve years later, on 20 November 1990, they fetched £14,000.

When researching Henderson's life in Paisley, the writer received assistance from a lady named Manan Smith; she was given a gold necklace by her grandmother, who was probably Henderson's fiancée. It was to be the last gift that he gave her.

D.P. HIRSCH

Near Wancourt, France, 23 April

Capt. David Hirsch was in command of Y Company, 4th Yorkshire Regiment (Alexandra, Princess of Wales's Own), of 150th Brigade, 50th Division. This battalion, also known as the 4th Green Howards, was to take part in the Second Battle of the Scarpe. The section of the front that it was involved with lay roughly between Wancourt Tower and the River Cojeul. The front line itself offered scant protection and any attack suffered severely from the German artillery. When the unit was in support it occupied Niger Trench. When in reserve it occupied recently captured deep German dug-outs in the position known as the Harp.

The British plan was to attack on a front of about 9 miles extending from Croisilles to the right to Gavrelle to the north. The German high ground positions at Chérisy were to be taken by three divisions, the 15th and 30th as well as the 50th. During the night of 22/23 April the Green Howards moved up into position for the attack on the following day.

With the support of two tanks the 1/4th East Yorkshires and the Green Howards captured their first objective, where a party of Germans was holding out in a small wood called Kestrel Copse on the Chérisy–Guémappe road, now the D38. It was here that Hirsch attempted to capture a machine-gun post.

The history of the Green Howards tells the story in greater detail, and to paraphrase it:

W, X and Z Coys. were in the front line from right to left and other troops were north of the railway. The barrage began at 4.45 a.m. and the German reply targeted the line of the River Cojeul and ground to the west of Wancourt. Progress by W Coy. was slow and German machine-gun and rifle fire caused many casualties. The Green Howards had to occupy shell holes for cover. When they were reinforced they captured the enemy trench in which there were many dead Germans.

X Coy. reached their objective with fewer casualties than W and Z. At 5.25 a.m. they reached a wide German support trench which was full of German

110

dead. Z Coy. continued their advance and dug in about 150 yards to the west of their original objective.

By 6.05 a.m. Hirsch was the only officer left with Y Coy. and he decided to make a defensive flank in line, parallel to the river, with half of the men left from Y Coy. He also decided to hold on to his position with the remaining men (150) and sent back for reinforcements. A Coy of the 5th Durham Light Infantry came up and extended the line on the right across the river and towards the 1/4 East Yorks still of the 150th Brigade.

To quote Hirsch's citation:

For most conspicuous bravery and devotion to duty in attack. Having arrived at the first objective, Capt. Hirsch, although already wounded, returned over fire-swept slopes to satisfy himself that the defensive flank was being established. Machine-gun fire was so intense that it was necessary for him to be continuously up and down the line, encouraging his men to dig and hold the position. He continued to encourage his men by standing on the parapet and steadying them in the face of machine-gun fire and counter-attack until he was killed. His conduct throughout was a magnificent example of the greatest devotion to duty.

Hirsch was killed at 7.15 a.m. and his place was taken by a Lt Luckhurst, who was in charge of a trench mortar battery. At 7.30 a.m. it was clear that the enemy was about to launch a strong counter-attack with one part of it coming from the low ground close to the river. A phased retirement was organized and on 24 April the Green Howards were back at the citadel in Arras.

As had happened so often in the past, the day was won by German machine-gunners and they had established a particularly strong post at Wancourt Tower, which had been captured and then lost in previous days. It stood on high ground and had a clear field of vision, so it was also used as an artillery observation post. The tower was later reduced to ruins, which are still visible (1997). Wancourt British Cemetery is down a track which leads to the village of the same name. The River Cojeul, which was so important in 1917, is now a mere stream,

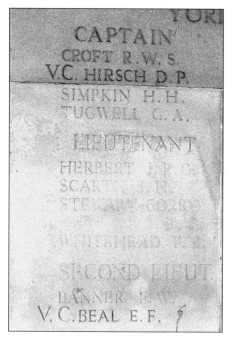

Hirsch's name on the Arras Memorial to the Missing (Photo: Donald Jennings)

and German blockhouses remain on the river banks giving visitors an indication of the importance of the position.

Hirsch was awarded a posthumous VC for his actions on 23 April 1917 and the medal was presented to his parents by the King in the forecourt of Buckingham Palace on 21 July 1917. At the time of his death Hirsch was unmarried. His name is listed on the Arras Memorial to the Missing.

David Philip Hirsch was born in Leeds on 28 December 1896; he was the eldest son of Harry and Edith Hirsch of Westwood Grove, Leeds. He entered Willaston School, Nantwich, in 1908 and became a star pupil. His favourite subject was modern history and he won an open exhibition in the subject at Worcester College, Oxford. He was also an accomplished athlete and a good cricketer. During his final year at school he was head boy. In December 1914 he left school and began army training with the Leeds University OTC.

On 7 April 1915 Hirsch was commissioned into the 11th West Yorkshire Regiment and in early 1916 he left for the front. He was attached to the 1/4th Yorkshire Regiment and was with them at High Wood on the Somme and in the capture of Eaucourt l'Abbaye in early October. In September Hirsch had been wounded and in the same month he was Mentioned in Despatches. He was also made a temporary lieutenant.

The 1/4th Yorkshire Regiment were in billets in Albert from 3 October 1916 and since mid-September they had suffered 399 casualties, including those men killed, missing or wounded. On 30 November the Green Howards marched with their brigade to the village of Contay and on New Year's Eve they moved into huts near the village of Bazentin-le-Petit. In the New Year the battalion moved again, first to Fricourt and then to Buire. The battalion was still understrength and saw very little front line service during this period.

On 10 February 1917 the battalion moved to Foucaucourt, where they relieved units of the French Army and became the extreme right battalion of the British Army line on the Western Front. In March 1917 Hirsch was made temporary captain and his battalion moved into the Arras area at the end of the month. Shortly before his death he was promoted to full captain.

In the late 1930s Hirsch's father declared open a Convalescent and Men's Holiday Home at Great Hucklow, Derbyshire, which was built as a memorial to the men of the Unitarian Church who had lost their lives in the First World War. Hirsch's parents paid for a swimming pool to be built in their son's memory at his former school, Willaston School, in London Road, Nantwich. The pool was open to the public and contained a plaque to Philip's memory. The school later became St Joseph's Community Home and subsequently closed.

Hirsch's VC became the property of his brother, Maj. Frank Hirsch, who died in 1995 at the age of ninety-seven. Frank's grandson, Philip Kilpin, later presented the medal to the Green Howards Museum in Richmond, Yorkshire, which holds thirteen VCs won by the regiment. Hirsch's Army file, which was weeded in 1935, does not even mention his winning the VC.

E. FOSTER

Villers-Plouich, France, 24 April

The 13th East Surreys of the 40th Division (XV Corps) moved to the village of Equancourt, to the south-west of Havrincourt Wood, on 16 April 1917. The village had been virtually destroyed by the Germans when they retreated to the Hindenburg Line.

However, sufficient shelter was found in the ruins for the battalion. In the evening of 18 April the battalion moved up to Gouzeaucourt Wood, to the south-east of Havrincourt Wood, to positions close to the present-day D917 road. There were no trenches and the men either gathered at one of four outposts or camped in bivouacs or small shelters.

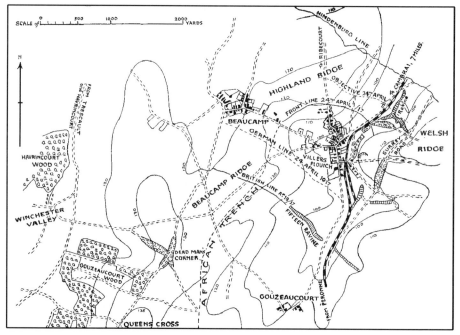

Map showing the area around Villers-Plouich. The village was captured by the 13th Battalion on 24 April 1917

Within twenty-four hours, however, the German artillery had 'found them out', although resulting casualties were very few. On the 21st the battalion moved with the 119th Brigade on their right and the 11th King's Own Royal Lancasters on their left to a line some 800 yards to the south of the hamlet called Beaucamp, via a position called Fifteen Ravine. During the night of the 22nd a 4½ ft trench was dug on the battalion's front in preparation for an assault on the village of Villers-Plouich, which was in front of the Hindenburg Line. The battalion was also to capture some of the high ground to the north of the village, which was called Highland Ridge.

At 2.00 a.m. on 24 April the 13th East Surreys occupied their new trench, which led in a north-westerly direction from Fifteen Ravine, with the Péronne–Cambrai railway on its right. Fifteen Ravine was so-named as it had once contained fifteen trees: these were cut down by the enemy as they gave the British artillery too good a ranging mark. The ravine had been captured by the 12th South Wales Borderers on 21 April after severe fighting. Four companies from the 13th East Surreys were involved in the initial attack on the 24th and at 4.15 a.m. the battalion moved forward in four waves towards the German wire, under the leadership of Capt. L.B. Mills and behind a barrage of fire. The German artillery replied, but did little harm to the attackers. After seven minutes the first enemy trenches were entered and after a short struggle the advance towards the village continued. During this advance Lewis guns dealt with various enemy strongpoints and machine-gun positions.

At 5.30 a.m. the village was reached and the battalion was then split up into three sections. The right party met with strong opposition, but still managed to reach a ravine 700 yards to the north-east of the village. Capt. Crocker was killed and Lt F.J.T. Hann took over. It was at this point that Cpl Edward Foster, with his two Lewis guns, attacked and captured the machine-gun teams that had been holding up the right company. The guns were 'entrenched and strongly covered by wire entanglements'. Foster succeeded in entering the German trench and engaged the enemy guns. One of his own Lewis guns was lost, but he rushed forward and, bombing the enemy, recovered the captured gun. He then put his two guns into action, killing the German gun team and capturing their guns, which allowed the advance to continue. For his bravery, Foster was later awarded the VC.

The middle party moved through the western side of the village and established themselves on the section of high ground known as the Highland Ridge. The party on the left of the battalion attack overpowered a strongpoint on the Villers-Plouich–Beaucamp sunken road. After a short fight for possession, a hundred Germans were taken prisoner. It was then discovered that Beaucamp had not yet been captured by the British according to plan and the captured strongpoint was subsequently consolidated. A defensive flank was established towards Beaucamp and the high ground to the north-east of the village.

At 6.30 a.m. the British barrage ceased and consolidation continued. However, the German artillery began a very heavy barrage ten minutes later which was accurately targeted on the right and centre parties. It was decided to move them to less dangerous positions to the east of the village. The two parties withdrew and their role was taken over by Lewis gunners who secured the entrances to the village.

An hour later the 14th Highland Light Infantry arrived as reinforcements, and the 13th East Surreys were able to advance once more and reach positions 300 yards east of the village where strong outposts were established. The enemy continued with a bombardment.

The next day Beaucamp village was at last cleared by the 11th King's Own Royal Lancasters and in the evening the 13th East Surreys were relieved by the 13th East Yorks. The battalion moved back to the village of Equancourt again and spent the next few days there. The capture of Villers-Plouich had been a successful operation. The casualties for the month totalled 223 dead, wounded or missing. Later, cemeteries were built on the site of Fifteen Ravine and at the sunken road.

On 21 July 1917 Foster was presented with his VC by the King in the forecourt of Buckingham Palace. Owing to the King's relative lack of height most soldiers appear to be taller than he; however, 'Tiny' Foster towers over his sovereign in the published pictures of the two men.

Fifteen Ravine, Villers-Plouich (Photo: Peter Batchelor)

Edward Foster was born in Tooting Grove, London, on 4 February 1886. As a child he received rudimentary education at Tooting Graveney School, the local elementary school. Prior to the First World War, Foster became known as 'Tiny' because of his height of 6 foot plus and his 20 stone weight. At the age of fourteen he found himself a job as a dustman, initially with a contractor called F.W. Surridge.

Foster enlisted at the beginning of the war and joined the 13th East Surreys, which was raised by the Mayor of Wandsworth in May 1915; his service number was 13290. The battalion was allowed to incorporate the motto 'We Serve' from the borough's coat of arms into its badge. Within two months 800–1,000 recruits had joined up and much of their initial training was carried out in Buckhold Road, which later became King George's Park. The battalion served in France for two years from 1916 to 1918. Foster was demobilized in 1919. On Armistice Day in 1920 he was one of the holders of the VC who attended the burial service of the Unknown Warrior.

On Michaelmas Day (29 September) 1920 Wandsworth Borough Council decided to adopt the devastated village of Villers-Plouich, under a scheme arranged by the British League of Help. Funds were sent to France from the borough which helped to rebuild the village school and reinstate the water supply. A marble plaque in the village commemorates the village's gratitude to Wandsworth. Each Armistice Day the village people honour the dead of the 13th East Surreys at their local cemetery where many of them lie.

In recognition of his valour in the war, a job was virtually created for Foster by Wandsworth Council. As Dustman Inspector, he covered Wandsworth, Putney and Roehampton and his duties were to see that the rubbish collections were being carried out efficiently. He regularly took part in VC and British Legion functions and was often a wreath-layer at the annual ceremonies. In 1931 he attended the opening of the new Town Hall in Wimbledon on 5 November and was a member of the guard of honour for Prince George (the Duke of Kent), to whom Foster was introduced.

Foster's grave in Streatham Cemetery, Tooting, London (Photo: Donald Jennings)

Foster lived until the end of the Second World War at 92 Fountain Road, near Tooting Broadway. After a short illness he died in St James's Hospital, Wandsworth, of bronchial pneumonia on 22 January 1946 at the age of fifty-nine. He left behind a widow, Alice Jane Foster, and a son, Dennis, who was a naval petty officer. Dennis was given special leave to attend his father's funeral which took place on 5 February. Foster's coffin was covered with a Union Jack and was taken to the Streatham Cemetery chapel in Garratt Lane, where the service was conducted. Many local dignitaries attended the funeral, together with his immediate family. His grave is No. 357 in Section F15. When she died twenty-six years later, on 20 October 1972, Alice Foster was buried in the same grave, having reached the age of 88.

On 8 May 1995 a new path alongside the River Wandle in King George's Park, Wandsworth, was named Foster's Way by the Mayor of Wandsworth, Beryl Jeffery, in honour of the former council employee. Dennis Foster attended the ceremony along with some forty members of the Foster family; a memorial commemorating the event was unveiled at the same time. In recent years the original links between Villers-Plouich and Wandsworth have been re-established and the annual wreath-laying service at the memorial of the 13th East Surreys in Wandsworth High Street has also been revived.

On 7 June 1997 a new headstone was unveiled at Foster's grave to replace the one put in place fifty years before. The grave had previously had a free-standing kerb around it, and permission had been granted to erect a permanent headstone. However, this had never been carried out and the cemetery authorities indicated that they would be happy to accept a copy of the standard Commonwealth War Graves Commission stone. The site was in danger of being 'tidied up' if the kerbstones were not removed. Obviously, this spurred the Foster family and friends into action as the necessary funds for the new stone were duly collected.

At the ceremony a guard of honour was supplied by a company of the regiment that is a successor of the 13th East Surreys, namely A (Anzio) Company of the 5th Battalion, The Princess of Wales's Royal Regiment.

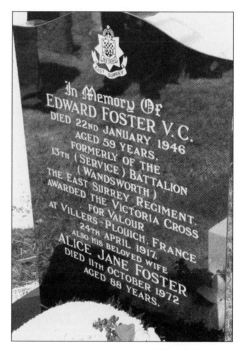

Foster's new gravestone (Photo: P. McCue)

Once again, Councillor Jeffery laid a wreath and addresses were given, including one by Dennis Foster. Later a reception was held for the families of men who had formerly served in the 13th East Surreys. Each year the junior NCOs of the current battalion hold a Villers-Plouich dinner to commemorate Foster winning the VC.

Foster's medals, which included the BWM, VM, George VI Coronation Medal, Médaille Militaire (French) as well as his VC, were offered for sale in July 1988 by Sotheby's with the expected price of between £8,000 and £12,000. They actually fetched £12,100.

E. BROOKS

Fayet, France, 28 April

The 2/4th Oxford and Buckinghamshire Light Infantry landed in France on 24 May 1916, having been previously on the east coast of England engaged in training and garrison duty. They were part of the 184th Brigade of 61st (South Midland) Division.

The battalion moved to the Laventie sector where the men received instruction in trench warfare. They first saw action in the Battle of the Somme on 19 July 1916 and four months later took over part of the Somme line in Grandcourt. In March 1917, when the German Army was beginning to fall back to the Hindenburg Line, the Ox & Bucks were near the village of Ablaincourt. A few weeks later the battalion was in action near the village of Le Vergier and three weeks after that they were at the village of Fayet near the German-held town of St Quentin.

It was at Fayet that a plan was proposed for a raiding party supplied by men from the 2/4th Ox & Bucks to pass through a known gap in the section of the enemy trench opposite the village of Fayet. The trench was thought to be unoccupied. The raid, timed to begin at 4.20 a.m. on 28 April, was also to pass through several copses which were also thought to be unoccupied.

C Company, under Capt. G.K. Rose, began to move up to their start positions at dusk on the 27th; it was later discovered that the enemy was contemplating carrying out a similar operation at the same time. Moving up from Holnon, the raiding party reached the sunken road leading to Fayet and found it full of troops. Reliefs and supports were being organized, and while all this activity was taking place the German artillery dropped five nines on the sunken road. Many of the men initially packed themselves under the banks of the road for safety. C Company continued across the Gricourt–Fayet road until they came to a large crater close to the gap in the German defences.

It was in this action that 201154 CSM Edward Brooks won his VC. At 3.00 a.m. on 28 April Capt. Rose led his company of about 150 men over open ground north of Fayet in order to reach its eastern side. It was pitch dark and the raiding party managed to capture one prisoner and two machine-guns. The supposedly deserted copses had not been left empty. The enemy attacked the Ox & Bucks in their flank and rear positions and the company managed to extricate itself as soon as it began to grow light. During the fighting Brooks saw that the front wave was buckling, because a German machine-gun was checking the attackers of the first wave at close quarters. Without waiting for orders, Brooks dashed forward from the second wave with the intention of capturing the gun. He killed one of the gunners with his revolver and bayoneted another. Seeing what had happened to their comrades, the rest of the machine-gun crew decided to make themselves scarce. This left the German gun in Brooks's possession and he promptly turned it against the fleeing Germans before carrying it back to his own lines. The raiding party returned to Holnon Wood and rested in a sandy railway cutting before continuing to Attilly.

Brooks's VC was gazetted on 27 June 1917 and the citation was as follows:

For most conspicuous bravery. This Warrant Officer, while taking part in a raid on the enemy's trenches, saw that the front wave was checked by an enemy machine-gun at close quarters. On his own initiative, and regardless of personal danger, he rushed forward from the second wave with the object of capturing the gun, killing one of the gunners with his revolver and bayoneting another. The remainder of the gun's crew then made off, leaving the gun in his possession. Company Sgt-Major Brooks then turned the machine-gun on to the retreating enemy, after which he carried it back into our lines. By his courage and initiative he undoubtedly saved many casualties, and greatly added to the success of the operations.

The battalion later moved to the Arras sector and took up positions south-west of Cambrai.

For four weeks from mid-August 1917 the 61st Division was involved in the Third Battle of Ypres. The battalion history describes Brooks at this period as a member of Company Headquarters: 'there was, of course, the redoubtable Sgt-Maj. Brooks, who besides being a great fighter possessed high organising powers.'

Edward Brooks was born in Oakley, Buckinghamshire, on 11 April 1883. Prior to the First World War he worked for Messrs Knowles & Sons, a building firm in Oxford, and lived in Windsor Street, Highfield. At some period he had been in the Grenadier Guards.

In October 1914 he decided to enlist and was posted to a battalion of the Oxford and Buckinghamshire Light Infantry as a private. For the first two months of the war he taught shooting to members of the Headington Miniature Rifle Club. He was a first-class shot and before the war had won prizes for shooting. He also taught army drill. He was soon promoted to lance corporal and in May 1915 he was made a sergeant. Shortly afterwards he left for France and in July he was made a company sergeant major. In November 1916 he went home for ten days' leave. In July 1917 *The Sketch* called on his wife, Elsie May Brooks, and the couple's children in order to take their photograph. Next day several newspapers reported on Brooks's feat in winning the VC and a committee was formed in Highfield to make arrangements for celebrations when Brooks returned from the front.

In 1919 he was discharged from the Army with the rank of company sergeant major. He attended the 1920 garden party for winners of the VC and GC, and the 1929 dinner at the House of Lords. On 18 November 1929 Brooks attended the unveiling of the 61st (South Midland) Divisional Memorial at Holy Trinity Church, Stratford. The memorial, in the form of a tablet, was unveiled by Sir Ivor Maxse, commander of XVIII Corps, to which 61st Division belonged. At the ceremony the divisional flag was raised by Brooks. On 6 May 1935 Brooks took part in a Silver Jubilee rally of over three thousand veterans from the First

Brooks's grave, Rose Hill Cemetery, Oxford (Photo: Donald Jennings)

World War, and at a Poppy Day appeal on 11 October 1935 Brooks was photographed shaking hands with Countess Haig. In 1944 he took part in a local Salute the Soldier Week in the Oxford area.

He worked for twenty-five years on the production line of Morris Motors of Cowley. Later, he became a fireman at the works and finally, when he had turned sixty, he worked in the stores for a short time. Lord Nuffield met him on a number of occasions and the press occasionally featured pictures of the two men. He lived at 42 Morrell Avenue, Oxford, and died on 26 June 1944, having been ill with thrombosis for five weeks. He was survived by his wife, Elsie May Brooks, two sons and three daughters. He was buried on 29 June in Rose Hill Cemetery, Oxford, in Plot G2, Grave 119, and Lord Nuffield sent a wreath. Brooks's former regiment was also represented at his funeral, which was not a military one, although the local British Legion presented a flag for covering the coffin of the former soldier. The fire brigade from Morris Motors was also well represented. A local newspaper described Brooks as a 'quiet home-loving man, he was a keen gardener and won the cup for gardens on the Council estates for two years'.

Elsie died in November 1958 and is buried in the same grave as her husband. Brooks's medals are in the Royal Greenjackets Museum, Winchester.

R.L. HAINE

Near Gavrelle, France, 28/29 April

In mid-April 1917 the 63rd (Naval) Division took over from the 34th Division, who were on the right of the 2nd Division in front of the village of Gavrelle. The division had artillery support from the 34th Division. Gavrelle was just to the east of the enemy Hindenburg Line, or German third position. The new positions were taken over by the 189th and 190th Brigades of the 63rd (Naval) Division. On 15 April the 4th Bedfordshire Regiment and the 10th Royal Dublin Fusiliers, both of 190th Brigade, made an attempt to get the brigade outposts into a straighter line. However, this proved to be a costly failure and on the 16/17th another attempt was made by the 1st Battalion Honourable Artillery Company (HAC) and 7th Royal Fusiliers, who managed to push their outposts forward, allowing the two brigades to link up.

These positions were far from ideal, as they were on a forward slope which looked down into the Gavrelle Plain and they were in full view of the enemy. To add to the problems, the weather was extremely cold and wintry with alternating sleet and snow.

On 22 April the 1st HAC was in the Black Line, preparing to take part in an attack the next day. The 37th Division was on the right flank and the three objectives of the Naval Division were the German trenches in front of the village, the north–south road running through the village from Oppy in the north to Roeux in the south, and lastly a line around 600 yards to the east of the village which would allow them to link up with the 37th Division to their right. Further south the 51st (Highland) Division was attempting to capture the chemical works strongpoint. After the first objective had been taken, the 190th Brigade was to form a defensive flank while their sister brigade, the 189th, took part in the next stage of the fight for the village.

The HAC, with whom we are especially concerned here, were in support of the 4th Bedfords and 7th Royal Fusiliers and were in positions about half a mile from Gavrelle at Point du Jour (a former miniature fortress in the German line). Machine-gun companies went forward with the infantry when the attack began at 4.45 a.m. on 23 April. The first objective was captured, but the advance was held up on the Oppy–Roeux road. At this point the British barrage lifted. Fighting in the centre of the village became intense and was organized by Commanders Asquith and Bennett. Progress was slow but the next north–south line was reached, which was the main Oppy–Gavrelle road. There was no sign of the 4th Bedfords, who had been given the task of capturing a windmill on the north side of the village.

Beyond the Oppy road was the mayor's house, which was a possible German strongpoint. It was captured with little loss, however, as it was found to be virtually empty. An enemy force at the windmill was nevertheless proving to be a problem, and as Asquith's force was by now very much reduced he wisely decided to withdraw to the western side of the village. It was considered that only a large force would be capable of capturing the mill. Initially the attack turned out to be a costly failure but later a foothold was secured in the village, and Capt. Alfred Pollard, in charge of the HAC B Company, managed to clear the German support trench and to occupy the whole of the enemy first line trench system.

Progress had been made further south and soon the whole of Gavrelle was in British hands; this proved an awkward salient that was overlooked by the Hindenburg Line. However, owing to the failure of the left-flanking 2nd Division, the men of B Company HAC found themselves sharing the same trench with the enemy, and a block in the trench line was quickly established. The two groups were divided by a railway line which ran across the trench at right angles. There was a strongpoint in the German section of the trench and B Company could do little about the situation except try to consolidate their own position. During the night C and D Companies moved up to take over from A and B Companies. The officer in charge of C Company was 2/Lt Reginald Haine.

On 24 April the Germans, specifically the Prussian Guards, through a very determined counter-attack and with the help of their artillery, managed to repossess Gavrelle and capture the positions lost by them the day before. Later the HAC were relieved by the 2nd Royal Marines.

The HAC remained in the Black Line until 27 April. In Gavrelle there had been little change in the situation. A new attack was to be carried out on the 28th against the German line that ran from the northern part of Gavrelle due north to Oppy Wood. Simultaneously with the initial attack, the HAC were to try to bomb out the strongpoint by working along the trench from the south part of the village. Haine's C Company was given this task, and D Company was to concentrate on the German support line at the same time. Unfortunately, a machine-gun at the German strongpoint next to the railway line took a very heavy toll of the HAC, but Haine decided to attack the strongpoint regardless of the considerable danger. Three attempts were made and the personnel of C Company dwindled in numbers. To help out, Haine sent a message back asking for Stokes mortar assistance for the next attempt to take the position. Meanwhile, D Company had made progress against the German support line and were able to see the rear of the German strongpoint.

However, time was running out and Haine decided not to wait for Stokes mortar support; with the help of D Company he managed finally to take the strongpoint, but was unable to hold on to it for long. He discovered that the position held about a hundred men as well as several machine-guns. It was a sort of 'honeycomb' which not only bristled with machine-guns but also contained a deep dug-out. Soon a counter-attack from the direction of Oppy forced C Company, which was then down to a couple of dozen men, back to the south of the railway line.

During the day the Naval Division hung on grimly and fought off at least seven attempts to shift them from the village, but they hardly lost a yard of captured ground. The two sides were so close that any artillery fire would have caused casualties to both sides simultaneously. Early the next day Haine was called back to battalion headquarters, which was in the same trench, further down the trench line. There he met up with Col. Osmond, who was then in charge of the operation and who told him to attack the strongpoint again. So Haine made a sixth attempt to attack the strongpoint across the railway. This time his party was successful and they took the position, capturing fifty Prussian guardsmen. According to an interview with Haine by Peter Liddle, the reason why the attack succeeded was that 'they panicked'.

To prevent a quick German recovery 2/Lt Pollard went through C Company's positions and established a post some distance to the north of the strongpoint. This allowed Haine to consolidate his position. Expecting the inevitable counter-attack, Pollard placed himself at the point closest to the enemy, together with a handful of men, all well supplied with bombs. The Germans began to move down the trench towards Pollard, but they had met their match for he was a very experienced bomber and was able to hold up the German advance with accurate throwing of Mills bombs. The Germans even retreated to get out of Pollard's range! Sensing that he had his adversary on the run, Pollard moved forward in pursuit and once he got moving there was no holding him. Fed by a continuous supply of bombs, Pollard managed to clear 300 yards of trench. He thus managed to capture territory which a whole brigade had previously failed to capture, and he and Haine were recommended for two very well deserved VCs which were both gazetted on 8 June 1917.

Haine's citation read as follows:

For most conspicuous bravery and determination when our troops, occupying a pronounced salient, would be surrounded. 2/Lt Haine organized and led with the utmost gallantry six bombing attacks against a strongpoint which dangerously threatened our communication, capturing the position, together with fifty prisoners and two machine-guns. The enemy then counter-attacked with a battalion of the Guard, succeeded in regaining his position, and the situation appeared critical. 2/Lt Haine at once formed a block in his trench, and for the whole of the following night maintained his position against repeated determined attacks. Reorganizing his men on the following morning, he again attacked and captured the strongpoint, pressing the enemy back for several hundred yards, and thus relieving the situation. Throughout these operations this officer's superb courage, quick decisions, and sound judgement were beyond praise, and it was his splendid personal example that inspired his men to continue their efforts during more than thirty hours of continuous fighting.

The HAC were relieved by a battalion of East Yorks from the 31st Division and marched back to Roclincourt where they rested under canvas. On 1 May the HAC were congratulated by their corps commander, Sir William Congreve VC. Eight days later the battalion moved to excellent billets at Mont-St-Eloi, remaining there for ten days. A draft arrived from England and on 20 May the battalion marched to St Catherine on the outskirts of Arras. At this time they returned to trench positions in Gavrelle, where they consolidated their positions for the five days of their tour before returning to a support line close to Bailleul. On 1 June they were relieved by the Nelson Battalion and returned to huts at Roclincourt. Any plans for capturing Gavrelle were abandoned for the time being.

On 6 June an announcement about the winning of the two VCs was made and, not surprisingly, a great reception was arranged in the evening which was attended by senior officers and many others. On 21 July 1917 both Haine and Pollard received their VCs in the forecourt of Buckingham Palace.

Haine was also presented with an Illuminated Address, and was informed of plans to set up a subscription on his behalf. He rejected this suggestion with great vehemence and the Richmond council officials were not pleased! Haine simply could not see any connection between money and his deed.

The City Press of 28 July 1917 wrote up Haine's and Pollard's investiture in the following way:

The investiture of VC heroes at Buckingham Palace on Saturday was followed by a rousing welcome at Armoury House to the two recipients belonging to the HAC – Capt. Alfred Oliver Pollard and 2/Lt Reginald Leonard Haine. The regimental flag was broken in line with the Union Jack and the Stars and Stripes, and all the available artillery and infantry mounted a guard of honour. Preceded by the regimental band, playing 'See the Conquering Hero Comes' and the Regimental March, the two officers walked through cheering lines to a platform in the middle of the drill ground, where they were accompanied by their parents and a group of distinguished officers, including General Sir Henry Mackinnon of C.I.V. fame, and Colonel the Earl of Denbigh, commanding the HAC. When the cheers had subsided, Lord Denbigh said that, during the many years he had had the honour of commanding the regiment, that day was one which made him feel more proud of it than any other event. He had seen various notable gatherings on that old ground, and the regiment when he first entered it 25 years ago was very different from what it was to-day. One never thought in those days that the HAC would become the magnificent fighting force it has now developed into, and that the regiment would have an opportunity of congratulating two of its officers on having won the most desired honour for bravery in the British Army. (Hear, hear.) He had just come away from a most remarkable investiture, by the King, and had heard recited the brave deeds which merited the honours bestowed by His Majesty. He did not wish to distinguish one from another, but when the Corps considered what those two HAC boys – for he would call them boys – had done, it had reason to be proud of them, not merely on account of their pluck and bravery shown on the field, but because of the coolness and initiative they showed, and owed to the valuable training they had acquired. (Applause.) It was one thing to be able to follow in the field, and quite another thing to organize and lead men in a difficult situation, to keep up its discipline, and to save the situation. The two winners were up against the Prussian Guards. Capt. Pollard had won the VC and the MC Bar for conspicuous bravery and determination at a place he was not allowed to mention. Troops of various units had become disorganized by shell fire, and Capt. Pollard dashed up to stop the retirement. With only four men, he started a counter-attack with bombs, and regained not only the ground that had been lost but more besides. He had already won the DCM and the MC (Applause.) 2/Lt Haine organized with the utmost gallantry six bombing attacks against a strongpoint which dangerously threatened our communications, and he captured many prisoners and guns. The enemy regained the situation, and the position was critical. Reorganizing his men the next morning, he again attacked, captured a strongpoint, and relieved the situation. (Applause.) Those feats gave some idea of the fighting that some of the HAC battalions had been doing in France for a long time. The two officers were to be congratulated on having come safely through, and on having been able to receive the honours they had won so well. One must not forget the men who were with and followed them, and those who followed and had not come back. (Hear, hear.) Fortunately, the losses on that occasion were small, compared with the importance of the gains, and the small losses were undoubtedly attributable to the excellent discipline and splendid training of the officers and men who took part in the fight. That showed the value of discipline and training. They were all very proud of being members of the old regiment, which had expanded during the war to an extent they never dreamt of. Whereas at the beginning of the war the HAC consisted of two horse batteries and half a battalion of infantry, it now contained four mounted batteries in the field, a siege battery, and two infantry battalions that had done some of the heaviest fighting which had taken place on the front. In that connection he would like to read an extract from an address given to the HAC Battalion in question by the Commander of the Army Corps to which they belonged. 'The fighting recently has been very severe, and, sitting behind, as I have to do, I admit at times that I was anxious, as it appeared that our position might possibly be worse than it was at the beginning. Then word came through that the HAC were bombing up the Hun trench, and afterwards further word that the HAC had driven the enemy out of the front line. This was indeed a great relief to me. Nobody hates the Bosche more than I do, but I admire him as a very fine soldier. You had against you the finest troops of the German Army – the Prussian Guard – and you beat them. That is enough. Your regiment has a very fine record in history, and you will now have added a page which is worthy of any page in that history. To thank you and to congratulate you, and to tell you how proud I am of you, is what I have come here for today.' . . . The King told him that morning to let the officers and men know how proud he was to be connected with the regiment as Captain-General and Colonel, and to decorate those two officers. His Majesty sent them all words of encouragement, and felt confident that they would do everything they possibly could to maintain the record of the HAC. (Applause.) With the utmost enthusiasm officers and men gave the HAC fire – Zay, Zay, Zay – for the two VCs, the King and General Sir Henry Mackinnon.

Haine's deeds were also written up in a rather breathless style in *The Scouts' Book of Heroes* by F. Haydn Dimmock.

Reginald Leonard Haine was born in Wandsworth, London, on 10 July 1896 and throughout his life he was known as 'Bill'. He was the son of Mr and Mrs H.J. Haine of Clipsham in Rigley Avenue, Horley, Surrey, and as a young man he became a keen Boy Scout. Having just turned eighteen years of age, he joined the Honourable Artillery Company on 24 August 1914, a few days after Alfred Pollard had done so. Both men went abroad on 16–18 September 1914.

In November 1916, when still a sergeant, Haine took part in the fighting at Beaucourt and at the end of 1916 he was commissioned as a second lieutenant.

When he was serving in the Indian Army in Afghanistan in 1919 he won the

The Honourable Artillery Company plaque at Gavrelle

MC, which he received on 10 March 1920. After serving with the Sikhs for some time, he returned to the HAC and in June 1929 was transferred as an officer to the Territorial Army Reserve. In civilian life he returned to a career in the City of London, where he worked with a firm of chartered accountants. During the Second World War Haine was a Colonel in the Home Guard and in 1956 he became a founder member of the VC/GC Association.

He was married in 1922 to Miss Dora Holder of Cherry Orchard, Woodcote Valley, Purley, at St Mark's Church, Woodcote, Purley, Surrey. In 1935 the survivors of the 1st Battalion HAC's crossing to France in September 1914 dined at Armoury House, City Road, London. The ship they sailed on was the *Westmeath* and the dinner was therefore called the Westmeath Dinner. Haine was the vice-president of the local branch of the Royal British Legion and he lived at Hollist Lane, Easebourne, Midhurst. He was described as a 'very quiet, happy and jovial person, full of fun and always most hospitable'. He died at St Thomas's on 12 June 1982 at the age of eighty-five, leaving behind him a widow from a 59-year marriage. He also left a daughter, Jan, and three grandchildren. His funeral was held at Easebourne parish church and he was cremated the same day. A plaque to his memory is on one of the church walls. His VC, MC and other medals are not publicly held.

Gavrelle was adopted by the City of Westminster after the war and a plaque to the Queen's Westminster Rifles is in the *Mairie*. To the north-east of the village can be found the remains of the famous windmill in a small circle of trees. To the south-west of the village is the Naval Trench Cemetery, which contains the remains of around sixty members of the Naval Division. It was named after a second line trench during the Battle of Arras. During the German

Haine's plaque in Easebourne Priory Cemetery, Midhurst, Surrey (Photo: Donald Jennings)

The Royal Naval Division Memorial at Gavrelle (Photo: Peter Batchelor)

offensive of March 1918 the Queen's Westminsters were here before the village was captured by the Germans who once more surrendered it at the end of August.

In recent years a memorial to the 63rd (Naval) Division has been built on the western side of the village of Gavrelle. It is not to everyone's taste, perhaps because some people consider it to be too arty, rather than being based on a classical tradition.

A.O. POLLARD

Near Gavrelle, France, 29 April

When 2/Lt 'Bill' Haine and Capt. Alfred Pollard won their VCs at Gavrelle on 28/29 April they worked so closely together that it might be sensible for the reader to have the biographies of both men consecutively. While Haine was holding the enemy at bay during the night of 28/29 April, Pollard was sleeping before he was woken with instructions to form a defensive flank.

In his autobiography Pollard described the events that followed:

> My instructions to them [his runner and a lance corporal] before I started were very simple. Each had a Mills bomb in his hand with the safety pin out. I told them that if I fired my pistol they were to throw bombs immediately to pitch about fifteen yards in front of me. This would land them in the next traverse in front of where we were. They only had two bombs each, at the time; I gave no thought as to where we might find a further supply.

In the 100 yards along the trench the small group encountered nobody and then suddenly, in a stretch between two traverses, they stumbled over a German who was immediately shot by Pollard. His bombers threw their bombs and two more Germans were dealt with before the enemy began to retreat. Pollard was able to replenish his bomb supply from the German trench and continued working up the line with his two colleagues. The Germans counter-attacked as expected, but just as quickly decided to retire once more, at a point when Pollard's supply of bombs was becoming low. Reinforcements who brought a supply of bombs with them came up and they, together with Pollard, consolidated the positions. The enemy tried one more counter-attack, which failed. Pollard and his colleagues were relieved that night.

On 30 April Pollard and Haine were both recommended for a VC. Pollard's citation was gazetted on 8 June 1917:

> For most conspicuous bravery and determination. The troops of various units on the left of this officer's battalion had become disorganized owing to the

heavy casualties from shell fire; and a subsequent determined enemy attack with very strong forces caused further confusion and retirement, closely pressed by hostile forces. 2/Lt Pollard at once realized the seriousness of the situation, and dashed up to stop the retirement. With only four men he started a counter-attack with bombs, and pressed it home till he had broken the enemy attack, and regained all that had been lost and much ground in addition. The enemy retired in disorder, sustaining many casualties. By his force of will, dash and splendid example, coupled with an utter contempt of danger, this officer who has already won the DCM and MC, infused courage into every man who saw him.

Haine and Pollard were bidden to attend an investiture which was to take place at Buckingham Palace on Saturday 21 July. In his book, Pollard describes the scene in the following way:

The investiture was a very impressive affair. It was for VCs only – twenty-four in all. Eighteen attended; the others were posthumous awards. We formed up in the courtyard in the front of the Palace. Each of us had a hook or hooks fastened into his tunic by an official on his arrival. The Grenadiers mounted a guard of honour. Until His Majesty arrived surrounded by a group of A.D.C.s, the band played as only a Guards band can.

At last a sharp word of command brought the Guard of Honour to rigid attention. We followed suit. 'Present arms!' The ensigns dipped. The band played the most stirring tune in the world – the National Anthem. His Majesty emerged from the Palace.

I stood with my arms straight down by my sides and my chest swelling my tunic. 'God save our gracious King.' Wasn't that what we were fighting for? To save the King and all he stood for – our great Nation? From the highest in the land whose representatives surrounded their monarch to the middle class and the lowest who formed the crowd pressed against the railings of the forecourt, all were epitomized in that gathering. We

Capt. Pollard receiving his VC from the King

represented the Navy, the Army and the Air Force. We even represented those who were fallen in the little group of relatives of those to be posthumously honoured at the end of our line.

'Send him victorious, happy and glorious.' Well, he would be victorious if human endeavour could make him so. Every one of us had done his damnedest and we were there to receive our rewards. Not that we needed them. People do not go into action with the idea of winning the Victoria Cross. They go with the bare intention of doing their duty. The decoration merely happens.

'Stand at ease!' The tension relaxed, the proceeding commenced. We were called out in order of seniority. I was the sixth. Ten paces forward and I halted in front of my King. Colonel Clive Wigram read out the particulars of my deeds as published in the *Gazette*. I stood stiffly at attention. When the recitation was concluded His Majesty hooked my medals on to their hooks.

'I've followed the doings of your battalion with the greatest interest,' he said. 'I'm very proud indeed to be your Captain-General and Colonel.'

He shook my hand with a grip of iron. I had scratched the back of my hand rather badly against a rock at the seaside and the scar had only just formed. His Majesty's hand clasp was so powerful that the wound had burst open afresh. I still have the scar. Every time I look at it I am reminded of the occasion when I was so highly honoured.

I stepped back, saluted, and returned to my place to watch Bill going through the same ordeal.

At last it was over and we were in a taxi speeding down the Mall. We were to be given a lunch at Armoury House, Regimental Headquarters . . .

A platform had been especially erected in the centre of the parade ground. The two officers were accompanied by the Colonel of the Regiment, the Earl of Denbigh, and preceded by the regimental band. Two long lines of troops cheered the two men vociferously. There were various speeches but Haine and Pollard kept their responses to the absolute minimum.

In the latter part of the war Pollard ceased to take much of an active part in proceedings and became employed in training members of the American Army who had arrived in France.

In May 1919 the cadre of the 1st HAC returned to London from the Continent. The party comprised just fifty-four men, including six officers, and the group marched from Waterloo station to battalion headquarters in the city.

Alfred Oliver Pollard was born in Wallington, Surrey, on 4 May 1893; he was the son of James Alfred Pollard, a man who lived in at least three different houses in

Wallington during the forty-five years that he spent there. His address in 1893 was Rycroft, Melbourne Road, and his son Alfred may have been born there (at least it was the address of the family home at the time of his birth). Later, Pollard senior moved to Tidbury, 2 Belmont Road. He was a Fellow of the Chartered Insurance Institute and he sent his son to the Merchant Taylors' School.

When war broke out in August 1914 Pollard was working as a clerk with the Alliance Assurance Company at their branch office at St James's Street. His employers told him that if he joined up they would keep his position open for him when the war was over. Pollard quickly decided to join up and as his elder brother had joined the HAC in 1907 he chose to join the same unit. When he first visited Armoury House, the battalion headquarters, he found a crowd of men waiting there. A notice was displayed stating that no further recruits were required. Most of the other men lost interest and drifted off, but Pollard decided to hang on and was rewarded when three hours later he found that recruiting had begun again. An hour later he was in the Army, with the service number 1023. The date was 8 August 1914. The recruits carried out initial army training for the rest of August until volunteers for overseas service were called for. The 42 per cent who wished to go abroad made up what was to become the 1st Battalion. After further training Pollard travelled to France with his unit, Number 1 Company, in mid-September.

His first jobs in the Army were those of batman and then officers' mess cook. His baptism of fire came at La Bassée in the winter of 1914. He was made a lance corporal in the spring and around six months later, still not an officer, he was put in charge of the battalion bombing platoon. Pollard won the DCM as a sergeant, in action at Sanctuary Wood at the end of September 1915. By this time he had acquired an excellent knowledge of bombs and had become a proficient bomber. He led a successful counter-attack and although he was wounded in the right arm he gave a 'fine display of leadership'. His wound made it difficult for him to use a revolver properly.

After a period in hospital in England he recovered from his wounds and his commission came through on 19 January 1916. He was made an officer almost a year before his chum 'Bill' Haine and went on a three-week training course. It was a rule of the HAC that all officers had to come up through the ranks. Pollard returned to France in May 1916 and was greeted by Col. Treffry, who asked him to become battalion bombing officer. His nickname at this time was 'Bombo'. The HAC joined the 63rd (Naval Division) in 1916. In February 1917 Pollard won his first MC, at Grandcourt, when in charge of a successful patrol and a dangerous reconnaissance. He also repulsed two strong German counter-attacks. Two months later, in April, during the Battle of Arras, Pollard won the MC a second time. Then on 29 April he won the VC on the same day as his colleague, 2/Lt Haine. No other man in the war held all three medals: the VC, MC and the DCM.

Pollard ended his military service as part of the Army of Occupation in Cologne. In 1918 he married Mary Ainsley of Trefilan, Purley. This marriage was a failure and ended in divorce six years later; then in 1925 he married Violet Irene Swarbrick from Ealing.

Pollard attended the garden party for winners of the VC at Buckingham Palace on 26 June 1920 and other VC functions, including the centenary celebrations in 1956 at Hyde Park. Between 1920 and 1925 he found it difficult to find employment although he was offered his old job back with the Alliance Assurance Company. He resigned after a few months, and at one time he tried his hand at being a salesman. In 1923 Pollard was fined for dangerous driving in Biggleswade when he knocked down a farm labourer. In 1925 he decided to take a short service commission with the RAF and after this he devoted most of the remaining part of his life to writing, including a book on the history of the RAF. His other hobbies were said to be dogs, gardening and handicrafts; at one time he worked on a model of a three-masted clipper, fully rigged. He was also involved in a new parlour game named Zodia, which was launched in time for Christmas 1932. He was 6 ft 2 in tall.

In 1949 he moved to Bournemouth and wrote many of his books while living in the seaside town. All told, he wrote about fifty books, many of them thrillers and adventure stories, but none of them has been in print for many years. In 1955 he was presented to the Queen when the HAC was presented with new colours. During his post-war life Pollard was not only a prolific writer but he also wrote a considerable volume of journalism, much of which reads rather oddly in the 1990s. A useful book for researchers is his autobiography called *Fire-Eater. The Memoirs of a VC*, published by Hutchinson in 1932, in which he states that he had enjoyed the war, especially walking around no-man's-land at night.

In the *Dundee Evening Telegraph* Pollard wrote a piece under the heading of 'VCs Don't Help to get Jobs'. Its subtitle was 'War Heroes are distrusted now: even the pawnbrokers set a low value on decorations'. He described how difficult it was for him to find a job and despite answering a great number of job advertisements he made little headway. Pollard also quotes the following advice given to him as a holder of the VC from a famous writer whom he did not name: 'Either get a job opening taxi doors outside a fashionable hotel, or take to literature.' In the same article Pollard talks of attempting to pawn his medals and says that he tried twenty or thirty pawnshops in London. 'The VC might be valuable. The others aren't worth bothering about.' When he asked how much he would be given for the VC, Pollard was told that the shop was not allowed to take them. The following comes from an article entitled 'The Battle of Life' that was published in 1933:

What happens to all the bright boys and girls who win scholarships at school? What happens to all the young men and women who enter the fight of life with brilliant prospects? Why is it that only a few fulfil their early promise? What is the powerful adversary who defeats them in the struggle for success?

Life is a battle from start to finish. Man sets forth to it with a perfectly equipped army. His weapons are youth, health, education, training, ambition, and the desire to succeed. He goes marching forward with confidence which thrills the older generation watching him with pride . . .

Pollard's father, James Alfred, died in February 1933 in Wallington. In 1934 in an article in the *Daily Mail*, Pollard also warned that London was severely threatened by a possible aerial attack: 'London possesses the biggest target in the world for air bombardment.' He died at his home at 18 Queen's Park Gardens in Bournemouth on Monday 5 December 1960 at the age of sixty-seven. He predeceased his wife. His body was cremated and he is commemorated at the Garden of Remembrance at Bournemouth Crematorium. His medals are with the HAC.

Pollard's remains lie here in the Garden of Remembrance, Bournemouth (Photo: Donald Jennings)

J. WELCH

Near Oppy, France, 29 April

The 1st Royal Berkshires (99th Brigade) formed part of the 2nd Division. At the end of April 1917 the 2nd Division was on the left flank of the 63rd (Naval) Division, who were in Gavrelle to the south, and the line of the 2nd Division was from near Gavrelle to Arleux in the north.

The operation in which the 99th Brigade participated was part of the Second Battle of the Scarpe and it turned out to be a costly failure. Even before zero hour the German artillery had managed to score a heavy blow on the attack when their guns blew up several dumps of bombs and small arms ammunition, as well as water dumps.

The brigade moved forward at 4.00 a.m. on 29 April accompanied by an artillery barrage, and six minutes later the German artillery responded with a very severe barrage. The experience of the 1st Royal Berks was as follows, according to the *History of the Second Division*:

> The left battalion of the 99th Infantry Brigade, the 1st Royal Berks, moved forward close on the barrage at 4 a.m. On the right the wire was imperfectly cut, but wide gaps were found on the left, and through these the troops rushed up the enemy's trench.

A quarter of an hour later they had reached a section of the Oppy Line, but found that neither of their flanks was in touch with adjoining battalions, except for a small group of men from the 22nd Royal Fusiliers. On the left, the gap between them and the 5th Brigade (2nd Division) was around 200 yards wide. The Royal Berks set up blocks and defences on their flanks and placed snipers in Oppy Wood. Three German machine-guns were used against a fleeing enemy and some prisoners were taken.

The right flank of the battalion was under considerable pressure but managed to beat off a counter-attack. Over a period of four-and-a-half hours the Germans launched no fewer than five counter-attacks and they were all repelled by the 'splendid marksmanship of the Berkshires'. At the fifth German attempt, the Berkshires' supply of bombs ran out but as they moved back they came across a German bomb dump which allowed them to continue the desperate fight.

However, it was only a matter of time before the Berkshires had to return to their original line, as their numbers were rapidly dwindling. Initially they moved back to the sunken road that ran south-westwards from the western corner of the wood. C Company, the left-hand company, was to the north of the sunken road and was down to thirty-five men; they were now able to join up with the 5th Brigade of their own division.

The remaining Berkshires, still with their left flank open, retired to their former front line and there they held their ground. It should be noted here, perhaps, that Oppy would not be captured by the British for another two months. It was during this intensive fighting that 8763 L/Cpl James Welch of B Company, who was in charge of a Lewis gun, won his VC. It was gazetted on 27 June 1917:

> For most conspicuous bravery. On entering the enemy trench he killed one man after a severe hand-to-hand struggle. Armed only with an empty revolver, L/Cpl Welch then chased four of the enemy across the open and captured them single-handed. He handled his machine-gun with the utmost fearlessness, and more than once went into the open fully exposed to heavy fire at short range to search for and collect ammunition and spare parts, in order to keep his guns in action, which he succeeded in doing for over five hours till wounded by a shell. He showed throughout the utmost valour and initiative.

However, despite this heroism and similar actions elsewhere in the line, the attack had failed to capture Oppy Wood. The Germans had fought very tenaciously and counter-attacked the 99th Brigade at least eight times. It is not that easy to retrace the Berkshires' actions as Oppy Wood is private, and the writer has not yet managed to identify the former German strongpoint in the wood.

At the end of April 1917 Welch was promoted to corporal, and he was decorated by the King with his VC in the Buckingham Palace forecourt on 21 July 1917. A few weeks later, in August 1918, he was made a sergeant. He had served for eleven years and four months when he was discharged on 24 April 1919, after being deemed no longer fit for service having been wounded in the war. He was thanked by brigade, divisional and battalion commanders for his service.

❖❖❖

James Welch was born at Stratfield Saye, near Silchester, Hampshire, on 7 July 1889. He was the son of Mr and Mrs D. Welch and was educated in Stratfield Saye. He was only 5 ft 2 in tall when he joined the Royal Berkshire Regiment on 25 January 1908 at the age of eighteen.

Welch was a first-class athlete and represented his battalion at cross-country running. When the war began in August 1914 he was serving in India. After he returned to Europe he went to France with his unit and was wounded at Neuve-Chapelle; he was sent home to England to recuperate. In 1916, during the Battle of the Somme, he was wounded again.

After the war Welch lived in Sheffield where he was employed by a cardboard box company. As the Second World War approached he decided to join the RAF Auxiliary Service in 1938; he was quickly promoted and served in the north-east of England. He attended many of the VC functions including

Welch's grave, North Cemetery, Bournemouth (Photo: Donald Jennings)

the 1956 centenary at Hyde Park. He had married Daisy Welch and the couple had five children, but only three survived, one of whom was called Daisy Victoria. In 1960 his family moved from Sheffield to Bournemouth. His wife died in 1968. Welch died at 80 Pinehurst Park, West Moors, Bournemouth, on 28 June 1978 at the age of eighty-eight and was cremated on 4 July. His ashes and his wife's remains share a grave in North Cemetery, Bournemouth.

Welch's medals include the VC, 1914 Star, BWM, VM, DM, 1939–45 War Medal, George VI Coronation Medal and Queen Elizabeth II Coronation Medal. In 1979 Welch's regiment bought his VC for £9,000 and it is on display in the Regimental Museum in Salisbury, next to the cathedral.

R.G. COMBE

South of Acheville, France, 3 May

Robert Combe, a drawing by Francis M.L. Barthropp

Just over three weeks after the main part of Vimy Ridge had been captured by the Canadians on 9 April 1917, they were still involved in local actions in the area of the town of Lens, due north of Arras. This time the target was a group of small villages incorporated in the German Third Line in the plains of Douai. The names of the villages, from right to left, were Fresnoy, Acheville, Méricourt and Avion.

The 1st Canadian Brigade had three battalions in front of Fresnoy, and on the brigade's left was the 27th Battalion and then the 31st Battalion, both of the 6th Canadian Brigade. We are concerned here with the part of the line at Acheville where the 27th Battalion was under orders to capture the northern part of the Arleux Loop and Oppy–Méricourt Line. Arleux, another small village, had only recently fallen to the Canadians.

Soon after 3.45 a.m. on 3 May the 27th Battalion attack had only gone forward around 200 yards before the enemy barrage was suddenly shortened. This had a disastrous effect on the Canadians, who suffered considerable initial casualties which led to the operation becoming a very costly one. On the left of the 27th Battalion, the men of the 31st Battalion were held up by dense wire on their front and as a result they were unable to advance on the 27th Battalion's flank.

In the right company of the 27th Battalion, Lt Robert Combe was soon the only surviving officer. Signalling to the small number of men who were still with him, he continued through the German barrage. However, he found that if his small party were to reach the German line, they would also have to run the gauntlet of the British guns as well. He steadied his men, but in the end only five men survived to reach the enemy line. When they entered the German trench they were accompanied by a few men from another company (from the 1st Battalion) whom they had picked up along the way.

The mixed group began to bomb along the trench, using German bombs as their own supply had dried up some time before. In all, eighty Germans were

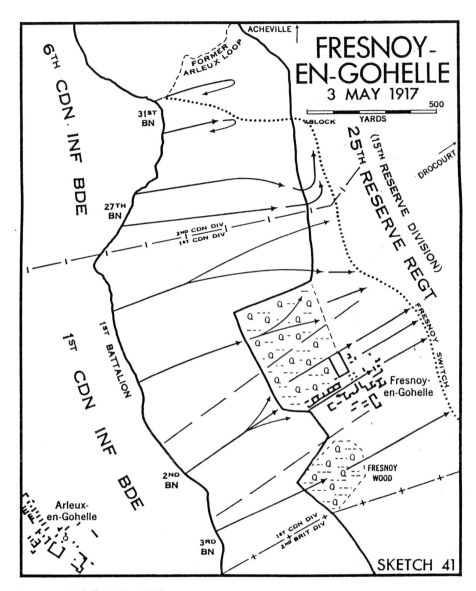

Fresnoy-en-Gohelle, 3 May 1917

captured and 250 yards of trench line taken. Combe's men charged the enemy several times with great courage. Combe was always the first man round the traverse and into dug-outs until a German sniper killed him, just as a party of reinforcements arrived to assist him. His citation was published in the *London Gazette* of 27 June 1917:

The Canadian memorial at Vimy Ridge
(Photo: Peter Batchelor)

For most conspicuous bravery and example. He steadied his company under intense fire, and led them through the enemy barrage, reaching the objective with only five men. With great coolness and courage, Lt Combe proceeded to bomb the enemy, and inflicted heavy casualties. He collected small groups of men, and succeeded in capturing the company objective, together with eighty prisoners. He repeatedly charged the enemy, driving them before him, and whilst personally leading his bombers, was killed by an enemy sniper. His conduct inspired all ranks, and it was entirely due to his magnificent courage that the position was carried, secured and held.

Although the Canadians had fought to a standstill, they were handicapped by their lack of numbers and by late evening they were relieved by the 29th Battalion. There had been 270 casualties during the day but, to offset this figure, 120 Germans had been taken prisoner and 400 yards of enemy trench had been captured.

As his body was not recovered, Combe's name is commemorated on the Vimy Memorial.

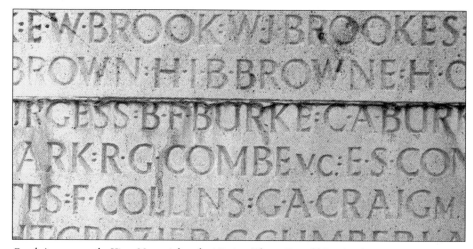

Combe's name on the Vimy Memorial to the Missing (Photo: Donald Jennings)

Robert Grierson Combe was born on 5 August 1880 in Aberdeen, Scotland. He was the youngest of six children of James Combe of 2 Millburn Street, Aberdeen; later, around 1892, the family moved to 24 Ferryhill Place. Combe's father was a hotel waiter and two of Robert's elder sisters later became schoolteachers. Robert was first a pupil at Ferryhill School, but in 1894 he became a pupil at the local grammar school, where his name appears on the Board of Bursary and Foundation Winners. After leaving school in 1897 he served an apprenticeship as a chemist in Aberdeen with William E. Hay, but then decided to emigrate to Canada, probably in 1906. He joined the staff of a drugstore in Moosomin, Saskatchewan, but later he ran his own business for several years in Melville, Saskatchewan.

In 1909, in Melville, Combe married Jean Donald of Moosomin. In 1915 he enlisted and was granted a commission; he was posted to the 53rd Battalion in Prince Albert, but actually went overseas with the 27th Battalion. He eventually rose in rank to major and became an instructor. However, at his own request, he reverted to the rank of lieutenant as he wished to be sent overseas. In January 1915 Combe wrote home to his former school at Aberdeen:

> I hope to call on you when the third Canadian contingent gets over in the spring and to become a Life Member. Training conditions here are sublime. I had fifty recruits out the other morning for a route march with the thermometer at 18 degrees below zero. I froze my chin and one cheek. Several of the men had frozen noses and cheeks. We all feel very fit, however, and the cold is most invigorating. We are all very anxious to get over. Many men like myself have not been home for nine or ten years, while others have never seen 'the old country'. We expect to concentrate at Regina or Winnipeg any day now, and after a short course there, hope to embark. I have a lieutenancy in the 95th Saskatchewan Rifles. I have been trying to get back for a visit to the old country for two or three years, but being a married man now it is not so easy to pick up one's traps and march. My wife has never been in Scotland, and one of the things she is most anxious to see is 'the old school'. I hope it will come up to my boastful accounts. I just notice one of my old class in the first list of volunteers – Hugh F. Mackenzie, Glasgow. I hope I shall meet many more and that we have a chance to have a little reunion – preferably at Potsdam.

In early 1916 he was invalided back to England suffering with rheumatism and then returned to France with the 27th Battalion. A life-size oil painting of him used to hang in Ottawa's Peace Tower and a lake in North Saskatchewan was also named after him. His medals are with the Saskatchewan archives.

The family of Jean Donald (Combe's future wife) had moved to Moosomin in 1889 and, after spending her school years there, she took up teaching at Riga, Coverdale and Moosomin. After she married she followed her husband to Europe and trained with the British Red Cross for a year. She was posted to Aboyne Castle Hospital, where she became quartermaster. She was then posted to Edinburgh War Hospital, working with the Voluntary Aid Detachment.

After her husband was killed in May 1917 Mrs Combe returned to Canada and trained as a physiotherapist at Hart House, Toronto. On completion of her training, she was posted to Tuxedo Military Hospital in Winnipeg. When the war finished she was demobilized and then joined the staff of Dr Galloway's Clinic in Winnipeg. While working there she was summoned to Regina in order to receive her husband's VC from the hands of the Prince of Wales at the Legislative Assembly. Owing to ill-health she had not been able to attend an investiture at Buckingham Palace during the time she was in Britain.

In 1925 Mrs Combe moved to Victoria where she set up home. In 1942 she was appointed supervisor of Blur Triangle Leave Center, a position which she held until 1946 when the center was closed. In February 1963 she was back in Victoria, but a short time later she became ill and died in hospital on 12 April. Members of the 27th Battalion, her husband's former unit, acted as her pall-bearers at her funeral. She had truly lived a very useful and Christian life.

J. HARRISON

Oppy, France, 3 May

The village of Oppy was one of the villages just behind the German Third Line, called the Oppy–Méricourt Line. The village was also the subject of a famous photograph which shows Oppy Wood as little more than a collection of what look like matchsticks, but were of course the remains of the trees, stripped of most of their foliage. The 92nd Brigade of the 31st Division was entirely made up from four battalions of the East Yorkshire Regiment, namely the 10th–13th Battalions. The divisional line in early May was unusually long: close to 2 miles. The village of Oppy was to the left of the divisional front.

The enemy opposite held Oppy village and its protective wood, along with a toehold of around 750 yards to the west of Oppy Wood. Many of the trees in the wood had been smashed and their fallen branches provided an admirable defence. Also, as the ground was very open between the two lines, it was difficult for the British artillery who had to fire at long range. Owing to the extent of their front, the 31st Division was given additional artillery assistance and had the use of extra machine-guns from the 63rd (Naval) Division.

Before the attack began, the 11th East Yorkshires were in position in trenches between Bailleul and Roclincourt. They moved off at 9.00 p.m. on 2 May using a narrow gauge railway which ran to the north of Bailleul and then due east for half a mile or so. They were then met by guides from the 13th Battalion who conducted them to their assembly positions around 200 yards in front of the western edge of Oppy Wood. It was as they were on their way to these positions that the moon behind them showed them up quite clearly to the vigilant enemy. To prove that they were well aware of the impending attack, the Germans fired off Very lights which further illuminated the 11th Battalion positions.

The target for the battalion was the wood, the village behind it and the Oppy Support Trench beyond. The 12th East Yorks moved up a little later and were in position to the left of the 11th Battalion. The 10th Battalion were to the right.

The British barrage opened at 3.45 a.m. on 3 May after the three battalions had been in their assembly positions for about two hours. The German artillery quickly replied and conditions now became totally confusing for the Yorkshire

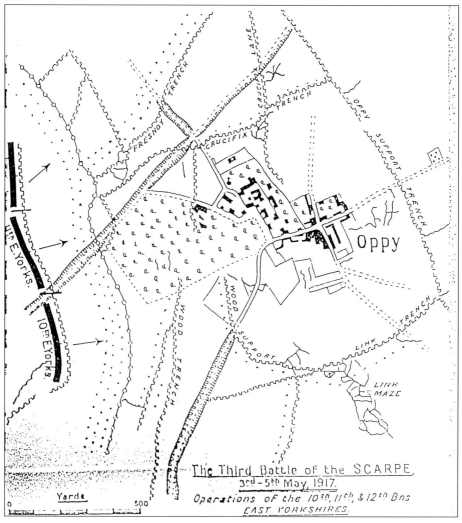

Map showing the operations of the East Yorks battalions during the Third Battle of the Scarpe, 3–5 May 1917

battalions – when their own barrage lifted they were unable to see, owing to the dark, smoke and dust that prevailed.

To the right the 10th Battalion found that the German front line was strongly defended and the attackers were held up by machine-gun and rifle fire. Despite this, however, a few men penetrated to the first objective. All four company commanders became casualties and the survivors withdrew to their start line in front of the wood, where they remained for twenty-four hours exposed to artillery and machine-gun fire. Snipers were also operating from Oppy Wood.

The experience of the middle battalion (the 11th) was very similar to that of the 10th, except that, in addition to the dark, they had to cope with the horrors of fighting in Oppy Wood as well. Despite machine-gun fire from the wood and fire from front line trenches, B Company to the right made some progress. Two or three attempts were made to advance, but they were repulsed. Number 6 Company was under 2/Lt John Harrison, who rallied his men and led them forward to negotiate three belts of barbed wire. All the time an enemy machine-gun from the southern edge of the wood played on the Yorkshire attackers. Harrison ordered his men to take shelter in protective shell holes and, taking a Mills bomb, he attempted to rush the machine-gun single-handed. Almost at the moment his bomb hit the machine-gun crew, Harrison fell dead. The gun did not fire again. Harrison had given his life in order to save others. He was awarded a posthumous VC and his citation was published in the *London Gazette* of 14 June 1917:

> For most conspicuous bravery and self-sacrifice in an attack. Owing to darkness and smoke from the enemy barrage, and from our own, and to the fact that our objective was in a dark wood, it was impossible to see when our barrage had lifted off the enemy front line. Nevertheless, 2/Lt Harrison led his company against the enemy trench under heavy rifle and machine-gun fire, but was repulsed. Reorganizing his command as best he could in no-man's-land, he again attacked in darkness under terrific fire but with no success. Then, turning round, this gallant officer single-handed made a dash at the machine-gun, hoping to knock out the gun and so save the lives of many of his company. His self-sacrifice and absolute disregard of danger was an inspiring example to all. (He is reported missing, believed killed.)

Inspired, Harrison's company rose to their feet and rushed on, but they found themselves isolated so again sheltered in shell holes and remained there until nightfall. Part of C Company passed through the wood and into the village by 6.00 a.m., but then became totally isolated. The 12th Battalion, on the left of the 11th, had a similar experience through the day to those of their sister battalions.

According to the official history:

> The right battalion failed completely; parties of the centre and left entered Oppy Wood in the darkness, but were either captured or driven out. The division suffered about 1,900 casualties.

After their drubbing at Oppy, the 92nd Brigade left for the Gavrelle sub-sector. Harrison's posthumous VC was presented to his widow, Mrs Lilian Harrison, at Buckingham Palace on 2 March 1918. She left Hull after the war to live in

The Arras Memorial to the Missing (Photo: Peter Batchelor)

London. Prior to winning the VC, Harrison had won the MC in May 1917. As his body was not recovered from the battlefield, his name is listed on the Arras Memorial to the Missing.

John Harrison (known as Jack) was born on 2 November 1890 at 20 Williamson Street, a terraced house in a road leading down to Earle's shipyard at Drypool, Sculcoates, Kingston upon Hull, in Yorkshire. He was the only son in a family of four of Mr and Mrs J. Harrison. He was educated at Hull Secondary School and St John's College, York. Harrison senior worked at Earle's as a boilermaker or plater. In 1912 Jack became a schoolteacher at Lime Street Council School, Hull, which was under the control of Hull Education Authority in the local dockland area close to the river.

In 1914 his family moved to Ainslie House, Sculcoates, Kingston upon Hull, and on 1 September of that year Harrison married Lilian Ellis, the daughter of a shipwright, and the couple had a son, another John, who was born in June 1915. They moved across the river to a house at 75 Wharncliffe Street, close to the local rugby club ground. Jack Harrison was well known as a sportsman in the north of England, and was one of the finest wing three-quarters in the Northern League game. Initially he played for St John's at York; later he began to play for Hull in around 1910 and became a consistent scorer. He scored the winning try in the 1914 Cup Final at Wakefield, when playing for Hull.

Harrison did not rush to join the swelling ranks of the local Pals battalions which later formed the 92nd Brigade of the 31st Division. On 4 November 1915 he joined the Inns of Court OTC TF with the number 7203 and reported for full-time training in November 1915. He trained with them until March 1916 before joining a cadet school at Berkhamsted, Hertfordshire, whence he was gazetted on 4 August 1916, exactly

Harrison's name on the Arras Memorial to the Missing (Photo: Donald Jennings)

two years after the First World War had begun. He joined the 14th Reserve Battalion East Yorkshire Regiment, then in training at Seaton Delaval near Newcastle. The battalion supplied drafts to the Hull Brigade. After a short period he was posted to France to join the 11th Service Battalion and at the end of February 1917 he won the MC, gazetted on 17 April 1917:

> he handled his platoon with great courage and skill, reached his objective under the most trying conditions and captured a prisoner. He set a splendid example throughout.

Oppy Wood remains in private hands and it should not be entered without permission. A few railway sleepers have been incorporated in the fence along one side of the wood. In the village, with its back to the wood, is a memorial to the men of Hull who lost their lives in the First World War; this was unveiled in 1927. The land on which it stands was given by the Vicomte and Vicomtesse du Bouexic de la Driennays, in memory of their son who had died in the war.

In May 1921 a bronze memorial plaque to the memory of Harrison was unveiled at Lime Street School. The school was bombed in the Second World War but the plaque was rescued by salvage men and taken to the Guildhall for

The Kingston upon Hull memorial, Oppy (Photo: Peter Batchelor)

151

safe-keeping. It was overlooked for more than thirty years until it was rediscovered in the roof in 1978. It was displayed in the Rugby League Centenary Exhibition and was then installed in the main ground floor corridor. St John's College also set up a memorial to its former students who gave their lives in the First World War, but at present a portrait of Harrison, together with his citation, is awaiting a suitable place for display.

In 1923 Lilian Harrison's plight as a war widow with a young son was recognized by the local community and a fund was set up to pay for her son's education. Unfortunately he, too, was killed in war – at Dunkirk in 1940.

Having lost her 'two men', Lilian was to spend a long and possibly lonely life, as she lived on until December 1977 when she died in Addlestone, Surrey. She bequeathed her husband's medals to the East Yorkshire Regiment which had by then been amalgamated with the Prince of Wales's Own. Their two historical collections were combined in their present home in Tower Street, York.

After Lilian's death a third memorial to her husband was erected; this time it was the turn of the Rugby Club in Hull to commemorate their former player. It was unveiled at the Boulevard, the Rugby Club ground, on 23 November 1979. Finally, a block of fifty-seven flats for the elderly were named Jack Harrison Court during the 1980s.

G. JARRATT

Near Pelves, France, 3 May

Cpl George Jarratt was in the 8th Royal Fusiliers (36th Brigade, 12th (Eastern) Division). Other battalions in the 36th Brigade were the 9th Royal Fusiliers, 7th Royal Sussex and 11th Middlesex.

On 3 May the 12th Division was to try to capture the village of Pelves to the south-east of Roeux across the River Scarpe. The strongly fortified village of Roeux was still in German hands and while it remained so it would be very unlikely that Pelves would fall to the British. This was proved to be the case and Roeux was not finally cleared until eleven days later on 14 May.

Meanwhile, at Pelves on 3 May the 37th Brigade, also of the 12th Division, attacked on the right and the 36th Brigade, with the two Royal Fusilier battalions, attacked on the left. The two Royal Fusilier battalions moved forward behind a creeping barrage and the leading units reached the Brown Line. However, the 8th Royal Fusiliers came under considerable pressure from the direction of Roeux. Thus they were only able to reach as far as Scabbard Trench, from which they were driven back as a result of a German counter-attack. In the confusion, the enemy had managed to conceal themselves and were passed over in the darkness, which led to some men being surrounded or cut off. An unconfirmed report stated that the enemy was holding Devil's and Scabbard Trenches.

Ten minutes after noon, following a brief bombardment, parties of two companies from the 7th Royal Sussex attacked under a howitzer barrage and managed to clear Scabbard Trench of its occupants and then passed the Brown Line. Thus the 36th Brigade gained its first objective. It was when the Sussex men were clearing the captured trenches that one of them threw a bomb into the dug-out which was sheltering Jarratt and a few others of the leading wave from the 8th Royal Fusiliers who had been taken prisoner. Without hesitating Jarratt placed both of his feet on the bomb in order to limit the explosion and thus save his comrades' lives. Both his legs were blown off and, although his comrades were safely removed to their lines, Jarratt died before stretcher-bearers could reach him.

Scabbard Trench was to the west of Pelves and south of Roeux. Reports of the day's fighting suggest that the British artillery was woefully inadequate and that many German infantrymen were simply standing shoulder to shoulder waiting for the attackers to advance. Withering fire kept the British pinned down until darkness. The 12th Division suffered 2,000 casualties during the day.

Jarratt's deed of self-sacrifice was gazetted on 8 June 1917 and won him a posthumous VC with the following citation:

> For most conspicuous bravery and devotion in deliberately sacrificing his life to save others. He had, together with some wounded men, been taken prisoner and placed under guard in a dug-out. The same evening the enemy were driven back by our troops, the leading infantrymen of which commenced to bomb the dug-outs. A grenade fell in the dug-out, and without hesitation Cpl Jarratt placed both feet on the grenade, the subsequent explosion blowing off his legs. The wounded were later safely removed to our lines, but Cpl Jarratt died before he could be removed. By this supreme act of self-sacrifice the lives of these wounded were saved.

The medal was presented to his widow on 21 July 1917 in the forecourt of Buckingham Palace by the King.

Jarratt's name is listed on the Arras Memorial so, although his body was removed from the battlefield, it must have been lost later.

❖❖❖

George Jarratt was born in Kennington, London, on 22 July 1891. As a young man he became a Scoutmaster. In 1914 he enlisted in the Royal Fusiliers with the service number 55295. He became a lance sergeant.

Among the letters of sympathy Mrs Jarratt received was one from her husband's former commanding officer, Lt-Col. N.B. Elliott Cooper, who was subsequently

Jarratt's name on the Arras Memorial to the Missing (Photo: Donald Jennings)

also awarded the VC. Jarratt's wife later remarried and became Mrs G.M. Pearce, having had one son by George. In 1964 she was living at 67 North Street in Southminster, Essex.

In 1963 Mrs Jarratt sold her first husband's medals, including the VC, BWM, and VM, to the trustees of the Royal Fusiliers Regimental Museum, where they are now held.

M.W. HEAVISIDE

Near Fontaine-lès-Croisilles, France, 6 May

In early April the 15th Durham Light Infantry (DLI) of the 64th Brigade, 21st Division, were billeted in Boisleux-St-Marc until 14 April 1917 when they moved further west to Blairville. Here they remained in a huge cave, which was a novel experience, and then moved via Mercatel and Boiry-Becquerelle to take over from a battalion of the 33rd Division.

On 3 May the 15th DLI were ordered to bomb down the section of the Hindenburg Line to the west of Fontaine-lès-Croisilles, a village to the south of the Arras–Cambrai road. This section of the line was called the Chérisy–Riegel Line and the attack began at 3.50 a.m. Communication proved to be very difficult owing to the width between the front and support lines. The company on the left of the attack moved down the support trench but was slowed by the strong wire defences and machine-gun fire. A tank which was to take part in the attack arrived an hour late. After a brief burst of firing down the trench, the tank was put out of action. The company on the right could make little progress down the front trench, mainly as a result of the number of men they had lost at the beginning of the assault, which had severely depleted their ranks. In the afternoon the battalion was relieved; the heat had become very oppressive and the assault party had become very dehydrated.

The battalion spent the next day in divisional reserve and there were no more plans to attack again. Three days after the attack went in, a man was spotted trying to attract attention by waving his water bottle from a shell hole about 40 yards from the German lines. Owing to the exposed nature of the ground it was decided not to send out a stretcher party, but to call for a volunteer to take the wounded man food and water. Having volunteered, Pte Michael Heaviside began to crawl from hole to hole dodging enemy machine-gun and sniper fire, and eventually he reached the man. When darkness came Heaviside returned and then guided a stretcher-bearer party out to where the man lay and brought him in. For this deed Heaviside was awarded the VC.

The citation reads:

When the battalion was holding a block in the line, a wounded man was observed about 2 p.m. in a shell hole some sixty yards in advance of our block and about forty yards from the enemy line. He was making signals of distress and holding up an empty water bottle. Owing to snipers and machine-gun fire it was impossible, during daylight, to send out a stretcher party. But Pte Heaviside at once volunteered to carry water and food to the wounded man, despite enemy fire. This he succeeded in doing and found the man to be badly wounded and nearly demented with thirst. He had lain out for four days and three nights, and the arrival of the water undoubtedly saved his life. Pte Heaviside, who is a stretcher-bearer, succeeded the same evening, with the assistance of two comrades, in rescuing the wounded man.

When Heaviside came home after winning the VC, the residents at his home turned out to greet him, bands played and choirs sang. A decorated tableau was arranged, along with a procession, and many civic dignitaries attended the ceremonies.He was presented with his VC in the forecourt of Buckingham Palace on 21 July 1917.

Michael Wilson Heaviside was the son of Annie and John Wilson Heaviside and was born in Durham City on 20 October 1880. On the 1881 Census form his father was listed as an unemployed grocer, while his mother was listed as a dressmaker. At the time of the census Michael was five months old and the family address was 4 Station Lane, St Giles. Heaviside was educated at Kimblesworth, Co. Durham, and after leaving school he became a colliery worker for a time, before serving in the Army in the South African war.

On 7 September 1914 Heaviside enlisted, initially serving with the 10th DLI before being transferred to the 15th; his service number was 4/9720. He was discharged in 1919 and for the remaining twenty years of his life suffered from gas poisoning, which possibly hastened his death. He was also a heavy smoker and sported a clay pipe. He was a friend of Pte Ernest Sykes VC. His home was at Bloemfontein Terrace, Craghead, Durham.

He died on Wednesday 26 April 1939 and his funeral at Craghead was attended by a large number of local people. The coffin, draped with a Union Jack, had Heaviside's hat, belt and bayonet resting on the lid. Surrounded with flowers, it was borne to St Thomas's Church on a horse-drawn cart. Members of the British Legion and soldiers from the 8th DLI provided bearers for the coffin. A firing party, also drawn from the 8th DLI, preceded the coffin and the procession was led by the Craghead Colliery Band playing 'Dead March in Saul'. The cortège stretched for nearly half a mile and the route to the church was lined with villagers. At the burial service three volleys were fired over the grave and the Last Post was sounded, followed by Reveille.

St John's Church, Craghead. Michael Heaviside was buried in an unmarked grave to the west of the church on 30 April 1939 (Photo: Jack Cavanagh)

Heaviside was a member of the Newcastle British Legion and used to attend VC functions. In 1957 his family gave his VC to the Durham Light Infantry for their collection. The museum also has his other medals, including the Queen's South African, King's South African, 1914–15 Star, BWM, VM and George VI Coronation Medal. His grave was lost and subsequently rediscovered; there are plans to repair it and to erect an appropriate stone.

G.J. HOWELL

Near Bullecourt, France, 6 May

On the third day of the Battle of Arras, 11 April, the 4th Australian Division attempted to capture Bullecourt, Riencourt and Hendecourt. Tanks and artillery assistance had been promised but did not materialize, and the Australians ended this disastrous day with a loss of 4,170 men, including 3,000 casualties. The village of Bullecourt is to the east of Croisilles and the A1 autoroute. Cpl. George Julian Howell (always known as 'Snow'), was a member of the 1st (New South Wales) Battalion, Australian Imperial Forces, which was part of the 1st Australian Brigade attached to their 2nd Division. Howell won a VC on 6 May 1917, which was gazetted on 27 June 1917.

In early May the German positions were pounded by artillery, and the enemy retaliated by firing 300 gas shells on the area behind the railway. The three villages were by then completely in ruins. An attack was planned which took place with the 2nd Australian Division on the morning of 3 May. It was a better planned operation than the previous one and the Australians made some early progress. However, as they did so, they came across the bodies of many of their comrades among the barbed wire from the disastrous attack of 11 April. They encountered strong opposition and the 1st Battalion took over part of the divisional line at Bullecourt in the evening of 3 May, which was the old German line known as 'OG1'. The battalion occupied the line with three companies from right to left, D, C and A, with B in reserve. Their position was such that they occupied a wedge into the enemy line with the two flanks still in enemy hands.

During the next three days very heavy fighting between the two sides took place. With the assistance of the 3rd Battalion, the 1st Battalion had extended its line to the left. However, at about 6.00 a.m. on 6 May Howell, who was in charge of a post on the right of the line, found that the battalion on the right flank was being forced out of its trench and was beginning to retire, which would threaten the whole position. Without delay Howell alerted battalion headquarters. Capt. A.K. McKenzie, in command of the battalion, immediately gathered up all available non-combatants from headquarters, together with signallers. He organized them along a road bank in order to try to fend off the expected enemy advance and then to make a counter-attack of their own.

The battalion's posts were heavily bombed with stick-bombs and egg bombs, but the Australians replied with a continuous flow of Mills bombs. This resulted in around eighty of the enemy becoming casualties, including the group's two officers. It was at this point that Howell took the direct action which led to his VC. Running along the open parapet of OG1 he threw his bombs down on the hapless Germans, who retreated under this treatment; when he ran out of bombs he used his bayonet until he was severely wounded and fell into the trench. Howell had been hit in both legs by machine-gun fire and he suffered at least twenty-eight wounds, but when he was brought in some hours later it was found he had no broken bones. Soon the ground which had been lost on the right of the line was retaken. The casualties had been high and totalled 281, including the killed and wounded. In winning the VC, Howell was supported by Lt T.J. Richards who had been operating a Lewis gun.

The citation reads:

> For most conspicuous bravery. Seeing a party of the enemy were likely to outflank his battalion, Cpl Howell, on his own initiative, single-handed and exposed to heavy bomb and rifle fire, climbed on to the top of the parapet and proceeded to bomb the enemy, pressing them back along the trench. Having exhausted his stock of bombs, he continued to attack the enemy with his bayonet. He was then severely wounded. The prompt action and gallant conduct of this NCO in the face of superior numbers was witnessed by the whole battalion, and greatly inspired them in the subsequent successful counter-attack.

Howell was sent to the Norfolk and Norwich War Hospital in England. He recuperated for a long time and as he was still not fit he was discharged from the Army on 5 June 1918. His VC was recommended on 14 May 1917 by Brig.-Gen. H.W. Bennett, commander of the 1st Australian Brigade, and approved by Lt-Gen. W.R. Birdwood, commander of the Anzac Corps. Howell was decorated with his VC and MM in the forecourt of Buckingham Palace on 21 July 1917 by the King. A picture of Howell with the King was published in the *Times History of the War*.

Bullecourt was finally captured by the Allies on 17 May and the second battle resulted in 7,000 Australian casualties.

George Julian Howell was born in Enfield, a suburb of Sydney, New South Wales, on 21 November 1893. He was the fourth son of a carpenter from

Brighton, Sussex, named Francis John Howell and his Australian wife Martha Howell, née Sweeny. He was educated at the Croydon Park and Burwood Public Schools and when he enlisted he was an apprentice bricklayer. On joining the AIF on 9 June 1915 Howell was given the service number 2445. According to his medical records he was 5 ft 7 in tall and weighed 14½ stone. He joined the 1st Battalion and sailed for Egypt on 14 July with the 7th Reinforcements for the 1st Battalion, which he joined at Gallipoli on 1 November. After the evacuation the battalion moved to Egypt, then to France in March 1916, and in April the unit entered the line in the Fromelles sector. During the Somme battles Howell was wounded at Pozières in the third week of July and evacuated to a hospital in Sheffield, Yorkshire, in early August. He rejoined his battalion on 26 November 1916. In December he was made a lance corporal.

On 6 February 1917 Howell was made a corporal and in April 1917 he won the MM for bravery during the battalion's capture of the village of Demicourt. On 3 May Howell's battalion was at Vaulx-Vraucourt to the south of Bullecourt and on 6 May it was relieved by the 44th Battalion. Two days later they were back at Vaulx-Vraucourt.

Howell's father, John Howell, also fought in the war along with two of 'Snow's brothers, one of whom was killed. On 1 March 1919 'Snow' Howell married Sadie Lillian Yates, a nurse, at St Stephen's Presbyterian Church in Sydney. They set up home in Coogee and Howell joined Smiths' Newspapers as a member of their advertising staff and later the Bulletin Newspaper Co. Pty Ltd. In 1933 Howell was the New South Wales representative for the *Standard* in Brisbane.

When the Second World War began Howell again offered his services to the Army and this time he joined as a staff sergeant at the headquarters of Eastern Command in Paddington on 14 October 1939. At the time he was living at 106 Brook Street, Coogee, and gave his occupation as journalist, a profession that had allowed his family, which now included a daughter called Norma, to live quite comfortably. However, he found Army life a trifle dull and he left in March 1941. He then joined the American Army and served with the United States Sea Transport Service in August 1944, which enabled him to take part in the invasion of Leyte at the beginning of the Allied campaign to drive the Japanese out of the Philippines.

In December 1953, after his wife had died, Howell moved from east Australia to the west coast, accompanied by his grandson; the journey on the old 'Overlander' train took four days. They settled in at Applecross, a suburb of Perth, to live with Howell's married daughter and then he moved to Gunyidi, via Watheroo, around 150 miles to the north of Perth, where he stayed for a couple of years. Being fond of pubs and of a gregarious nature, he found the lack of a nearby local bar was a heavy price to pay. He was also a bit of a ladies' man, and could be very charming. He lived on a 90 per cent ex-service-man's pension. Financially, this was a fairly tough time for Howell and his family, and he later moved back to Perth where he used to stay with friends. He greatly missed his chums back in eastern Australia, including another holder of the VC, Bede Kenny.

In 1956 he was a member of the Australian VC contingent that visited London and paraded in Hyde Park for the centenary review. He was photographed with other holders of the VC including Jack Carroll, Tom Axford and Clifford Sadlier.

Howell died at the Repatriation Hospital in Perth on 23 December 1964 and, after a military funeral and Anglican service, his body was cremated

Ronnie Baker wearing his grandfather's miniature medals, Grandcourt, 1997 (Photo: Peter Batchelor)

and his ashes buried at Karrakatta Cemetery, Hollywood, Perth. His name is commemorated on the Australian War Memorial in Canberra.

In July 1997 the writer was privileged to meet Mr Ron Baker, a grandson of Howell on his grandmother's side, who was in France on the trail of his grandfather at Bullecourt eighty years before. Ron had memories of his grandfather from when he was a child: he used to be taken to pubs when still very young and 'Snow' used to sit his grandson on the bar and buy him soft drinks and chips. He also recalled his grandfather being a bit of a disciplinarian. Ron wore his grandfather's miniature medals at the annual ceremony at Lochnagar Crater on 1 July 1997, and earlier in the year he had visited Gallipoli.

The fighting in Bullecourt in April and May 1917 will always be associated with the Australian Army and in recent years a local historic trail has been organized for visitors which takes in the main points of the battles and

George Howell's miniature medals (Photo: Peter Batchelor)

Signposted trail
through the Australian
battlefield

An historic trail

A walking tour
Starting Point : Bullecourt
a 8 km lap - 2 hours
a 13 km lap - 3 hours and 15 min.

includes the villages of Riencourt and Hendecourt. A memorial erected by the Souvenir Français called 'The Slouch Hat' was unveiled in 1981 in the village and a caterpillar track of one of the tanks used in April 1917 can also be seen. On the Bullecourt–Riencourt road is another memorial erected in 1992–3 by the Australian Government, called the 'Diggers' memorial'. A third on the same road was put up in 1982 on the former German second line in tribute to the 2,423 men killed in the two Bullecourt battles of 1917.

*The plaque to George Howell in Karrakatta
Cemetery, Perth, Western Australia
(Photo: E.W. Bullock)*

T. DRESSER

Near Roeux, France, 12 May

Prior to 9 April the 7th Green Howards belonged to the 50th Brigade of the 17th (Northern) Division, who were busy training for the forthcoming Battle of Arras. The division was in XVIII Corps in the Third Army, which was responsible for a line that stretched from the village of Croisilles in the south to Thélus in the north. By the end of April the French initiative on the Aisne–Champagne Line had collapsed and as a result the German Army was able to concentrate even more on the defence of the Hindenburg Line and its satellite villages.

Pte Tom Dresser of D Company of the 7th Yorkshire Regiment (Alexandra, Princess of Wales's Own), also known as the Green Howards, won his VC on 12 May 1917 close to Roeux, probably the most heavily defended German-held village to feature in the Battle of Arras in 1917. This stage of the battle was later designated the Third Battle of the Scarpe, named after the river of the same name.

On the night of 10/11 May, having taken over from the 9th Division, the 17th Division moved into the area facing the German trench line on the western slope of Greenland Hill, to the north-east of Roeux. An attack on the enemy positions in front of the hill was scheduled for 12 May at 6.30 a.m. On the right of the 17th Division was the 4th Division, facing the outlying defences of Roeux which were taken, according to plan, on the 11th. The village itself, which protected the River Scarpe flank of the enemy line in front of Greenland Hill, was the target for the 4th Division on

An artist's impression of Dresser winning his VC

163

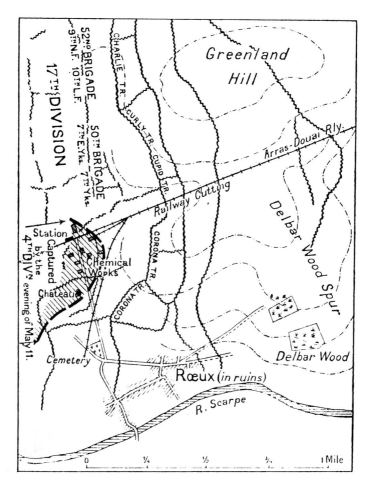

Map showing operations east of Arras, 12 May 1917]

the 12th. The village had been captured nine days before, but the Germans had won it back again.

On the 12th, the 52nd Brigade of the 17th Division attacked the trench line known on the maps as 'Charlie'; on the right the 50th Brigade had as its objectives the lines known as Curly and Cupid, to the north of the Arras–Douai railway. The 7th Green Howards were on the right of the 50th Brigade attack. The day dawned bright and sunny, and any chance of making a surprise attack was spoilt by observant German aeroplanes making low flights over the British front.

The British artillery opened fire and was quickly answered by the German guns; a dense fog of smoke and dust settled over the lines of the British advance. The attacks against Charlie and Curly Trenches were a failure but the 7th Green

Howards, close to the railway line, managed to enter Cupid Trench; once there they attempted to bomb their way to the left into Curly Trench. It was at this point that Dresser won his VC. Overall, the fighting had been inconclusive and after the wounded from both sides were recovered, the Green Howards established a post at around 10.00 p.m. at the junction of Cupid and Curly Trenches. There was to be little progress by the British on this front for the next few weeks.

Dresser's citation was published in the *London Gazette* of 27 June 1917.

For most conspicuous bravery and devotion to duty. Pte Dresser, in spite of being twice wounded on the way and suffering great pain, succeeded in conveying an important message from battalion headquarters to the front line of trenches, which he eventually reached in an exhausted condition. His fearlessness and determination to deliver this message at any cost proved of the greatest value to his battalion at a critical period.

In the *Northern Echo* of 11 June 1979 Dresser was quoted as saying the following of the occasion when he won the VC:

'We went over the top in a charge but accidentally ended up in one of the German trenches.

'Our Captain wanted Mills bombs and he sent me back to headquarters to get some.

'When I reached HQ I was given two men strapped up with the bombs and the three of us had to make our way back to the unit but the enemy had seen me leave the trench and they were ready for us.'

Having survived one hail of bullets he had to face another plus heavy guns which were concentrating on the section.

Twenty yards from the trench Tom was shot in the shoulder but the ammunition was delivered.

On his return to England Dresser was taken to hospital at Fazakerley, near Liverpool, before later returning to Middlesbrough.

He was presented with his VC by the King in the forecourt of Buckingham Palace on 21 July 1917, which was also his 25th birthday. Dresser, who was accompanied by his mother, still had his

Tom Dresser receiving his VC from the King at Buckingham Palace

arm in a sling. A photograph of the King talking to him was published in *The Times History of the War*.

Dresser was the first Middlesbrough-district man to win the VC but accounts differ concerning how his home town responded to his feat. One source says that the townspeople gave him a hundred guineas and a gold watch and chain, and another that the Hull Soldiers' Club presented him with a silver watch and chain. A third account says that Dresser was honoured on 23 September 1917 by a civic procession along with the gift of a cheque for one hundred guineas from the local war heroes fund.

❖❖❖

Tom Dresser was born in Westgate, Pickering, Yorkshire, on 21 July 1892. He attended St John's School and completed his formal education at Hugh Bell Central School. For his first job he was put in charge of one of the branches of his father's group of newsagents in a shop in Linthorpe Road. He was also quite an accomplished artist and contributed work to the local *Sports Gazette*. When he enlisted he was given the number 242697.

Before Dresser won his VC, on 19 February 1917 the 7th Green Howards marched to the village of Méaulte, near Albert, on the Somme. They remained there until 1 March when they moved to the village of Warloy and on the 14th they moved again to Viel-Hesdins.

Tom Dresser in later life

On 13 May 1944 Dresser and Maj. Edward Cooper VC were both presented with the Freedom of Middlesbrough. In 1956 Dresser attended the VC/GC centenary celebrations in London.

Dresser spent much of his life as a newsagent, in fact around seventy-five years. He closed his shop in Marton Road, Middlesbrough, where he also lived, for the last time in June 1979 as the council wanted the site for redevelopment. Dresser was compensated and he bought a house in nearby Errol Street. Shortly after he retired, Dresser, who had attended many of the VC and GC receptions during his life, was invited, together with members of his family, to a reception provided by the Mayor of Middlesbrough and the local council in the Mayor's Parlour.

Dresser died on Good Friday, 9 April 1982, in his home in Errol Street, three months short of his ninetieth birthday. He was given a military funeral and members of the 1st Battalion Green Howards carried the coffin from St John's Church, Middlesbrough. At the graveside at Thorntree Cemetery, the Last Post and Reveille were sounded. Among those who paid their respects were Maj. Edward Cooper VC, then eighty-six years of age, the Mayor of Middlesbrough and other local dignitaries. Tom left three children including two sons, Tom and Brian, but his wife Teresa had died in 1965.

In the year following Dresser's death, his family presented his VC to the Green Howards Museum at Richmond, North Yorkshire.

R.V. MOON

Near Bullecourt, France, 12 May

On the night of 9 May 1917 the 15th (Victoria) Brigade of the 5th Australian Division took over a section of the line at Bullecourt. The plan was for them to capture the village, together with the 7th British Division. If successful, the Victoria Brigade would then be able to 'join hands' with the British at the crossroads in Bullecourt.

Lt Rupert Vance Moon of the 58th Battalion (15th (Victoria) Brigade) won his VC three days later on 12 May when he was commander of C Company in the later stages of the fight for possession of the village. A section of the Australian battalion was assigned to assist the 7th British Division. The rest of the battalion was to attack the centres of enemy opposition on the left of their line, the closest being a substantial dug-out and a concrete machine-gun shelter situated between the opposing trenches. Beyond this shelter, further to the left, was another German position which was the battalion's third objective.

The 60th Battalion, also of the 15th (Victoria) Brigade, joined the 58th to assist. The Australian positions were bombarded the night before, but the attack went in on time and Moon's group of twenty-eight men stormed the concrete shelter in the OG1 line and captured it after a twenty-minute battle, driving the Germans back into the main trench. A Lewis gun team was organized in order that this trench could be enfiladed. This encouraged the Germans to run back to a position called the Diagonal Road, a continuation of the OG2 line, pursued by Moon and his men. However, the Germans began to throw bombs and Moon's group took shelter in a railway cutting. Moon then arranged for the enemy to be showered with grenades which killed some of them and drove others into nearby dug-outs, where they became trapped: 186 men were captured. Moon and two other officers had already moved away from the cutting to take up positions on the side nearest their own lines. Moon had no link with his left flank and set up a Lewis gun to consolidate the position. Enemy sniping fire was on the increase and Moon was shot in the jaw. This was the fourth time that he had been hit: the first was in front of the concrete shelter, the second in the shoulder when in the rear trench, and the third in the foot and leg during the fighting in the cutting.

Moon's VC citation was published in the *London Gazette* on 14 June 1917:

> For most conspicuous bravery during an attack on an enemy strongpoint. His own immediate objective was a position in advance of the hostile trench itself, and thence against the hostile trench, after the capture of which it was intended that his men should co-operate in a further assault on a strongpoint further in rear. Although wounded in the initial advance, he reached his first objective. Leading his men against the trench itself, he was again badly wounded and incapacitated for the moment. He nevertheless inspired and encouraged his men and captured the trench. Lt Moon continued to lead his much diminished command in the general attack with the utmost valour, being again wounded, and the attack was successfully pressed home. During the consolidation of the position, this officer was again badly wounded, and it was only after this fourth and severe wound in the face that he consented to retire from the fight. His bravery was magnificent, and was largely instrumental in the successful issue against superior numbers, the safeguarding of the flank of the attack and the capture of many prisoners and machine-guns.

On 10 June Moon rejoined his battalion from hospital. A few weeks later he attended an investiture at Buckingham Palace on 3 August 1917 after he had recovered from his wounds. In March 1918 he went back to Australia but in May he returned to Europe. After the Armistice he was made a temporary captain on 5 February 1919. A few months later he returned home and was demobilized on 4 October. His name was then placed on the officer reserve list with the rank of honorary captain.

Rupert Vance Moon was born in Bacchus Marsh, Victoria, Australia, on 14 August 1892. He was the son of Mr and Mrs Arthur Moon of Kinaird, Toorak, Victoria. He spent much of his childhood in the Gippsland district and went to school at Kyneton Grammar School, Kyneton, Victoria. Moon's father was a bank inspector and a position was procured for Moon in the National Bank in Melbourne, where his father worked.

Prior to the war Moon trained with the 13th Light Horse and 8th Infantry Regiments and he joined the colours when he enlisted in the Australian Imperial

Forces on 21 August 1914 shortly after he embarked on his banking career. On enlistment he expressed a preference to join the light horse and he was posted to the 4th Light Horse Regiment. Two months later he sailed overseas as a trooper attached to the Light Horse Regiment as part of the 1st Australian Division. He served in Gallipoli for seven months from May to December 1915, where the Light Horse was used as dismounted infantry.

Moon was made a lance corporal in November 1915 and sergeant in March 1916. In May he arrived in France and was recommended for a commission which was gazetted in September 1916; he then joined the 58th Battalion.

After his demobilization Moon returned to his banking career, but after a few years he resigned his position and joined a firm of accountants, Dennys Lascelles, of Geelong. Later he became the firm's managing director and was general manager from 1948 to 1959. When he retired, an annual horse race handicap was named after him; this is still run every September.

On 18 December 1931 Moon had married Susan A.M. Vincent, and the couple had a son and daughter. The home of the Moon family was Calder Park, Mount Duneed, Victoria. On 25 February 1954 Moon was present at the Melbourne Cricket Ground along with nine other holders of the VC, who were all presented to the Queen and the Duke of Edinburgh. In 1956 he was a member of the Australian contingent to London for the VC centenary. In March 1957 he attended, along with six other holders of the VC, the funeral of William Dunstan VC. On 28 February 1986 he died at Bellarine Private Hospital, Whittington. His funeral was held on 4 March 1986, at Baron Heads, All Saints' Anglican Church. When he died he was the last but one surviving Australian VC from the First World War: William Joynt outlived him by only nine weeks, dying on 5 May 1986.

Moon's VC was presented to the Australian War Memorial's Hall of Valour by his family. At that time a portrait of Moon by W.B. McInnes was also on display.

A. WHITE

Monchy-le-Preux, France, 19 May

On 12 April 1917 the 2nd South Wales Borderers (SWB) of the 87th Brigade, 29th Division, helped to relieve troops in the village of Monchy-le-Preux. The 87th Brigade took over the right-hand section of a new line from Monchy southwards to the River Cojeul. The 2nd SWB were facing the village of Guémappe. Although during the relief the area had been shelled with gas shells and the positions were difficult to locate, the companies eventually found them and then proceeded to push out patrols. Two days later the enemy counter-attacked from a position called Bois du Sart to the north-east of Infantry Hill. This attack overwhelmed the 1st Essex and Newfoundland Regiment of the 88th Brigade.

The 87th Brigade was continuously shelled, but the enemy infantry attacks did not materialize in their sector. In the evening, however, and owing to the losses incurred by the 88th Brigade, their support lines had come up to relieve the 4th Worcesters (88th Brigade). The 2nd SWB remained in the front line for a few more days until 17 April. It was then in support and reserve for six days and on the 22nd the battalion returned to the front line in time for a new attack, to the north-east of Monchy.

On 19 May Sgt Albert White, a member of the 2nd SWB, won a posthumous VC in an act of great gallantry. D Company was on the left of the 1st Border Regiment and their objective was a part of a position called Devil's Trench, astride Bit Lane beyond Monchy. The position formed a sharp angle. D Company was given partial protection by a rifle grenade section which also gave covering fire. D Company bombers were very active in Devil's Trench and were managing to work in a northerly direction, and at the same time were trying to protect the building of a strongpoint. Two other companies, A and B, moved into trenches named Snaffle and Shrapnel which allowed D to move further forward. In addition, A supplied the attacking company with additional bombs and other supplies.

When the British barrage opened, the enemy began machine-gunning from the left of Bit Lane and despite the British barrage they maintained their fire. Casualties were becoming heavy, especially when D Company reached the waterlogged Arrow Trench, to the right. The attack was led by Capt. Davies and

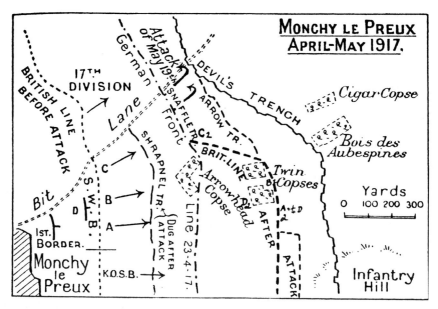

Map showing the area around Monchy-le-Preux, April–May 1917

2/Lt V. Jones, but they were both killed, to and it was left to Sgt White to try to destroy the menacing machine-guns that were holding up his company's advance. He decided to take on the nearest machine-gun post, which was the one causing the most damage. Followed by Cpl Newell, White dashed at the gun party and covered it, shooting three men and bayoneting a fourth. He managed to get within a few feet of the gun itself before he was riddled with bullets. Sadly his self-sacrifice, though presenting a wonderful example of heroism to his colleagues, did not lead to a successful outcome to the attack. The soldiers who remained waited until darkness before crawling back to their own lines. Out of the 116 men and officers involved in the abortive attack fewer than half of them survived, and many of those were wounded. To the right of the SWB the Royal Inniskilling Fusiliers were cut off by a German barrage and were mostly either killed or captured. The SWB were relieved the next day, but they had not seen the last of Monchy; they returned there about ten days later.

White's posthumous VC was gazetted on 27 June 1917:

> For most conspicuous bravery and devotion to duty. Realizing during an attack that one of the enemy's machine-guns, which had previously been located, would probably hold up the whole advance of his company, Sgt White, without the slightest hesitation, and regardless of all personal danger, dashed ahead of

his company to capture the gun. When within a few feet of the gun he fell, riddled with bullets, having thus willingly sacrificed his life in order that he might secure the success of the operations and the welfare of his comrades.

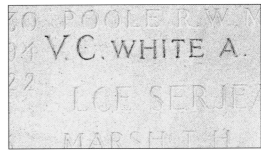

White's name on the Arras Memorial to the Missing (Photo: Donald Jennings)

White's father was presented with his son's VC in the fore-court of Buckingham Palace on 21 July 1917. As he has no known grave, White is commemorated on the Arras Memorial in Bay Six.

Albert White was born in Kirkdale, Liverpool, in 1896; he was the son of Thomas White and Susan White, née Percival. His father was a merchant seaman and worked as a ship's carpenter. White was educated at a reform school, Everton Terrace School, Liverpool, and before the war followed in the steps of his father and became a merchant seaman.

When the war began in August 1914 White was ashore and he enlisted in the Royal Army Medical Corps on 23 October 1914. A few months later, on 1 June 1915, he transferred to the South Wales Borderers with the service number 24866, and became a member of the 2nd Battalion. The battalion arrived on the Gallipoli Peninsula as part of the 89th Brigade, 29th Division, on 25 April 1915, and White joined them on 30 June as one of the unit's reinforcements. Two months later the battalion was involved in the assault on Suvla Bay and in October, after suffering very high casualties, they were back at Helles. In January 1916 the battalion, still with the 29th Division, was evacuated to Egypt and in March they sailed to France, where they undertook intensive training. The division was subsequently involved in the disastrous attempt to capture the village of Beaumont-Hamel at the beginning of July. In the same month White was promoted to the rank of sergeant.

The 2nd SWB was so depleted that it had to be reformed and White was offered a commission, but after beginning his officer training he had to withdraw as he could not afford the lifestyle of an officer. White's closest relation was Jessie White, his sister, who used to live in the family house at 54 Lamb Street, Kirkdale, which was later demolished.

White's medals, which include the VC, 1914–15 Star, BWM and VM, are not publicly held.

T.H.B. MAUFE

Feuchy, France, 4 June

When he won his VC on 4 June 1917 at Feuchy, 2/Lt Thomas Maufe was serving with the 124th Siege Battery, Royal Garrison Artillery. Feuchy is about 4 miles east of Arras, south of a canalized section of the River Scarpe and was captured on 9 April – the opening day of the Battle of Arras. Maufe's citation was gazetted on 2 August, as follows:

For conspicuous bravery and initiative. Under intense artillery fire this officer on his own initiative repaired, unaided, the telephone line between the forward and the rear positions, thereby enabling his battery to immediately open fire on the enemy. 2/Lt Maufe further saved what might have proved a most disastrous occurrence by extinguishing a fire in an advanced ammunition dump, caused by a heavy explosion, regardless of the risk he ran from the effects of gas shells which he knew were in the dump. By this great promptitude, resource and entire disregard of his own personal safety, he set an exceptionally fine example to all ranks.

At the time of Maufe's death, twenty-five years later in 1942, Judge Frankland wrote the following appreciation which was published in the *Ilkley Gazette* of 3 April 1942:

When he performed the deeds which were later rewarded by the Victoria Cross I was serving in the same area on the Headquarters Staff of the Heavy Artillery under whose command was the battery in which Maufe was serving.

Maufe's gallantry was not chiefly the repair of telephone lines under fire – that was done hourly by scores of brave men – but his coolness in dealing with a fire in a forward ammunition dump. This dump had caused us much anxiety, being of necessity placed in a forward and exposed position.

The great peril was the presence of a number of gas shells. Had these been involved in the fire a whole area east of Arras would have become lethal for some considerable time and most probably have caused a temporary withdrawal in a vital sector. To attempt to deal with ignited ammunition is ever a terrible thing; when gas shells are included, it demands complete disregard of self and an entire devotion to the welfare of others. Maufe did his task with calculated courage, and saved the lives of many.

Then, as since, his distinguishing characteristic was quietness. I remember that when we entertained him in our mess at Arras after he had received his decoration he appeared terrified. The one subject on which he kept complete silence was himself, and it was typical of Maufe's modesty that many years later a fellow member with me of Maufe's club was astonished when I informed him that Maufe had received the Victoria Cross.

Having lived through many and great dangers he died as a result of accident. High irony and sadness are here, but we remember that significantly he died in his own land preparing for its defence. Truly of him it shall be said that he lived by the artillery motto, 'Quo Fas et Gloria Ducunt' (Whither Right and Glory Lead).

Maufe was decorated by the King at Buckingham Palace on 29 November 1917. By the end of the war he had become a major and was one of the youngest men in the Army to hold that rank.

Thomas Harold Broadbent Maufe was born on 6 May 1898 in Ilkley, West Yorkshire, the youngest of four sons of Mr and Mrs F.B. Maufe. He was educated at Ghyll Royd School, which had been established in 1889 by Mr A. Wooldridge Godby. The school offered places to the sons of gentlemen between the ages of eight and fourteen to prepare them for public schools, and promised an all-round liberal education. Maufe left the school when he was fourteen and went on to Uppingham School, where he boarded at West Deyne House; his three brothers also attended the school. The family home at that time was Warlbeck, King's Road, Ilkley.

In October 1915 Maufe left Uppingham and entered the Royal Military Academy at Woolwich and on 10 May 1916, when he had just turned eighteen years of age, he was commissioned in the Royal Garrison Artillery and left for France in July 1916.

After the war Maufe returned to Ilkley; the town awarded him with a silver casket in recognition of his VC and bravery, and when the town's war memorial was dedicated he was invited to unveil it.

Maufe decided to complete his interrupted education and went to Cambridge University where he became a member of Clare College. He graduated and then went on to the Royal School of Mines at South Kensington. At some period he was involved with tin smelting at Gravesend and with tin mining in Cornwall. He subsequently became a director of Brown, Muff & Co. Ltd of Bradford.

He was married at St Margaret's, Ilkley, on 4 June 1932, fifteen years to the day after he won his VC in 1917. His bride was Mary Gwendoline Carr of Low Wood, Ben Rhydding, who was well known locally as a tennis player. A reception was held for the couple at the Wells House, Ilkley, and their honeymoon was spent in Scotland.

Mr and Mrs Maufe were later to have a son and daughter and the family lived at North Hill, Ilkley. In 1935 Maufe resigned his commission because of continual ill-health, having been on the Reserve of Officers since the war. On at least one occasion Maufe played a prominent role in the local Remembrance Day commemorations when a United Service took place at St Margaret's and afterwards a parade was organized followed by a march to the town's war memorial. Col. J.H. Hill, formerly of the 6th West Yorks, took the salute, attended at the saluting base by Maufe.

Later the Maufes lived at Whitethorn, Myddelton, Ilkley. A tragedy occurred on 28 March 1942 when Maufe was killed in an accident at Manor Farm on Blubberhouses Moor. Maufe was serving as a private in the Home Guard at the time. A practice mortar shoot had been arranged to take place near Manor Farm and two trench mortars were set up there. Initially five rounds of practice shells were discharged and then a further five with half charge, followed by one with full charge. This last shot did not explode on impact and another round was prepared. The *Ilkley Gazette* of 3 April 1942 described what happened:

The exercise was being carried out near Manor Farm at Blubberhouses. The trench mortar shell is in the form of a bomb which is fired by charges of varying strengths. The minimum charge is a primary cartridge containing half an ounce of black powder at the tail of the bomb, a half-charge consists of the primary cartridge and two half-ounce bags of black powder and the full charge of the primary cartridge and five half-ounce bags of black powder. The bomb is placed tail end first in the muzzle of the trench mortar, and is discharged when the percussion cap of the cartridge is detonated by contact with a steel pin.

The final bomb exploded in the barrel of the gun, and Maufe and a colleague, Henry Galloway, standing beside the gun, were both killed instantly. A third man was injured. Maufe's funeral service took place at Ben Rhydding Church. Although neither he nor Galloway was given a military funeral, their coffins were placed on a gun-carriage and draped with a Union Jack. A detachment of the Ilkley Home Guard provided an escort and Maufe was buried in Ilkley Cemetery, Grave A768.

At the inquest held at Otley a verdict of accidental death was recorded and in his will Maufe left £24,797 gross, £20,546 net. A memorial to the two dead men was erected close to where the accident occurred, on 27 May 1946. It is a simple stone from Heber's Ghyll bearing a bronze plaque with the following inscription:

> To the honoured memory of Henry Galloway and Thomas Harold Broadbent Maufe, VC, who gave their lives for King and country, 28th March 1942. This stone was erected by the Ilkley Company Home Guard.

Describing the stone, the *Ilkley Gazette* of 17 May 1946 published the following information:

> The stone is to be placed some twenty yards from the place where the accident occurred, and the ceremony will take the form of a service conducted by the Rev. E.B. Alban, Vicar of Ben Rhydding, and Chaplain to the Ilkley Company of the Home Guard. The singing will be led by the choir of the Ilkley Parish Church.
>   The service will begin at 8 p.m. and transport has been arranged to take those wishing to attend. Buses will leave the Brook Street car park for Manor Farm, at 7.15 p.m. Friends, members of the Ilkley Home Guard and the Ilkley Home Guard Ladies Association are invited to attend and the Ilkley British Legion has been invited to send a representative party.

T.H.B. Maufe's grave in Ilkley Cemetery, Yorkshire (Photo: Donald Jennings)

For readers wishing to visit the site of the memorial, it can be approached from the main Harrogate–Skipton road, to the north-east of Ilkley. An unclassified road leading southwards to Otley goes close to Manor Farm and cars can be parked in the church car park. Visitors to the memorial should seek permission from the owners of Manor Farm.

On 16 May 1993 a service of commemoration was held at Uppingham School in Rutland to honour the five former pupils of the school who won the VC. A memorial tablet in Galilee Chapel was dedicated by the Archdeacon of Northampton and unveiled by Gen. Sir Martin Farndale. Members of the families of the VC winners were among those who attended the service and an exhibition of VC memorabilia was organized by the school.

Maufe's medals are not publicly held.

J. CARROLL

At St Yves, France, 7–12 June

Pte John Carroll was a member of the 33rd (New South Wales) Battalion, Australian Imperial Forces, and gained his VC in the period 7–12 June during the Battle of Messines. On 7 June his battalion, which was in the 9th Brigade of the 3rd Australian Division, was on the extreme right of the Anzac positions, to the south of the River Douve.

When nineteen mines exploded in the small hours of 7 June, the last men of the attacking 3rd Australian Division were reaching their points of assembly. The 9th Brigade on the right was to be part of the attacking force and the Australian units, taking full advantage of the confusion on the enemy front, moved off across no-man's-land. According to C.E.W. Bean, the Australian Official Historian: 'The local German garrison, already overstrained by the week's bombardment, was entirely unstrung.' The exploding of the mines created vast craters, and German resistance was almost completely absent. As the Australians moved into the enemy trenches they found only a few Germans, who appeared quite keen to surrender rather than make a fight of it.

However, on the extreme right the fight was more severe, and to quote Bean again:

> The 33rd Battalion, an especially fine unit commanded by a young veteran of Gallipoli, Lieutenant-Colonel Morshead, had been picked for this position, and its advancing troops were from the first under the fire of distant Germans, who took long shots at them from safe trenches many hundreds of yards beyond the flank. Almost immediately also a party of the enemy at local headquarters in the support trench, just beyond the edge of the attack but closer than the barrage, turned a machine-gun upon the nearest men of the 33rd as they were 'mopping up'.

The crew of the machine-gun were killed and the gun was captured. Another gun to the extreme right was also captured with the help of a Stokes mortar. Soon the first stage of the 3rd Divisional advance was complete.

Later that day and during the next two days the enemy made greater efforts to resist by the use of sniping, machine-gun fire and shelling. The 33rd Battalion strengthened their positions and handed them over to another battalion three days later. Although the fighting had been a bit of a walkover for the battalion, nevertheless it was made easier by the role played by Carroll.

His VC was gazetted on 2 August 1917 and the citation was as follows:

For conspicuous bravery. During an attack immediately the barrage lifted, Pte John Carroll rushed the enemy's trench and bayoneted four of the enemy. He then noticed a comrade in difficulties, and at once proceeded to his comrade's assistance, and killed one of the enemy. He continued working ahead with great determination until he came across a machine-gun and team of four men in a shell-hole. Single-handed he attacked the entire team, killing three of the men and capturing the gun. Later on two of his comrades were buried by a shell, and in spite of very heavy shell and machine-gun fire, he managed to extricate them. During the ninety-six hours the battalion was in the line Pte Carroll displayed most wonderful courage and fearlessness. His magnificent example of gallantry and devotion to duty inspired all ranks in his battalion.

John Carroll was of Irish extraction and was born in Brisbane, Queensland, on 15 August 1892. He moved to Western Australia as a young man, and worked in the Kalgoorlie gold mines and in Karrawang which was close by. He continued as a miner until he decided to enlist on 27 April 1916 when he joined the 44th Battalion, which was mainly composed of men from Western Australia. His service number was 1804. He transferred from the 44th to the 33rd Battalion on 14 November 1916 when the battalion was about to leave their training area at Larkhill Camp on Salisbury Plain, Wiltshire, for France.

After winning his VC, Carroll was wounded in July 1917 and again in the following October. On 23 March 1918 he was presented with his medal by the King at Buckingham Palace. In July he was transferred to AIF Headquarters in London and he returned to Australia for discharge in August 1918.

On 23 April 1923 Carroll married Mary Brown, daughter of Mr H. Brown. Four years later Carroll had a serious accident at Yarloop, which necessitated a foot amputation after it had been crushed at a timber mill where he was working as a truck examiner.

In 1956 he travelled to London for the VC review in Hyde Park.

Carroll's home was 184 Shaftesbury Avenue, Bedford Park, a suburb of Perth, Western Australia. He died on 4 October 1971 and left his VC to the Kalgoorlie branch of the Returned Soldier's League (RSL), where it was kept in a safe and a

replica was displayed. In October 1989 the branch presented the original medal to the Australian War Memorial in Canberra, where almost all the Australian VCs are on permanent display. This decision upset certain members of his family, who considered that the medal should remain in Kalgoorlie. However, the local RSL was convinced that they were only carrying out Carroll's own wishes in allowing the nation to see the medal instead of having it hidden from sight in a bank safe.

John Carroll's grave in Karrakatta Cemetery, Perth, Western Australia (Photo: E.W. Bullock)

S. FRICKLETON

Messines, Belgium, 7 June

The battle to capture Messines Ridge and the extensive German lines beyond it was planned to begin in the small hours of 7 June 1917. The ridge was the first objective and the village was part of the second objective for II Anzac Corps. Having been in German hands for a considerable time, the village itself had been converted into a virtual fortress by the enemy, to be held at all costs. It was surrounded by a strong trench system of deep wire entanglements and was also protected by five concrete strongpoints. In addition, many cellars had been converted into dug-outs.

When units of II Anzac Corps, including tanks, attacked the edge of the village two machine-gun posts were rushed immediately. It was at this point that 6/2133 Cpl Samuel Frickleton (3rd Battalion, 3rd New Zealand (Rifle) Brigade) won his VC and the citation was later published in the *London Gazette* of 2 August 1917:

> For most conspicuous bravery and determination when with attacking troops which came under heavy fire and were checked. Although slightly wounded, Cpl Frickleton dashed forwards at the head of his section, pushed into our barrage, and personally destroyed with bombs an enemy machine-gun and crew which was causing heavy casualties. He then attacked a second gun, killing the whole of the crew of twelve. By the destruction of these two guns, he undoubtedly saved his own and other units from very severe casualties, and his magnificent courage and gallantry ensured the capture of the objective. During the consolidation of this position he received a second severe wound. He set throughout a great example of heroism.

Col. H. Stewart wrote a popular history, *The New Zealand Division 1916–1919*, and described Frickleton's action in the following way:

> The 3rd Battalion companies, with the 2 platoons attached from the 2nd Battalion, reached the neighbourhood of the Brown Line without opposition, but here they came under intense fire from a well-posted machine-gun on the edge of Messines. The officer commanding the company opposite the gun was

killed. Men fell rapidly, and the line was checked. Then Cpl Samuel Frickleton, although already slightly wounded, called on his section to follow him and dashed through our barrage with his men. Flinging his bombs at the gun crew, he rushed and bayoneted the survivors and then, still working within our barrage with the utmost sang-froid, attacked a second gun some 20 yards away. He killed the 3 men serving the gun and then destroyed the remainder of the crew and others, numbering in all 9, who were still in the dug-out. The infantry at once swept on to the trench. Frickleton, who was later severely wounded, was awarded the VC for the magnificent courage and leadership which prevented many casualties and ensured success. . . .

Frickleton's wounds were in his right arm and hip. He also suffered from the results of gas poisoning. A few weeks after Messines he was fit enough to rejoin his unit and was made up to acting sergeant on 11 August, a promotion which was confirmed in early November.

Frickleton received his VC from the King at Ibrox Park, Glasgow, on 17 September 1917. Two other recipients of the medal were also at the investiture: Pte H. Christian and Pte G. McIntosh of the Gordon Highlanders. The King had earlier spent the day touring Scottish firms and factories and went to the football ground in the afternoon before returning to the Royal Train at Kirklee. At the investiture, in addition to the VCs, he had presented other medals to a number of officers, non-commissioned officers and men, together with the next of kin of some of the men who had been killed in the war. At the end of the ceremonies the Chairman of Rangers Football Club was presented to the King by the Lord Provost.

In October 1917 Frickleton was back in hospital in England again and in the following month he was sent to Cambridge for Officer Cadet Training. He was commissioned on 26 March 1918. However, he became unfit again and returned to New Zealand, sailing from Avonmouth in May and arriving home on 12 June.

Frickleton was a consumptive; his medical records show that he was suffering from pulmonary tuberculosis as well as from gas poisoning and he was no longer fit for active service. This did not prevent him from attending a public welcome on 15 June in Wellington Town Hall to honour his winning the VC. Initially a band played 'See the Conquering Hero Comes', which was followed by three loud cheers from the audience in the hall as well as from the people crowded outside, not able to squeeze into the hall. The Mayor of Wellington presided and he apologized for the hall not being large enough to accommodate all the people who wished to catch a glimpse of Frickleton and to welcome him back to New Zealand. Mrs Frickleton, Samuel's mother, was publicly thanked and had a place on the platform. Several more congratulatory speeches were made and then Frickleton spoke a few words to the assembly himself:

You will have to excuse me. I am not much of a speaker; but I would like to express my thanks for the way you have treated me. I can tell you that it doesn't feel too good to be a hero, as you people may think. (Laughter and cheers.) I haven't got much to say regarding the honour I got. I just went out to do my bit – I did'na go looking for medals. When you go looking for them you usually get something else. Dozens of New Zealand boys have done equally as well. They only wanted the opportunity to take the chance. Hundreds of our boys would do the same thing if they had the chance and many a boy has won a distinction out there that has never been awarded. I thank you for your kind reception to myself and my mother! (Loud applause.)

Frickleton spent much of the rest of 1918 recuperating in hospitals or sanatoriums, but the military authorities made sure that he was given maximum publicity in order to drum up interest in the New Zealand war effort. He left the Expeditionary Force on 20 December.

Samuel Frickleton was born in Slamannan, Stirlingshire, Scotland, on 1 April 1891, the son of Elizabeth Logan Frickleton, and arrived in New Zealand in 1913, at the age of twenty-two. He became a coal-miner at Blackball, near Greymouth on the west coast, but gave this job up in order to enlist in the Army on 12 February 1915. His attestation papers describe him as being 5 ft 10 in tall, with brown eyes, dark hair and weighing 11 stone 4 lb. He also spoke with a broad Scottish burr.

He embarked for Egypt with the 5th Reinforcements as a corporal in the Canterbury Infantry Regiment and he served overseas in the Middle East for two months between 13 June and 10 August. It is likely that it was during this period that he contracted venereal disease, which was the reason for his medical discharge on 11 November 1915. He returned to New Zealand for treatment.

On 13 April 1916 Frickleton re-enlisted and was sent to England with the 15th Reinforcements with the rank of sergeant, but he was demoted at some point and was sent to join the New Zealand (Rifle) Brigade, 4th Australian Division. He arrived in France as a rifleman in November 1916 and joined the 3rd Battalion on 7 December. In February 1917 he became a lance corporal and then corporal in March. In early May he was detached to the Grenade School and rejoined his unit after nine days on 12 May.

After completing his service with the Expeditionary Force on 20 December 1918, Frickleton served as a temporary staff officer and was appointed Assistant Provost Marshal, Wellington Military District, from 21 December until 30 June 1919. On 1 July he was transferred to Canterbury Military District. He was sent to the New Zealand Staff Corps in October 1919 as a lieutenant and served in this position until he was placed on the Retired List on medical grounds on 1 April 1927.

Frickleton took up business in Wellington and tried his hand at farming in Wakanae. He then became what was known as a house manager and entered private employment. In 1934 he resumed active service with the Territorial Force and was promoted to captain. The following year he was awarded the New Zealand Long Service and Efficiency Decoration Medal and in December he was in charge of a guard of honour for the Duke of Gloucester, the King's younger brother, when he visited New Zealand. In May 1937 he was part of the New Zealand contingent to London for the coronation of King George VI. The party consisted of nine officers and forty-one men, including three holders of the VC. The party's ship docked at Tilbury and then the group travelled to St Pancras station where they were met by the New Zealand High Commissioner. Later in the day they marched to Waterloo and entrained for Pirbright in Surrey, where they were to camp before taking part in the coronation parade on 12 May. Also in 1937 Frickleton reverted to the Officer Reserve. In 1939 he was recalled as Inspector New Zealand Forces and in 1948 he was posted to the Retired List for the final time. In June 1956 he was also a member of the parade of four hundred VCs at Hyde Park.

He was one of nine brothers who had all enlisted in the war; one was killed and three were wounded. Frickleton's home was Glen Flats, Rara Street, Naenae, a suburb of Lower Hutt, 10 miles from Wellington. He died in Wellington on 1 September 1971 at the Hutt Hospital, Naenae, after a long illness. He was buried in Taita Servicemen's Cemetery, Naenae.

In November 1977 Frickleton's widow Mrs Valeska Frickleton (née Gambitsky), whom he had married on 12 January 1922, presented her husband's VC to the New Zealand Army Memorial Museum. Apart from the VC, his other medals were the 1914–15 Star, BWM and VM.

The New Zealand memorial at Messines (Photo: Peter Batchelor)

R.C. GRIEVE

Messines, Belgium, 7 June

The plan for the capture of Messines involved an assault on a line which stretched from St Yves to Mount Sorrel. The advance was to penetrate for a depth of between 1 and 2 miles into enemy-held positions. With the use of about twenty mines the ridge was to be captured in the morning and in the afternoon supporting battalions were to move down the eastern slope of the ridge in order to secure positions.

Before Messines the 37th (Victoria) Battalion, Australian Imperial Forces, had not taken part in any major action but at Messines they were to experience blockhouse fighting which became such a feature in the Passchendaele campaign later in the year. The slopes of Messines Ridge were covered by these concrete strongpoints, which became known as 'pillboxes'.

On the eve of the Battle of Messines, 6 June 1917, the 37th Battalion left Romarin camp on the main Ploegsteert–Messines road and began their approach march, but they were soon exposed to an intensive German gas shelling attack. The Australians donned their masks, but wearing them while marching was extremely uncomfortable. The route allocated to the battalion cut across the western side of Ploegsteert Wood to Heath Trench and continued down the long communication avenue and over Hill 63. It then went downhill to 'Donnington Hall', a subsidiary line. Other units in the Anzac Corps were moving to Messines via other routes.

The 37th Battalion was at the rear of the moving columns and reached the assembly trenches just before dawn. The men moved off at 11.00 a.m. on 7 June towards their objective, then came under heavy shell fire and suffered casualties.

The initial mine explosions had certainly done considerable damage to the German positions and had killed many, but by midday the enemy had recovered from the shock. The decision was made to delay zero hour for the battalion attack on the Green Line: the time was now to be 3.10 p.m. instead of 1.10 p.m. However, the men of the 37th Battalion were already moving across no-man's-land and beyond recall. They moved along the left bank of the River Douve and soon ran into a barrage of German 5.9s. When they were within 100 yards of the 38th Battalion on the German Black Line they halted and took up positions in the numerous shell

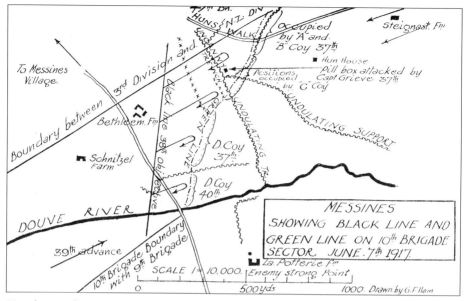

Map showing the area around Messines, June 1917

holes. A counter-attack by the enemy from Messines now began which was followed by a bombardment half an hour later. The counter-attack was repelled.

Just before 3.00 p.m. the attacking companies of the 37th Battalion moved forward to the 38th Battalion's positions and when the barrage began ten minutes later they followed in its wake. A Company was on the left flank in touch with the 47th Battalion. From the main road called Hun's Walk the 37th line moved back at an angle which connected up to the Black Line at the River Douve. However, the two-hour delay had given the enemy valuable breathing space and allowed them to rush forward to the Oosttaverne Trench with a series of counter-attacks.

The 47th Battalion had already captured a pillbox in their attack on the Green Line, and a second was outflanked and bombed from the rear. A third pillbox was causing considerable havoc though, and Grieve's A Company was in position on the left flank, with a thick belt of wire in front of it. As Grieve's men sought gaps in the wire, they came under heavy fire from the pillbox. An attempt to call up the assistance of a Stokes mortar failed, as the crew had all been killed. Furthermore, a Vickers gun team had also been hit. Grieve therefore decided to 'go it alone' and, taking a supply of Mills bombs, he set off to try to knock out the enemy strongpoint. Moving from shell hole to shell hole, he somehow avoided the pillbox's arc of fire. His aim was accurate and he advanced close enough to thrust two bombs through the firing slit. Grieve then moved quickly to the rear of the post, but the gun crew were already silenced, so he signalled to the rest of A Company to come up and take over the trench. The enemy could be seen moving down their communication trench and Pte W.E. Babington shot them down. The section of the Oosttaverne Trench was thus duly captured. Grieve was hit in the shoulder by a sniper and was severely wounded; his assailant, firing from trees 75 yards away, was promptly shot down.

The pillbox which Grieve captured was close to a position named Uncanny Trench, and was between Bethleem Farm and Steignast Farm.

The winning of a VC always has to be witnessed by at least one officer; on this occasion, however, there were none and the reports of the other ranks who witnessed the deed were accepted as authoritative.

Capt. Robert Grieve's VC was gazetted on 2 August 1917 and read as follows:

> For most conspicuous bravery. During an attack on the enemy's position in the face of heavy artillery and machine-gun fire, and after all his officers had been wounded and his company had suffered very heavy casualties, Capt. Grieve located two hostile machine-guns which were holding up his advance. He then, single-handed, under continuous fire from these two machine-guns, succeeded in bombing and killing the two crews, reorganized the remnants of his company, and gained his original objective. Capt. Grieve, by his utter disregard of danger and his coolness in mastering a very difficult position, set a splendid example, and when he finally fell wounded the position had been secured and the few remaining enemy were in full flight.

After Grieve won his VC, eighty-eight NCOs and men of his company wrote a congratulatory letter to him:

> We, as men of your company, will cherish with pride your deeds of heroism and devotion which stimulated us to go forward in the face of all danger, and at critical moments gave the right guidance that won the day and added to the banner of Australia a name which time will never obliterate. We trust that your recovery may be a speedy one, and we can assure you that there awaits you on your return to the boys a very hearty welcome.

The shoulder wound that Grieve suffered at Messines resulted in a four-month stay in an English hospital and he then rejoined his unit, but a serious illness required him to return to hospital for further treatment. He was suffering from acute trench nephritis and double pneumonia, and was sent back to Australia in May 1918.

Grieve was decorated with his VC by the King at Buckingham Palace on 20 October 1917. His VC was the first to be won by the 3rd Australian Division.

Robert Cuthbert Grieve was born in Brighton, Melbourne, Victoria, on 19 June 1889. He was the son of John and Annie Deas Grieve and was educated at

Caulfield Grammar School and Wesley College in Victoria; he was known as 'Bob'. He was an enthusiastic footballer and cricketer. On leaving college he became an interstate commercial traveller in soft goods but when he entered the Australian Army, in early June 1915, he gave his occupation as warehouseman. He had spent part of the previous nine months with the Victorian Rangers and was posted to the 37th Battalion, receiving his commission on 17 January 1916. On 1 May he was promoted to lieutenant and in the following month the battalion embarked for training in England.

When the 10th Light Trench Mortar Battery was organized Grieve was seconded to it. On 19 April 1917 he returned to the 37th Battalion in France with the rank of captain and was given command of A Company. His men admired him as an officer and had a respect for his 'quiet, understanding style of command'. His division, the 3rd Australian, left for France in November 1916 after training in England. During the First World War Grieve served at Armentières, Bois Grenier, L'Epinette, Ploegsteert Wood, Messines, La Bassée Ville and Warneton.

He was discharged from the Australian Imperial Forces on 28 June 1918 as medically unfit and at that time held the rank of captain in the Australian Army Reserve. A few weeks later, on 7 August 1918, Grieve was married at Scots Church, Sydney, to May Isobel, daughter of Mr and Mrs A.C.M. Bowman Plinlimmon, of Kurrajong, New South Wales. He had come to know May, a former nurse, when she nursed him through a serious illness after she met him at a casualty clearing station.

After the war Grieve returned to the soft goods trade. He founded the firm of Grieve, Gardner & Co., a soft goods warehouse of Flinders Lane, and became a well-known city businessman. He served as a captain in the 4th Victoria Battalion of the Volunteer Defence Corps from June 1942 to 18 September 1944, when he was placed on the Retired List. In February 1954 he was presented to Queen Elizabeth at Heidelberg Repatriation Hospital, where he was a patient.

Grieve's wife predeceased him, dying during a visit to London, and there were no children from the marriage. Grieve himself collapsed and died in his Melbourne office on 4 October 1957. The cause of death was cardiac failure; he had also suffered from nephritis since 1917. He was buried with full military honours in Springvale Cemetery. His name is commemorated at VC Corner in the Australian War Memorial at Canberra. In addition, a scholarship in his memory is awarded at Wesley College, Victoria, and his VC was presented to the college in 1959. Grieve had been a lifelong supporter of the college.

The grave of Robert Grieve in Springvale Cemetery, Melbourne, Australia (Photo: Bob Archer)

W. RATCLIFFE

Messines, Belgium, 14 June

The Battle of Messines began at 3.10 a.m. on 7 June 1917 and ended a week later. During the early stages the 2nd South Lancs (75th Brigade, 25th Division) was in brigade reserve. However, on 12 June the battalion was called upon to relieve the 16th Australian Battalion. The 2nd South Lancs found that no trenches had been dug and companies had to provide their own protection. The next day the battalion was to move forward to a new line between Ferme de la Croix and Steignast Farm. The capture of the former was the immediate task allotted to the battalion and, if successful, would help to clear the left bank of the River Douve.

The attack, which began at 7.30 p.m. on the 14th, was over open ground which thus afforded very little protection. The 8th Borders were on the left of the 2nd South Lancs and the latter unit worked forward in small groups. The artillery brought down a curtain of fire on the enemy trenches beyond Ferme de la Croix and the Lancashire companies hurried to keep up with the barrage. The enemy was initially surprised by the suddenness of the attack and yet their machine-guns were still very active, especially some close to Ferme de la Croix. D Company was given the task of outflanking the defenders and pursuing them with grenades. One group of Germans decided to retreat into the farm buildings, where they put up a strong resistance before being outflanked.

It was at this stage of the attack that Pte W. Ratcliffe (2251) won his VC:

For most conspicuous bravery. After an enemy's trench had been captured, Pte Ratcliffe located an enemy machine-gun which was firing on his comrades from the rear, whereupon, single-handed and on his own initiative, he immediately rushed the machine-gun position and bayoneted the crew. He then brought the gun back into action in the front line. This very gallant soldier has displayed great resource on previous occasions, and has set an exceptionally fine example of devotion to duty.

The commander of the 75th Brigade, Brig. Sir Douglas Baird, said this of the deed:

Private Ratcliffe was an old soldier with the South African Medal. He was a stretcher-bearer and had done distinguished service on the Somme, where he had earned the Military Medal. In this attack he was following his platoon and, on reaching the first objective, saw a Boche machine-gun in action that had not been 'mopped up' and was firing into the flank and rear of his advancing comrades. He at once dropped his stretcher and seizing a dead man's rifle went straight for the machine-gun and bayoneted the German officer and five of the crew. He then picked up the machine-gun and some ammunition and ran after his company, and when they had got the final objective he brought the gun into action against the enemy. He then went back and got his stretcher and spent the rest of the night bringing in the wounded through a heavy barrage.

Soon all objectives for the day were taken and all companies were in contact. The day had been very successful for the battalion and, in addition to Ratcliffe's VC, thirty-three other medals were awarded.

The Battle of Messines ended on 14 June and the 2nd South Lancs were relieved three days later and moved to St Omer.

William Ratcliffe was born in 5 Linden Street, Liverpool, on 21 March 1882; his parents were William Ratcliffe and Ellen Ratcliffe, née Atkinson. His father was a carter who worked with various Liverpool haulage firms. Linden Street ran between Oliver Street and Dinorben Street, and was at the top end of Parliament Street. St Anne's Roman Catholic Infants' School, which Ratcliffe probably attended, was bombed and no records of it now exist.

After a brief period working in the local docks, Ratcliffe, at the age of seventeen, decided to join the Army. He served in the South African War with the South Lancashire Regiment and was with the colours for fifteen years, which included a posting to India. On leaving the Army he returned to working in Liverpool Docks. However, as soon as the First World War broke out he rejoined his old regiment in August 1914 and served from Mons to Messines.

During his war service Ratcliffe gained the reputation of having complete disregard for his own safety. In addition to winning his VC in June 1917, he had been awarded the MM two months before. On 14 April well-positioned enemy snipers were taking a heavy toll of Ratcliffe's company; he decided to do something about it and managed to shoot down seven German marksmen. This action took place when the 25th Division was out of the line, and was providing working parties in the Wulverghem sector.

On 26 September Ratcliffe was decorated by the King at Buckingham Palace. A couple of weeks later, on 13 October, in the presence of Lord Derby, he was rewarded with a presentation from the National Union of Dock Labourers in Liverpool at a special dinner held in his honour. Lord Derby made a speech and referred to a monetary presentation to be given to Ratcliffe when the war was over, 'as it was against military regulations to reward a man with money for doing his duty'.

During the war he was wounded twice and won three service chevrons. He was discharged in 1919. By this time he had become known as the Dockers' VC, and he once more returned to the docks to work. However, in the 1920s he fell on hard times. He used to lodge with his sister and her husband in Brindley Street, which ran between Grafton Street and Caryl Street. They later moved to 29a St Oswalds Gardens, Old Swan Brindley Street, of which there is no trace today.

Ratcliffe attended various VC functions, including the 1956 centenary review at Hyde Park where he was assisted by his niece, and a local Liverpool tailoring firm presented him with a fifteen guinea suit to wear for the occasion. Ratcliffe was also kitted out with a new black trilby, together with new shoes and gloves.

Ratcliffe, who remained a bachelor, died in his early eighties on 26 March 1963 and a requiem Mass was celebrated at St Oswald's Church. He was buried in Allerton Cemetery, Liverpool, in the grave (19-274 0/5) of Sarah and John Hume, his sister and brother-in-law, with whom he had lived for several years.

In the local offices of the Transport and General Workers' Union there used to be a stone tablet commemorating the life of William Ratcliffe, but there is no trace of it now. His medals are not publicly held.

William Ratcliffe's grave in Allerton Cemetery, Liverpool (Photo: Donald Jennings)

J.S. DUNVILLE

Near Epehy, France, 24/25 June

On 24/25 June 1917 2/Lt John Dunville (1st Royal Dragoons) won a posthumous VC. Although he was a member of a cavalry unit, he won his medal for his role as an infantryman in a 'quiet' sector held by the cavalry near Epehy, during a raid on the enemy trenches north of St Quentin. The purpose of the raid was to obtain identification of their German opponents. Dunville's citation, gazetted on 2 August 1917, reads as follows:

> For most conspicuous bravery. When in charge of a party consisting of scouts and Royal Engineers engaged in the demolition of the enemy's wire, this officer displayed great gallantry and disregard of all personal danger.

In order to ensure the absolute success of the work entrusted to him, 2/Lt Dunville placed himself between an NCO of the Royal Engineers and the enemy's fire, and, thus protected, this NCO was enabled to complete a work of great importance. 2/Lt Dunville, although severely wounded, continued to direct his men in the wire-cutting and general operations until the raid was successfully completed, thereby setting a magnificent example of courage, determination and devotion to duty to all ranks under his command. This gallant officer has since succumbed to his wounds.

Dunville died in the small hours of 26 June and a few days later, on 30 June, his commanding officer, Col. Wormald of the Royal Dragoons, wrote to his mother:

Dear Mrs Dunville,
I feel I must write to you to express my deep sympathy, and that of all ranks of the regiment, to you and your husband in your irreparable loss.

Since writing first to your husband the sad news, much has come to light to emphasize your boy's gallantry and devotion to duty. We, his brother officers, whilst we shall always mourn the loss of a cheerful companion and friend whom we could ill afford to lose, are justly proud of the gallant way in which a brother officer met his death. The record of his daring and devotion must always remain an incident in the history of the regiment of which all connected with it will look back with pride.

All this is, I am afraid, small consolation to you and his father, and I can add that you have my whole-hearted sympathy in your sorrow.

I must give you an account of what happened to enable you to appreciate his bravery.

A raid was ordered to be undertaken on the German lines about 800 yards in front of our outposts, and 'The Royals' were detailed to carry it out. Two parties, each consisting of 50 Royals and two parties of three Sappers carrying torpedoes for destroying the enemy's wire, were told off. The right party consisted of men of Johnie's squadron and were under command of Ronnie Henderson. The left party of similar numbers consisted of men of 'B Squadron' under Bernard Helme. Each party had to march on a compass bearing to the point in the wire to be attacked. The parties moved through our lines at one a.m. on the morning of the 25th, and under cover of our artillery barrage moved on to to their objectives. Johnie, who was Scout Officer, had the direction of the right party, and brought them right up to the place to be attacked, arriving there punctually at the scheduled time. Having got to the wire, it was his duty to direct the Sappers where they were to place the torpedo, and lay a tape to the gap made by the explosion to show the assaulting party the way through the gap. Just before reaching the main wire the advanced party came upon a narrow belt of low wire, which Johnie and his scouts cut by hand. Johnie then ran forward with the three Sappers, and when they reached the main wire they found that one of the joints of the torpedo had got bent in some way, and it could not be put together and had to be repaired. This occasioned some delay, and the operation, which in practice had taken under two minutes, took them over five minutes. Meanwhile the enemy had detected our intentions, and opened fire with rifles and hand grenades. The Sapper Corporal, a very gallant boy, states that during the whole of this time Johnie was urging him to keep cool and kept assuring him that he was in no danger. He further stated that Johnie deliberately interposed his own body between the enemy and himself, and that by his example and bravery he gave him the necessary confidence to carry out his task. The whole party then withdrew until the bomb exploded, when Johnie told them they could go back. The assaulting party then advanced, but, owing to increase in the enemy's fire, were unable to get through the gap. As the leading men got up to the gap Johnie was wounded, his left arm being badly shattered by a bomb, it is thought. He then had to be taken back. And despite a dreadful wound, he walked back the whole distance – to the outposts. A man of less grit could not have accomplished it. He was quite calm when he reached my headquarters and talked cheerfully to the doctor who attended to his wounds, and apologized to me for not having been able to get into the trenches. I saw him again that morning in hospital about three miles back; the doctors held out very little hope of his recovery, so I got the division to send a wire to your husband. The doctor told me that he had another wound in his chest, which might have been caused by a fragment of the bomb which wounded him in the arm, or might have been from another bullet. Capt. Miles saw Johnie that evening; he was quite conscious, and the doctors were more hopeful. That night a clever surgeon called Lockwood was called in. The poor boy passed away at three a.m. on the morning of the 26th, quite painlessly. I don't think he suffered much pain at any time; and when I last saw him, he only complained of not being able to get his breath. This discomfort passed off during the afternoon and he slept peacefully for some time.

I won't go into details of what happened to the other party. They got through the wire and killed some Germans, and obtained valuable identifications, but poor Bernard Helme was killed.

Poor little Johnie, I feel his death very deeply. I had seen a great deal of him lately, and realized what a splendid boy he was. Quite apart from his gallant end, he had been working indefatigably with his scouts in 'No Man's Land' for a week before the raid, and was out nearly every night making himself acquainted with the ground over which the raid was to take place. He did everything that human power could do to make a success of the raid, and I cannot put into words the admiration which we all feel for him, and the respect in which we shall always retain him in memory.

I can only repeat how truly sorry I am for you and his father.

Yours very sympathetically,

[Signed] F.W. Wormald.

The distance that Dunville walked back with his arm practically blown off and a hole in his chest was nearly 800 yards. After being attended to by Billy Miles, his squadron commander, he was placed on a stretcher and taken back by motor ambulance to Villers-Faucon where his left arm was soon amputated. He was seen by the 'best Consulting Surgeon in France', who was brought over from a large Casualty Clearing Station at Tincourt, and a second operation was performed in order to beat the poison, but the gallant officer died at 3.00 a.m., without coming round.

In the book *Scarlet Fever*, John Cusack and Ivor Herbert described the raid from another standpoint. They had practised the raid for three nights for three weeks:

We studied aerial photographs of the German trenches, we had lectures, and we practised day after day on the ground behind our own lines. We were given twenty-five rounds of ammunition each in a cloth bandolier. Our faces were blacked and we wore cardigan jackets. At dusk the two raiding parties assembled and we were all given a ration of rum. . . . The right [*sic*, left] group was commanded by a fine big chap, Lieutenant Helme, a friendly but quiet fellow, about twenty-four, who had joined the Royals from Sandhurst with our first reinforcements in 1915. He was a South African who spoke good German. . . . As we were about to set off, Major Wilson Fitzgerald took me to one side and said to me quietly, 'Whatever you do, stay firm with Mr Helme.' . . . One point was hammered into us: there was going to be no such word used as 'retire', if the raid ran into serious trouble . . .

We went up silently in a long file. Half a dozen sappers headed our party, carrying bangalore torpedoes, with which to make a breach in the German wire. Lieutenant Helme and I were at the rear of our single file. The engineers were unrolling the tape at our feet . . .

Unfortunately, the tape ran out and Helme whispered to Cusack that they must be near the wire. Soon afterwards there was a minor panic as some of the party began to retire, but this order was mistaken for an instruction to cut the wire. Then there were two loud bangs as two of the torpedoes blew holes in the enemy wire. The raiding party burst through the wire and fanned out in all directions searching for German trenches. Not surprisingly, the Germans had 'woken up' by this time and began sending up red and white flares from their lines. The raiding party was now being illuminated and the enemy artillery began soon afterwards. The attackers were still trying to collect one of the enemy in order to return with the 'evidence' of who was occupying the opposing lines. The ground was full of shell holes and many Mills bombs were thrown in all directions but, alas, with no successful results. Cusack never even saw a German. However, Cpl Jewel did manage to find a dead German from whom he took a shoulder-flash. Soon after this, Cusack almost fell over the body of Lt Helme, who was easy to identify as he was wearing size ten riding boots. Cusack began to drag the body to his own wire where he handed him over. It appeared that Helme had died of a head wound and there was nothing that could be done.

Cusack wrote that on the other flank there were four men dead and seven missing. Their officer, too, was dead:

[the] baby-faced officer, only a boy, called J.E. Dunville, who had only arrived with the regiment in the last few months. He was a small, slightly built, fair lad of about five foot six. He looked nothing more than a young schoolboy, and a quiet, friendly one. His family came from Ireland, where they had a whiskey firm.

Dunville's grave in Villers Faucon Communal Cemetery (Photo: Donald Jennings)

Letters for Dunville were brought up from regimental details while he lay wounded in hospital, but he was not up to reading them or to having them read to him. They were put with his revolver and compass and placed in a small bag, which was later sent back to his parents. Before he died, Dunville received Holy Communion.

Dunville was buried close to Lt R. Helme in Villers-Faucon Communal Cemetery, Row A, Grave 21, one of 227 British graves and 90 German. The cemetery is on the north-west side of the village of Villers-Faucon, which is about 10 miles to the north-east of Péronne. The village was captured by the 5th Cavalry Division on 27 March 1917, lost nearly a year later and retaken by III Corps on 7 September 1918. An extension cemetery is close by, as is a French civilian cemetery. Also buried in the communal cemetery is 2/Lt Parsons VC.

Dunville's parents received a considerable number of letters of sympathy concerning the death of their son and these included a telegram from the King. Most spoke of Johnie's considerable charm and popularity; put in simple terms 'he was loved by all'. To quote a letter from J. Burgon Bickersteth, son of the Bishop of Leeds and a brother officer who joined up with Dunville:

To me his death is a tremendous blow. He joined the same day at York as I did, and many are the days hunting and cheery evenings we have had together. Of course in the regiment he was a general favourite from the day of his arrival – and I don't think there was a dry eye yesterday when the last post was sounded at his graveside. It must be some comfort to you to know that he died as he did, the whole regiment admiring his pluck and mourning his loss.

After the war Dunville's brother 'Bobby' visited his younger brother's grave and cut the letters VC on to his brother's wooden cross.

Dunville's posthumous VC was presented to his father, Flt Cdr John Dunville RNAS, on 29 August – the same day as Billy Bishop was awarded his. Dunville was the fifth man from the Belfast district to be awarded the VC in the First World War.

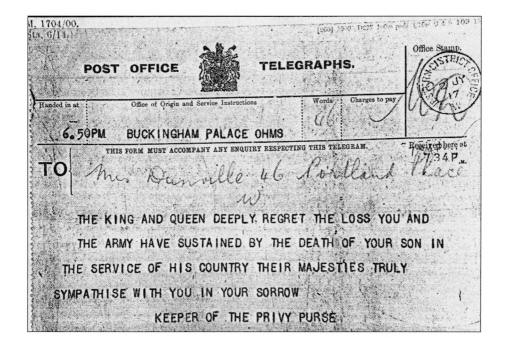

John Spencer Dunville was born at 46 Portland Place, Marylebone, London, on 7 May 1896. He was the second son of John Dunville CBE, and of Violet Dunville. Both Dunville's parents were aeronautical pioneers. In addition, John senior had at one time been private secretary to the Duke of Devonshire. John's elder brother, Lt Robert Dunville, who was in the Grenadier Guards, was wounded by the Sinn Fein in Dublin during the Irish rebellion at Easter 1916.

Johnie Dunville was educated at Ludgrove School and Eton College, where he was a member of Mr Williams's house and then with Mr Robeson until the summer of 1914. He was a member of the Eton OTC from May 1912 to July

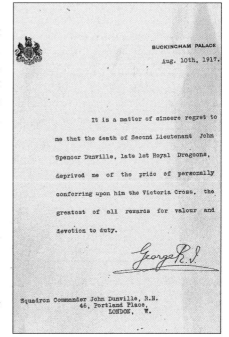

1914. He passed matric for Trinity College, Cambridge, but joined the Army soon after leaving Eton, in June 1915. He was gazetted Second Lieutenant Special Reserve D on 16 September 1914 and served with the 6th (Inniskilling) Dragoons. He took part in the battle of Loos, and there is a note in his Army file to the effect that 'he did excellent work at Loos, September 26/27 1915'. On 4 January 1916 he was transferred to the 1st Royal Dragoons. He served in France and Flanders from 6 June 1915 and took part in the Battle of Loos in September. On 19 April 1916 he was invalided to England for eight weeks with trench fever. He renewed his foreign service on 22 December 1916 until his death in June 1917, having taken part in the Battle of Arras in April. According to his file, he had planned to join the RFC, and although there were no objections, the transfer did not take place and the request was subsequently cancelled. His reason for the request was 'his interest in engineering, ballooning and motors and motoring'.

After the war a wreath used to be laid annually at the war memorial at Hollywood, Co. Down. The family had a house at Redburn, Hollywood, and an office address in Belfast. Dunville's VC is with the Household Cavalry Museum in Windsor, which also provided the majority of the information in this brief biography.

Johnie's mother left £196,569 and part of this money was used to set up a trust to provide funds for the needy on Armistice Day.

F.B. WEARNE

East of Loos, France, 28 June

On 28 June 1917 the 11th Essex Battalion and the 2nd Durham Light Infantry (18th Brigade, 6th Division) were involved in a raid in which a company was selected from each battalion, accompanied by one officer and twenty men from the 3rd Australian Tunnelling Company. The Essex personnel were drawn from C Company under Capt. S.E. Silver and consisted of three parties: A under Lt M.R. Robertson with 30 other ranks in three squads, B under 2/Lt Frank Wearne with 20 other ranks in two squads, and C with one non-commissioned officer and six men. The raiding party had undergone training at Le Brebis and personal reconnaissance was undertaken by the company leaders in preparation for the raid itself. A box barrage began and was quickly replied to by the German artillery. The raiding party assembled in a large dug-out at the junction of Scots Alley and the British reserve line, to the east of the mining town of Loos. At about 7.12 p.m. on 28 June A Party left the trenches and moved into the German line at a junction with Nash Alley. They rushed a block in the German trench, captured it and bombed the dug-outs there, into which the Germans occupying the post had retreated. A Party's role was then to collect prisoners and 'mop up' any opposition.

B Party, under the leadership of 2/Lt Wearne, moved off at the same time as A Party; they were to attack on A's left and their objective was a section of enemy front line. They were to hold it against counter-attacks, thus preventing the rest of the raiding party from being attacked from the left sap in the enemy line. The left squad of B Party made a block and held it against strong opposition. The fighting was intense and the enemy attacked down the trench, throwing bombs as they did so. Several of Wearne's B Party were killed or wounded, and it was at this point that Wearne leapt on to the parapet, ran along the top and threw bombs down on the enemy beneath him. This example inspired his men and the Germans were pushed back. Unfortunately, Wearne was wounded in the leg. He refused to leave his men and he was then wounded again, in the back of his neck, and died a few minutes later.

C Party rushed the position to the right of B Party, having set off a few minutes after A and B. The Australian miners followed C Party; their role was to destroy dug-outs and mine-shafts, and they succeeded in destroying two dug-outs and three mine-shafts in total. The fighting went on for about an hour and the raid was considered a success, although about 80 men out of the 100 involved on the British side had become casualties.

Wearne's posthumous VC was gazetted on 2 August 1917 and the citation for his deed on 28 June was as follows:

> For most conspicuous bravery when in command of a small party on the left of a raid on the enemy's trenches. He gained his objective in the face of much opposition, and by his magnificent example and daring was able to maintain this position for a considerable time, according to instructions. During this period 2/Lt Wearne and his small party were repeatedly counter-attacked. Grasping the fact that if the left flank was lost his men would have to give way, 2/Lt Wearne, at a moment when the enemy's attack was being heavily pressed and when matters were most critical, leapt on the parapet, and, followed by his left section, ran along the top of the trench, firing and throwing bombs. This unexpected and daring manoeuvre threw the enemy off his guard and back in disorder. Whilst on the top of the trench 2/Lt Wearne was severely wounded, but refused to leave his men. Afterwards he remained in the trench directing operations, consolidating his position and encouraging all ranks. Just before the order to withdraw was given, this gallant officer was again severely hit for the second time, and while being carried away was mortally wounded. By his tenacity in remaining at his post, though severely wounded, and his magnificent fighting spirit, he was enabled to hold on to the flank.

On the eve of the raid Maj. H.S. Roberts and three other officers including Wearne had met in a cafe in Le Brebis where they ate boiled rabbit with vegetables and drank a poor wine. During the evening a reference was made to K.M. Wearne, one of Wearne's brothers who had been killed by shell fire near Monchy-le-Preux while serving with the 1st Essex on 21 May.

Wearne's VC was presented to his father, Frank Wearne, by the King at Buckingham Palace on 20 October 1917. Frank junior's name is listed on panel 85 (or niche 1153), the Essex Regiment, of the Loos Memorial to the Missing.

Frank Bernard Wearne was born in Kensington, London, on 1 March 1894. His father, F. Wearne, was a wine merchant living at Manor Lodge, Worcester Park. Frank was the second of three brothers who served in the First World War. He

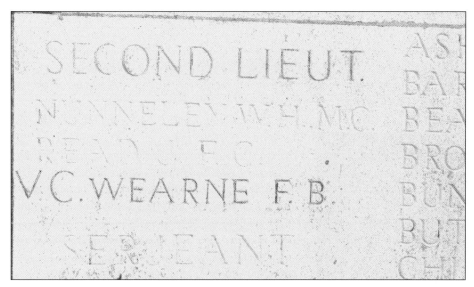

Wearne's name on the Loos Memorial to the Missing (Photo: Donald Jennings)

went to Bromsgrove School in 1908 when he was fourteen and left four years later for Oxford. His younger brother, G.W. Wearne, also attended Bromsgrove before entering the Army; he served with the Canadian Army and later suffered from severe shell shock. Frank joined the Army in 1914 when he volunteered for service in a Public School Battalion. His elder brother, Capt. Keith Morris may have had a hand in this as he was a regular Army officer in the Essex Regiment. He was killed in action on 21 May 1917. Frank began his army career with the 18th Royal Fusiliers and the number 2214. He was promoted to lance corporal on 22 November 1914 but on 30 December he was made a private again. He was discharged to a commission on 15 May 1915 and was gazetted second lieutenant in the 3rd Essex Battalion and was later attached to the 10th Battalion on 5 June 1916, when the battalion was in the region of Carnoy. As a scout officer, Wearne, together with three of his scouts, managed to capture a member of the German 62nd Regiment, and it was thought that the 12th Division to which he belonged had the left of the front opposite the 53rd Brigade.

Wearne's name is mentioned in the Essex unit history several times and he was considered to be a 'plucky and resourceful officer'. He was badly wounded on 3 July on the Somme and never returned to the 10th Battalion, but joined the 11th Battalion when his wounds healed in May 1917.

Wearne's VC passed into the hands of his surviving brother, G.W. Wearne, who lived in South Africa and in January 1977 it was auctioned at Sotheby's, fetching £7,000. His medals are not publicly held.

F. YOUENS

Near Hill 60, Belgium, 7 July

On 6 July 1917 2/Lt Frederick Youens of the 13th Durham Light Infantry (68th Brigade, 23rd Division) was in the trenches close to Klein Zillebeke on patrol with three other men when they came across a group of about thirty of the enemy. The Germans quickly tried to surround the four men but after a short and fierce bombing fight, the Durham patrol managed to escape to its lines. However, in the fighting Youens had been wounded, as had one of his men.

In the early hours of the next day the 13th Durham Light Infantry began to suffer from German artillery and under its cover about fifty of the enemy infiltrated the Durham's trenches. It was at this point that the wounded Youens won his VC, which was gazetted on 2 August 1917. The citation reads as follows:

For most conspicuous bravery and devotion to duty. While out on patrol this officer was wounded, and had to return to his trenches to have his wounds dressed. Shortly afterwards a report came in that the enemy were preparing to raid our trenches. 2/Lt Youens, regardless of his wounds, immediately set out to rally the team of a Lewis gun, which had become disorganized owing to heavy shell fire. During this process an enemy's bomb fell on the Lewis gun position without exploding. 2/Lt Youens immediately picked it up and hurled it over the parapet. Shortly afterwards another bomb fell near the same place; again 2/Lt Youens picked it up with the intention of throwing it away, when it exploded in his hand, severely wounding him and also some of his men. There is little doubt that the prompt and gallant action of 2/Lt Youens saved several of his men's lives, and that by his energy and resource the enemy's raid was completely repulsed. This gallant officer has since succumbed to his wounds.

A brother officer wrote to Youens's mother:

He did one of the finest acts of bravery that has been done in this war, and I only hope you will be awarded what he deserved. He was on a patrol; and was wounded. While he was being dressed in a dug-out, with his tunic and shirt off, the word came down that his company was being attacked. He immediately rushed out as he was, and rallied a Lewis gun team, and commenced firing at the Boche. They threw a bomb into the middle of the team, and he picked it up and threw it away. The Boche threw another in the same place, and your son picked it up and threw it away again. Unfortunately, the bomb burst very near to your son and severely wounded him. He died two days later. He undoubtedly saved the situation by his display of coolness and disregard for danger.

The major in Youens's battalion wrote as follows:

He was an ideal soldier, keen, efficient and brave, and was earmarked for early promotion. On several occasions his gallant work has been noted, and I sincerely hope that his last feat will be duly recognized. He was exceedingly popular with his men, who would cheerfully follow him anywhere.

Finally, the chaplain who conducted his burial service, wrote of him as follows:

As I wished him good luck, one of the senior officers said to me, 'That's a fine chap, just the sort of fellow we want in the battalion.' The first and almost only thing taken from him after his wound was a little diary, and in it a card bearing the words: 'Christ is risen.' I felt, as I conducted the service, surely death had no terrors for him.

Youens was buried in Railway Dug-outs Burial Ground, close to the village of Zillebeke near Ypres, both of which can be seen from the cemetery. The cemetery is between the south-west corner of Zillebeke Lake and the Ypres–Comines railway line. Youens's grave is close to the railway embankment that runs along one side of the cemetery. The date of death is shown as being 7 July on his stone, although he died of wounds two days later. Burials in the cemetery began in April 1915 and continued for the rest of the war. Advanced Dressing Stations were set up in dug-outs and at the farm on the west side of the cemetery, which was known as Transport Farm or Railway Dug-outs during the war. In the summer of 1917 the cemetery suffered considerable damage from shell fire before many of the graves could be marked.

Youens's mother received her son's VC from the King at Buckingham Palace on 29 August 1917.

Frederick Youens, the son of Mr and Mrs Vincent Youens, was born in High Wycombe, Buckinghamshire, on 14 August 1892. He first attended the local

Lt Youens remains lie in the Railway Dugouts Military Cemetery (Photo: Donald Jennings)

National School and later obtained a scholarship which allowed him to enter the Royal Grammar School in High Wycombe. He became a scholar of distinction and passed, in succession, the Junior and Senior Oxford Locals, both with honours.

In 1910 Youens passed the London Matric in the first division. He was also a prominent member of the school debating society and a member of the OTC; in addition, he took part in the school amateur dramatics. In 1912, at the age of nineteen, he was an assistant schoolmaster in St Peter's School, Rochester, and was a member of the Medway Swimming Club.

As soon as the war began Youens left his job at St Peter's in order to enlist as a private in the Royal Army Medical Corps, which he did in August 1914 at Aldershot. On 12 May 1915 he transferred as a private to the 7th East Surrey Regiment with the number

G179019. On 28 July 1916 he was transferred to the 3rd Battalion. On 1 August he was made a lance corporal, and acting corporal on 4 October. On 23 January 1917 he was discharged to a commission and was made a second lieutenant with the Durham Light Infantry. He was severely wounded in the arm when serving at Loos. He worked in the field all night after the battle, carrying out first aid and bringing the wounded in and under cover. He remained convalescing in England for about a year.

After his death in July 1917 a brass plate was put up in his parish church in High Wycombe and a prayer desk has been devoted to his memory in St Andrew's Chapel. A road on a new housing estate in the town has also been named after him. At some time Spinks sold his medals for £3,300; the lot included a Durham Light Infantry cap badge, photos, letters and other items. On 5 February 1977 Youens's VC was sold at Sotheby's and the Durham Light Infantry managed to raise £4,900 to purchase it for their museum; it was the sixth VC that they had acquired.

T. BARRATT

North of Ypres, Belgium, 27 July

The 7th South Staffordshire Battalion (33rd Brigade, 11th Division) was in the line to the west of Steenbeek stream, north-east of Ypres, on 27 July 1917, four days before the beginning of the Third Battle of Ypres; the division was due to be relieved shortly.

In the late afternoon aerial reconnaissance provided the information that the enemy positions opposite the 7th South Staffs were now empty and five patrols were organized in order to check what was actually happening in the enemy lines.

Pte Thomas Barratt, in his role as a scout, took part in a patrol consisting of twenty-five men and an officer of B Company. It was quickly discovered that the Germans had not entirely left their positions and that a number were still *in situ* on the British side of the Steenbeek. As the patrol reached the remains of a farm, the men were harassed by enemy snipers, several of whom Barratt dispatched. But the patrol had stumbled into an ambush and, without warning, the enemy suddenly opened up from a strongpoint in some ruined houses and pinned down the patrol. The officer in charge of the platoon covered the withdrawal of his two rifle sections, but his Lewis gunners were wiped out in the process.

Barratt noticed that the enemy was trying to work around the back of the patrol in order to cut off its retreat. He remained behind on his own to cover the withdrawal of the rest of the patrol and, in doing so, shot at least six of the enemy; all the time he was having to avoid heavy machine-gun and rifle fire. Once his colleagues were back in their lines Barratt managed to make his own way back. It was then that he was killed by a stray shell, after reaching his lines. His VC was gazetted on 6 September 1917 and written up in the Battalion War Diary on 8 September.

Barratt was buried in Essex Farm, Boesinghe, Plot 1, Row Z, Grave 8. The cemetery, close to the Yser Canal, is named after a farm on the site which contained a dressing station during the war. It is halfway between Boesinge and Ypres, and is where John McCrae wrote his poem 'In Flanders fields'.

Barratt's platoon officer wrote home to his grandmother (who was unable to read):

Your grandson was killed in the evening while on his way back to the front line to the battalion head-quarters, after doing some of the most splendid work that has ever been done by any man in the regiment, or for that matter, the Army. By his bravery and skill he accounted for a considerable number of the enemy and practically saved the platoon to which he was attached from being surrounded.

He got back safely to his own lines, and was proceeding down a communication trench with two others when a shell burst and buried them under a bridge, which was smashed on top of them. They were all killed instantaneously.

Barratt's remains lie in Essex Farm Cemetery, Boesinghe, Belgium (Photo: Donald Jennings)

His company captain wrote as follows:

Barratt, when very young, went to [*sic*, had?] bravery, coolness and courage. I have known him intimately for two years. He was a member of the draft I took from Mudrus to Suvla Bay, when I was in the ranks. At Suvla he acted as my runner.

Brig.-Gen. A.C. Daly, commander of 33rd Brigade, wrote to Barratt's next of kin on 18 September 1917:

I am writing these few lines to tell you how proud everyone in the brigade is that his majesty the King has recognized the great devotion and gallantry displayed by Private Barratt by the award of the Victoria Cross. No reward can compensate his relatives and friends for his loss, but the fact that his bravery has not passed unnoticed and that he did not give his life in vain for our great cause will, I trust, prove a consolation to you. The decoration which Private Barratt earned will no doubt be handed to you soon, and will keep his memory green in Coseley whose inhabitants will always think of him with pride.

Thomas Barratt was born at 9 Foundry Street, Darkhouse, Coseley, in the District of Dudley, Worcestershire, on 5 May 1895. He was the third child of

James Barratt and Sarah Ann Barratt, née Caddick; he had an elder brother and sister. James Barratt had been employed at one time by Deepfields Iron Company as an iron puddler. Barratt's mother, who could not read or write, died when her youngest child was three years old. His father was in very poor health and suffered from some sort of paralysis, which led to him and his young son having to go to the Dudley Workhouse (later Burton Road Hospital). Thomas remained there for about nine years and often ran away to the other members of his family who were living at Albert Street, Princes End. They clearly did not want to bother with him and he had to return to the workhouse. Finally, when he was twelve, he decided to try his grandmother at 35 Darkhouse Lane, Coseley, and she agreed to adopt him legally. She used to sell fruit in Tipton and she was married to a Mr Sam Haynes, a widower who had a young son called Joe. Thus Joe and Tom became great friends and the Haynes's home became Barratt's home for the next few years.

Thomas Barratt attended church day schools and was considered to be an unruly child. When he left school he worked at the Cannon Foundry for a shilling a day and he then moved on to Thompson Brothers, the boilermakers, at Lower Bradley, Bilston. He was a regular attendant at Bible classes, which were held in connection with Darkhouse Baptist Chapel.

James Barratt senior died in the workhouse at Burton Road Hospital in 1914, and a few months after war broke out Thomas enlisted (with the number 17114), on 14 January 1915. Four days later he began his military service with the South Staffordshire Regiment; he was nineteen years of age and about 6 ft 4 in tall. He served with the 7th Battalion at Suvla Bay in the Gallipoli campaign and remained with them when they moved to the Western Front. At some point he was wounded or became ill as the standard photograph of him before he was killed on 27 July 1917 shows him wearing hospital blues. On 20 October 1917 his VC was presented by the King at Buckingham Palace to James, his brother, and not to his grandmother who had taken Thomas in when his elder brother 'shut the door on him'.

As a result of local publicity after her grandson won the VC, Mrs Haynes received many visitors who wished to congratulate her on 'her lad'. Barratt is commemorated in a number of ways: his name is listed on the local war memorial, and there are memorials at Coseley parish church and Darkhouse Baptist Chapel. The latter was unveiled on 9 December 1917 and later, when the building was demolished, the memorial was transferred to the Garrison Church at Whittington Barracks. Thompson's erected a memorial tablet in the firm's canteen to commemorate Barratt and other members of staff. When the building was closed the memorial was offered to the Staffordshire Regimental Museum. In 1962 a block of flats, Barratt Court in Batman's Hill, Coseley, was named after him, and his former employer at Whittington Barracks already owned a

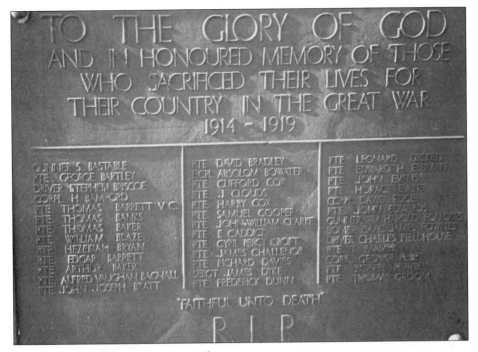

The centre plaque of Coseley war memorial

'Killed in Action plaque' that had been given to them by a member of the Barratt family in 1968. A plaque dedicated to all the members of the South Staffordshire Regiment who won the VC is on display at the Garrison Church at the barracks.

Barratt's medals, which included the 1914–15 Star, BWM and VM as well as the VC, were acquired by the Staffordshire Regimental Museum on 12 March 1987. They were purchased for the museum with the aid of a grant from the Museum and Galleries Commission Purchase Grant Fund and from grants from other regimental funds.

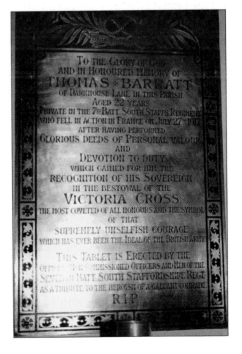

A plaque inside Coseley parish church, in honour of Thomas Barratt VC

SOURCES

The sources used in the preparation of this book include the following:

The Lummis VC files at the National Army Museum, London
The Victoria Cross files at the Imperial War Museum, London
The Public Record Office, Kew, Surrey
Regimental Museums and Archives
The London Gazette 1914–1920 (HMSO)

E.J. Mott
Oxford & County Newspapers
PRO WO 95/2305

H.W. Murray
Reveille, 1 February 1966
PRO WO 95/3491

F.W. Palmer
West London Observer, 20 July 1917

G.E. Cates
Lloyds TSB Group plc

C.A. Cox
Bedfordshire County Record Office
PRO WO 95/2043

P.H. Cherry
Reveille, 1 May 1968

F.M.W. Harvey
The Calgary Herald, December 1943, 23
  August 1980, 15 September 1980

J.C. Jensen
Australian War Memorial Newsletter, April 1987
The Canberra Times, 4 February 1987
PRO WO 95/3522

F.W. Lumsden
Bristol Grammar School
G.H. Dixon
Michelle Young

W. Gosling
Sheila Andrew
Daily Sketch, 13 July 1964
D. Hicks (Wroughton History Group)
Sue Knight

J.E. Newland
Reveille, n.d.
PRO WO 95/3252

T. Bryan
St George's Gazette, 30 June 1917
Sunday Pictorial, 22 July 1917
PRO WO 95/2467

H. Cator
Eastern Daily Press, 9 April 1966, 15 April
  1966, 26 April 1985, 14 June 1996
*Journal of the Queen's Royal Surrey
  Regiment*, 1966
Spinks Catalogue, June 1985

T.J.B. Kenny
PRO WO 95/3218

T.W. MacDowell
Department of Public Records & Archives
  (Historical Branch), 24 August 1970
Esprit de Corps, n.d.
MacLean's Magazine, 15 February 1929
Reveille, 1 October 1939
The Sunday Times, 17 September 1939
PRO WO 95/3908

W.J. Milne
Ottawa Citizen, 31 July 1989
PRO WO 95/3781

E.W. Sifton
Department of Travel and Publicity, 16
  May 1961
Esprit de Corps, vol. 2, no. 8
The Legionary, December 1968

E. Sykes
A VC is Remembered (no details)

J.W. Whittle
Reveille, n.d.
PRO WO 95/3252

J.G. Pattison
MacLean's Magazine, 15 February 1929

Letter to Canon Lummis from Henry Pattison, 30 September 1953

H. Waller
The Dewsbury Greats, November 1992
Morley Observer, 6 March 1980
PRO WO 95/2162
Yorkshire Post, 26 February 1980

D. Mackintosh
Ministry of Defence Army Records Centre

H.S. Mugford
The Essex Chronicle, 20 June 1958
Essex Weekly News, 20 June 1958
Bill Fulton

J. Cunningham
PRO WO 95/221B

J.W. Ormsby
The Dewsbury Greats, November 1992
The Dewsbury Reporter, 2 August 1952

C. Pope
PRO WO 95/3251

A. Henderson
Symon Allison
Douglas Gillespie
Clara J. Leckie
Scottish Record Office
Manan Smith
Alan R. Wilson

D.P. Hirsch
The Guardian, 22 June 1917
Yorkshire Evening Post, 11 November 1986, 22 September 1995
PRO WO 95/2836

E. Foster
The Western Front Association *Bulletin,* no. 45, June 1996
Daily Express, 7 October 1937
Evening News, 5 February 1946
Mr P. McCue
South Western Star, January 1946
Wandsworth Borough News, 8 February 1946
PRO WO 95/2612

E. Brooks
Mr C.M.V. Cooper
Ox and Bucks Regimental Chronicle, n.d.
PRO WO 95/3067

R.L. Haine
Midhurst and Petworth Observer, 27 June 1982
Times History of the War, vol. 13, pp. 364–5
PRO WO 95/3118

A.O. Pollard
Dorset County Library, County Library Service
Miscellaneous newspaper cuttings and reviews

J. Welch
Echo, 1 July 1978
PRO WO 95/1371

R.G. Combe
Aberdeen Grammar School Magazine
I.H. Brown
J.M. Cameron
Friends of the Canadian War Museum, Ottawa
MacLean's Magazine, 15 February 1929
Anne Park
PRO WO 95/3831

J. Harrison
A.D. Gerrard, *The Road to Oppy Wood.* Private publication, 1997
The Sapper, June 1954
PRO WO 95/2357

G. Jarratt
PRO WO 95/1857

M.W. Heaviside
Jack Cavanagh
Stanley News, 4 May 1939
PRO WO 95/2161

G.J. Howell
Australian Military Forces: Records for G. Howell
Ron Baker
Jean Letaille
Reveille, n.d.
The West Australian, 25 December 1964
PRO WO 95/3217

T. Dresser
Evening Gazette, 10 March 1965, 3 May 1979, 11 June 1979, 21 July 1979, 9 May 1983
PRO WO 95/2004

R.V. Moon
Australian War Memorial Newsletter, nos 46 and 48
'Stories of the VC, 1914–18: Capt. R.V. Moon', *Melbourne Argus,* 9 July 1941
PRO WO 95/3648 and 3649

A. White
Liverpool Daily Post, 20 and 21 March 1973

T.H.B. Maufe
Mr J.M. Shepherd of Ghyll Royd School, Ilkley
Mr J.P. Rudman of Uppingham School
Leicester Mercury, 15 May 1993
The Dedication of a Memorial in Chapel to Five Members of the School who have been awarded the Victoria Cross, Sunday 16 May 1993
Miscellaneous newspaper cuttings

J. Carroll
Daily News, 10 October 1989
PRO WO 95/3221

S. Frickleton
Daily Sketch, 19 September 1917
National Archives of New Zealand, Wellington
PRO WO 95/3710

R.C. Grieve
PRO WO 95/3414

W. Ratcliffe
Miscellaneous newspaper cuttings

J.S. Dunville
Household Cavalry Museum, Windsor
PRO WO 95/1161

F.B. Wearne
Nicholas Lovell, *VCs of Bromsgrove School: The Stories of Five Victoria Crosses Won by Old Bromsgrovians.* Bromsgrove School Enterprises, 1996
PRO WO 95/1616

F. Youens
PRO WO 95/2182

T. Barratt
Black Country Bugle, January 1981
Express & Star, 7 September 1917
The Stafford Knot, October 1970 and October 1987
Mr S.T. Smith
PRO WO 95/1816

BIBLIOGRAPHY

The following is a short selection of the published sources used in this book and does not include individual unit histories.

Australian Dictionary of Biography
Bean, C.E.W., *The Official History of Australia in the War*, vol. IV. University of Queensland Press, 1982
Boraston, J.H., OBE (ed.), *Sir Douglas Haig's Despatches (December 1915–April 1919)*. J.M. Dent & Sons, 1919
Canadian War Records Office, *Thirty Canadian VCs*. Skeffing & Son, Canada, 1919
Creagh, O'Moore and Humphris, E.M., *The VC and D.S.O.*, 3 vols. Standard Art Company, 1924
Edmonds, J.E. (ed.), *Military Operations France and Belgium, 1914–1918*. Macmillan/HMSO, 1922–49
Lindsay, Sidney, 'Merseyside Heroes' (unpublished manuscript)
Michelin Illustrated Guides to the Battlefields 1914–1918. n.d.
Nicholls, J., *Cheerful Sacrifice – The Battle of Arras 1917*. Leo Cooper, 1990
Nicholson, G.W.L., *Canadian Expeditionary Force 1914–1919*. Ottawa, 1962
Oldham, P., *Battleground Europe. The Hindenburg Line*. Leo Cooper, 1997
Pillinger, D. and Staunton, A., *Victoria Cross Locator*. 2nd edn, Australia, 1997
The Register of the Victoria Cross. This England Books, 1988
Sheffield, G.D. and Inglis, G.I.S., *From Vimy Ridge to the Rhine – The Great War Diaries of Christopher Stone DSO MC*. Crowood Press, 1989
Smyth, J., *The Story of the Victoria Cross*. Muller, 1963
Times History of the War
Wigmore, L. (ed.), *They Dared Mightily*. Australian War Memorial, Canberra, 1963

INDEX

INDEX